revealing art

'. . . a fine discussion of one of the most important topics in aesthetics: the value of art. Its arguments and conclusions are both original and accessible to a broad audience.'
Robert Stecker, *Central Michigan University, USA*

'Matthew Kieran offers an urbane, broad-minded, humanistic vision of the enduring values of art from Poussin to Matisse to conceptualism, delighting in the multi-facetedness of art and quietly admonishing those with moralistic or fashion-driven prejudices.'
Peter Lamarque, *University of York, UK*

Matthew Kieran is Lecturer in Philosophy at the University of Leeds. He is the co-editor of *Imagination, Philosophy and the Arts* (2003) and the editor of *Media Ethics* (1998), both published by Routledge.

revealing art

by Matthew Kieran

Routledge
Taylor & Francis Group

LONDON AND NEW YORK

First published 2005 by Routledge
2 Park Square, Milton Park, Abingdon, Oxon, OX14 4RN

Simultaneously published in the USA and Canada
by Routledge
270 Madison Avenue, New York, NY 10016

Reprinted in 2006, 2008

Routledge is an imprint of the Taylor & Francis Group, an informa business

© 2005 Matthew Kieran

Typeset in Janson and N Helvetica by
Keystroke, Jacaranda Lodge, Wolverhampton
Printed and bound in India by
Replika Press Pvt. Ltd.

British Library Cataloguing in Publication Data
A catalogue record for this book is available from the British Library

Library of Congress Cataloging in Publication Data
Kieran, Matthew, 1968–
    Revealing art / Matthew Kieran. — 1st ed.
        p. cm.
    1. Aesthetics. 2. Art—Philosophy. I. Title.
    BH39 .K5 2004
    701'.17—dc22   2004006196

ISBN 10: 0–415–27853–8 (hbk)
ISBN 10: 0–415–27854–6 (pbk)

ISBN 13: 978–0–415–27853–9 (hbk)
ISBN 13: 978–0–415–27854–6 (pbk)

Contents

Illustrations

Acknowledgements

I would like to acknowledge the University of Leeds for granting me a one-semester sabbatical in 2003 to help finish this book and the University of British Columbia, Vancouver, Canada, for having me as a visiting professor during that period and the following summer. I had such a wonderful time there it was rather difficult to leave, for which I thank all I came to know. I originally published some material in this book in the *Journal of Aesthetics and Art Criticism*, *Journal of Philosophy and Phenomenological Research*, *Philosophy* and *Philosophy and Literature*. I thank the editors of these journals for their permission to use it.

Aesthetics has always been my first love in philosophy, owing in no small part to Andrew Harrison, an inspirational teacher of mine whilst at Bristol. Berys Gaut, my PhD supervisor an age ago at St Andrews, helped to sharpen up my enthusiasm. In addition there are many people over the last few years whose interest and comments have helped prompt my thought in these matters. I am grateful to them all, and in particular to Darren Brierton,

Noël Carroll, David Davies, Berys Gaut, Peter Lamarque, Jerrold Levinson, Dominic Lopes, Andrew McGonigal, Seiriol Morgan, Peter Millican, Bob Stecker, Roger White and several anonymous referees for discussion, comments, criticisms and suggestions which have all helped immeasurably to improve the book. The weaknesses that remain are my own. I would also like to thank my students over the years in the philosophy of art at Leeds, whom I have enormously enjoyed teaching and have myself learnt from. It was Tony Bruce's idea that I write this book for Routledge and I'm glad that he persisted with it despite my initial scepticism. Both he and his ever efficient, personable team at Routledge have been very patient. To my friends and family I can only say it is an honour and a privilege. Lastly, since she introduced me to the wonders of art at an age I can barely remember, I dedicate this book to my mother Patricia.

Matthew Kieran, 2004

Introduction

In the Tate Modern there is a version of Auguste Rodin's *The Kiss* (1901–4) which can be seen on the cover of this book. A couple emerges from the block of marble in a rapturous embrace, the meeting of their lips deliberately concealed from the viewer. The woman leans into the embrace, turning and pulling the man down. Her leg presses over his thigh, gently prising his legs apart, whilst his right hand rests tentatively on her thigh and his left rests round her torso, barely holding on to the discarded book they have been reading. What is it that makes this work special? Why are we inclined to savour the form of their caress as beautiful? Should knowing more about the couple and the sculpture affect our appreciation? Perhaps you think it shows us something about the nature of erotic love or that if it commends immoral passions we should think less of it as art. Do you think we can demand or expect that other people appreciate it as art as we do? The ways we treat art works, describe them, discuss them, argue about them, painstakingly care for and restore them, award prizes or put prices on them, involve assumptions about these questions.

Think about how you're inclined to appreciate and value *The Kiss*. Would it matter if it turned out not to be by Rodin at all but by one of his pupils or a forger? Rodin's sculpture and drawings both remould the nineteenth-century tradition of classicism, with its emphasis on formal ideals of the nude, and look forward to the modernism of the twentieth century, with its explicitness regarding both the materials of art and subject matter. Does knowing this matter to your appreciation? Would it matter if Rodin had been working in the 1930s instead of from the 1880s on? What do we take such art historical facts to signify? After all, whatever the truth is with respect to them, the sculpture will still look the same. Or is there something apart from your experience or the look of the thing that matters? When we say *The Kiss* is beautiful, we seem to expect other people to agree with us. Yet someone might fail to see what the fuss is all about or maybe they don't get why people go to art galleries except to appear sophisticated and pretentious. Does this mean they're failing to look at the Rodin in some special way? How else would you explain their being nonplussed when looking at it?

The original model for *The Kiss* was an embracing couple Rodin sculpted into his famous bronze doors of the gates of Hell, now at the Rodin museum in Paris, which fused figures and scenes from Dante's *Inferno* with his artistic obsessions. The doors are so thick and heavy that they couldn't function, but the scenes he sculpted on to them provided a well of inspiration for the rest of his life. The story of Paolo and Francesca, *the* adulterous couple of Dante's second circle of hell, was familiar to Rodin's contemporaries in the way in which we know the story of Romeo and Juliet today. Francesca was given by her father in marriage to Gianciotto, Lord of Rimini, who though deformed was a man of great courage. Paolo, his brother, possessed the graces and beauty Gianciotto lacked. One day they were reading alone together about Lancelot, the lover of Guinever who was the wife of Arthur, his friend and king. Whilst Paolo and Francesca read of Lancelot's love, they were drawn together, observing each other's expressions as they read of forbidden passion and sealed their fates with a kiss. The couple were later discovered and then put to death by the enraged Gianciotto. As described in Dante it was Paolo who took the lead, pulling Francesca trembling into a kiss, but in Rodin's sculpture it is the other way round. Paolo's posture is somewhat rigid as if only just starting to relax from a state of shock and surprise. The hand on her thigh is rather tentative whilst the other hangs loosely around her body, book in hand. By contrast she presses her body into his, pulling his face and shoulders downwards and round as if about to roll him over. What at first glance we might take for the representation of innocent passion seems to take on a much more shaded and complex meaning. Our responses to the piece start to take on a different character once we know more about the couple represented. How should the deeper meaning of the piece interact with our responses to it as art? Perhaps it should still be understood as a romantic celebration of erotic love, but the undertones are much darker and more dangerous. In conveying to us the pull of prohibited sexual desire it may show us something about ourselves, but according to some if it glorifies that which should be condemned it is a worse work of art for all that. The first version was shown in Paris in 1898 and this version was produced in 1901–4, commissioned by Edward Perry Warren for his house in Lewes, Sussex. When the piece was stored in Lewes

Town Hall in 1914 a tarpaulin was thrown over it in case it inflamed the priapic passions of soldiers billeted there during the war. Yet it might be that the true achievement of the piece is that it gets us to respond sympathetically and even approvingly to that which, in the last analysis, would be condemned. How should the complex moral character of the piece affect our responses and evaluation? Should everyone agree on what the appropriate evaluation of the piece is? Can our artistic disagreements be blameless or is there some objective ordering of value and worth we all imperfectly aim at? And how can we know if we're in a good position to make the right kind of judgement?

It's just these kinds of questions that this book aims to explore in relation to visual art in general. But many of these considerations apply across all fields of artistic endeavour. In emphasising the continuities between contemporary or modern art and the art of our more distant past I am not seeking to flatten out the differences. In fact the continuities are often underestimated and they help to explain the ways in which much contemporary art remains in touch with the aims, if not the methods, of the cultural practice of art. Throughout the book I use the term 'art' to mean good or great art unless explicitly stated otherwise, with the exception of the last chapter where I'm interested in the status of artistic judgements. I do not directly address what makes something art, though that question is of interest in its own right. The focus of my concern is the nature and status of artistic value, the form and depth of our responses to art works, the ways in which art can be insightful or can cultivate our inner lives.

What distinguishes good or great art works from the mediocre or downright bad? An attempt to answer that question should illuminate just why we attach such significance to the creation and appreciation of art. Whether you agree with my conclusions or not, I hope you find the book beneficial in exploring your own reactions to art and that this critical process is as enjoyable and provocative as the art that inspired it.

Chapter One | Originality and Artistic Expression

Priceless

Leonardo da Vinci's *Mona Lisa* (1503–6) is housed in the Louvre behind plastic glass, some distance away from where its audience must stand. The viewing conditions are atrocious, and usually compounded by the gaggle of spectators crowding round to look at one of the most famous paintings in the world. Most of them have seen endless reproductions, but somehow the draw of the original is intensified rather than lessened. Why is this? Why do we assume that the original work is so precious? That we do seems clear, from the huge sums paid on the art market for original works to the lengths some people will go to to see particular exhibitions. If we could see a copy that was just as good would we really be missing out on anything? Why do we presume that forgeries and pastiches can't be as artistically worthwhile?

It is a commonly held view that an art work has no worth other than the value of the experiences it affords us. Does experiencing a work give pleasure? Do we gain insight or understanding? How can we distinguish between the values tied up with experiencing the work and those only loosely connected? As important as such questions are, assuming that only the experience counts sits uneasily with the thought that artistic originals matter. Perhaps a forgery or pastiche could give us experiences just as good as an original, in which case why bother? But it also seems to be in tension with the way we appreciate certain kinds of art, from contemporary conceptual art to recognising the innovations of cubism. Historically the importance of the original, and originality, is tied up with the Romantic idealisation of the artist. Central to Romanticism was the claim that distinctive, imaginative expression in art constituted one of humanity's highest achievements. It is a rarefied view and much out of favour. Is artistic value always just a function of valuable experiences? Or does there lie, in the shadows of the Romantic view, a clue as to what else artistic value can consist in?

Faking it

In the twentieth century, with its explosive developments in reproductive technology, many thought that the aura surrounding original art works would evaporate. Artists had been influenced by photography since the late nineteenth century, and in the 1920s, particularly within the Dada and surrealist movements, it came to be used in a distinctively artistic manner. Max Ernst used photomontage to unsettling effect by combining distinct photographic images and engravings, ranging from mundane adverts to landscapes superimposed with amorphous figures. John

Heartfield's vicious satire juxtaposed figures ranging from a member of the Nazi SA superimposed on to the image of a murdered body to Hitler saluting whilst gobbling huge amounts of money. From Duchamp and Man Ray through to the 1960s, with work by artists like Andy Warhol and Richard Hamilton, up to contemporary artists such as Jeff Wall, there is a common thread which seems to suggest that the original work of art is, strictly speaking, irrelevant. What matters is whether what you are looking at, be it the original or no, gives you the same kind of rewarding experience. In Walter Benjamin's suggestive phraseology, the work of art had entered the age of mechanical reproduction. Our fetishism of originals was supposed to diminish in proportion to the fidelity of copies realised by our use of machinery. For the age of photography (and no doubt cinema and now the world of computer generated imagery) was held to usher in an age when 'for the first time in world history, mechanical reproduction emancipates the work of art from its parasitical dependence on ritual'.[1] Only eleven years later, in 1947, André Malraux was to imagine and look forward to a museum full to the brim with photographic reproductions of the great art works of mankind.[2] Viewing the reproductions would not just please the eye but enhance our understanding of the complex relationships amongst the photographed works.

In a way we already move within Malraux's imaginary museum. There is no end of beautifully reproduced art works in monographs on particular artists, movements or epochs. Images of past masters, contemporary artists, great works and not so great works can be found on lavishly produced posters, postcards and even mugs. We're lucky to find ourselves in such a position. For the many of us who can't afford to buy original works can still enrich our lives with copies of works we find beautiful or intriguing. We can see how particular artists developed or the summation of the glories of the Renaissance without having to go to an exhibition – which may or may not ever be put together and which, even if it is, may or may not even be in our country.

It is easy to decry the ubiquity of images such as Monet's *Water Lilies*, yet we should be wary of snobbery – it's no different in principle from a Fornassetti mug or a Rothko poster – or the accretions of cliché from blinding us to great artistry. It is true that the ease of mass reproduction can lend itself to purposes that render banal even the greatest of artistic achievements. A few years ago I was in a fashionably monochromatic bar which had various art prints hung on the walls. One of them happened to be from Monet's *Water Lilies* series and, if giving it more than a brief glance, you could see it was hung upside down – the shifting pool of water reflecting the lilies was where the sky should be. Thus was a copy of Monet's *Water Lilies* reduced to coloured wallpaper. But all this shows is that people can misuse or fail to appreciate what the images are copies of, not that mass reproduction of such images is bound to lead to a cheapening of our appreciation of art.

Given the virtues of the mass reproduction of art works, and their quality, what is the point of going to see the originals? The answer by some is thought to depend on the nature of the artistic medium we're dealing with. In photography it is often assumed that, art market reasons apart, whether a photograph is an original print or a photographic reproduction doesn't matter. Photographs are, it is thought, utterly transparent with respect to what they are images of. Indeed, this has led some to claim that photography cannot even be an independent representational art.[3] Another reason is the belief that a photographic reproduction of a photo-graphic image, at least one which preserves the image's size, will preserve the relevant appreciable qualities of the latter. By contrast this is held not to be the case in painting, since the artist can choose how to represent the scene before him, hence every brushstroke matters, and reproductions fail to keep the relevant qualities intact.

However, this is a mistake. It's true in photography that 'the work' is usually a kind of which there can be many instances. Consider the work of Bill Brandt. One of the great photographers of the twentieth century, Brandt originally worked with Man Ray, then moved on to produce social commentary images of 1930s Britain. Some of his best work consists in images of dark, industrial northern towns, his poetic yet often bleak landscapes and his abstracted nude studies (for which he is most well known). Now for any one of his works, since it is a photograph, there can be many instances. On taking a photograph the image is captured on film and can be developed many, many times over. So, in principle, the same work could be sold to as many buyers and museums as possible. Hence I could see the same work in London, though not the same particular print of it, at the same time as you see the work in New York. They are two different versions of the same work. Now it is often assumed that photographers aim to make identical prints of the same photograph. Yet though this is often the case it isn't always true. Thus the print on display in London might be artistically different, darker lighting, blacker shadows, a more flecked and grainy tone, because the artist intended it to be so. This is just one way in which photography's representational qualities can be chosen and altered by the artist.[4] It is like listening to two different versions of Beethoven's *Choral Symphony* which vary in tempo, emphasis of tone and lyrical interpretation in performance. So though viewing the original in the case of photography admits of many instances or prints, which may vary, seeing an instance of the original matters for the same reason it matters that we're listening to a performance of Beethoven's score. Photographers usually try, though not always successfully, to limit the number of prints available of one of their images and often make sure there are subtle differences in the development of each print. This is partly for aesthetic reasons. Just as we value different performances of the same piece of music so too we often value different versions of the same image. It is also partly for economic reasons. If there are too many versions of the same image available then the exclusivity of the work diminishes and their prices plummet. If the artistic reason isn't sufficient motivation to limit the number of prints made, then the economic reason usually is. The same kind of characterisation applies to lithographic prints, etchings, screen printing and sculptures produced from mouldings. Even if in many cases the exact look of each version of the work is aimed for, it needn't always be the result, or the intended aim of the artist. It's true that in some cases the possible instances of a work are not limitless; in that of etchings, for example, the metal plating degenerates with each imprinting. None the less, such works are kinds of which there can be many instances – and lithographs, etching plates or sculpture mouldings are often destroyed by artists to limit the numbers of the work that can be reproduced.

Now, by contrast, we might think that originals matter in painting because we are dealing with a unique particular object. Take the work of the seventeenth-century Dutch painter Johannes Vermeer. There are only about thirty-six of his paintings left in existence and most of them focus on people in domestic scenes, mainly indoors, often with allegorical or religious significance. Vermeer's work is rightly celebrated both for the sheer smoothness of his painted surfaces and for the subtle interplay of light, shadow, colour and proportion. But the formal techniques are used to give a sense of the vivid reality of his subjects and finely express their moods and attitudes, as in, for example, the realism of his *The Little Street* (1657–8). This is a masterly street scene with the painterly delineation of bricks, mortar and houses serving as the background for ordinary household activities. But there is more to it than this. One starts to take in the blank, mute façades, the closed or half-open shutters and empty windows of the house on the right, and occasional female figures of whom we can only identify their external activities. An impression builds up that there is animating, interior life, within the figures themselves and behind the mute façades; yet we cannot know the exact nature of that life just in virtue of their appearances. So the quality of the painting and its formal virtues embody an insight into how difficult it may be to understand others – what a person is thinking and feeling cannot just be perceived from observing them. Had Vermeer's brush-strokes been different, the smoothness of the surface would be lacking; had the structural composition been different, the sense of scale would have been lost; had the grouping of figures been rendered differently then the sense of isolated figures going about their private, solitary, human activities would have been lost. In the painting each particular feature makes a difference to the composition as a whole, from the particularly fine brushstrokes characterising the brickwork to the echoing of each figure by the others. Given that every painterly feature matters in this very particular way, then looking at the original matters hugely. No matter how good the painted copy, the photograph, or the lusciously reproduced plate in a book, features of the painting which are crucial to appreciating it properly are bound to be lost – whether it be the brushwork, the sensuous surface or the light – and its proper impact thereby diminished. Interestingly, one can also get a false impression of how good certain paintings are because of the way they are reproduced. I remember being at an exhibition at the Georgia O'Keefe museum in Sante Fe a few years ago and was astonished at how comparatively small much of her work actually is. When one looks at reproductions of her flower studies, one imagines that they are painted on an epic scale. The formal structuring, the use of line and colour, the lack of detailing, suggest a vivid impact partly based on a contrast between the grand size of the paintings themselves and the fine, small-scale nature of the flowers depicted. In fact they are painted on a much smaller scale than the reproductions suggest and their impact is subsequently much less than one would imagine. Painting seems intrinsically particular, and no matter how good even the most painterly copy or forgery is, something will always be lacking.

There is good reason to think that no reproductive copy or forgery is likely to be as good but it is a mistake to think this is necessarily the case. In principle both a painting and a photograph could be copied perfectly. Consider modifying Malraux's imaginary museum. Imagine that it houses not good-quality photographic copies of original works but, instead, photographs and paintings which are visually indistinguishable from the originals. By some fantastic yet to be discovered cloning technique, any and every work can be exactly reproduced in the very same materials as perfectly as any original. Then painting would be in a similar position to photography and lithographs. We might be tempted to deny such a thing is or could be possible. But that's either because we are thinking about what can actually be done with our present technology or because we are just assuming that there could be no perfect copy. But just imagine that there could be such a thing. Would we then have any reason to value the original? At least, would we have any reason to value the original more than its perfect copies? It is tempting to assume that the answer is no – which helps to explain why people have fought over whether paintings are necessarily particular or not in contrast to photographs, books or musical works. But this would be a mistake. There is no good reason to hold that paintings couldn't be just the same. The crucial point is, even if we did have perfect copies, we would still have reason to value the originals more than the perfect copies. It is neither irrational nor sentimental to do so, since the reason runs very deep indeed.

What is the reason then? It concerns the essentiality of origin. What this opaque phrase picks out is the idea that what matters regarding our attitudes to something is not just a function of what its inherent qualities are, but also a matter of the relations in which the object stands to us.[5] It's easier to grasp the point if we consider a concrete case. Imagine that there are two young girls who are in every qualitative respect the same but one of them is a clone of the other – they look exactly the same, they act the same, they even think the same thoughts and one is a genetic copy of the other. Yet only one of them is your natural daughter whilst the other one is an exact copy of her, so they stand in different relations to you. Should we treat them exactly the same? If the only thing that matters is the nature of the girls then the answer is yes. But this is not so. For you have good reason to care about, and act differently towards, one of the girls because she is your daughter (which is not to say you can treat her clone any old way). Similarly, there could be two paintings that are exactly the same in terms of appearance but the relations in which they stand both to each other and to their origins may be different: one of them was created by the artist we credit with the work; the other was perfectly copied from that original by someone else. The copy may happen to give you exactly the same rewarding experience that the original gives when you look at it (just as both the girls can do exactly the same things). But it is none the less a copy of the original work rather than another version of the original (just as only one of the girls is your daughter and the other an exact replica). What this shows is that the relations in which a particular work stands make an essential difference to the nature of the work – and thus to how it should be treated. For without recognising the importance of such relations we could not explain why certain attitudes towards works of originality, pastiches and fakes are appropriate. Now, it could be asked why this really matters. Sure, whether a painting is really a Vermeer or a photograph a Brandt depends on the relations of the work to its creator. But why should that be relevant to artistic value? To answer that question we have to examine why originality matters.

Originality

One of the things we prize highly in good or great art is originality. By that I don't mean merely doing something novel. After all, someone can be novel by producing something spectacularly bad and awful (there was a good reason why no one had done it before), or by reproducing someone else's thoughts or techniques with minor variations. Mere novelty does not make for originality. Rather, originality consists in a certain kind of artistic achievement – for example, the independent and remarkable realisation of a solution to an artistic problem, the development of a new artistic technique, the strikingly fresh treatment of overly familiar subject matter. Caravaggio's claim to greatness partly lies in his revolutionary treatment of familiar religious subjects and scenes. Born in 1573, Caravaggio turned on its head the previous hundred years' tradition of idealising human and religious experience. In formal terms what is most striking about his work is the intense contrasts between darkness and light, through the use of vivid chiaroscuro effects, so that shadowy scenes are strikingly illuminated, often from an unknown source, to highlight the dramatic focal point of the depicted scene. Yet the most revolutionary aspect of his work is the way in which biblical characters are represented as ordinary, contemporary people. Biblical characters had more traditionally been represented in highly conventionalised, ethereal ways, marking them out as distinct in kind from those gazing upon the scene. Thus they were presented as people to be idolised and worshipped because their nature, whether by divine grace or by saintly goodness, was so much more perfect than our own. But Caravaggio rejected convention and strove for radical naturalism. Not only are his incidental figures represented in highly naturalistic ways, but his Christ, his Madonna, his St Matthew, are all represented in just the same way. They are of the same flesh, the same blood; they are part of the very same world as the viewer, not set apart from it. Thus do they partake of the same nature. In the Contarelli Chapel in the Church of San Luigi dei Francesi, Rome, for example, is Caravaggio's *The Calling of St Matthew* (1599–1600). Here St Matthew is represented seated at a table with four others in the process of counting money, probably from their tax collecting duties. Christ stands on the right with St Peter, backlit from the window on the right, the light straining through to pick out St Matthew who is pointing at himself in surprise. The two boys counting on the left fail to notice and the two other figures seem afraid or threatened. The dramatic point of the picture concerns St Matthew's shock of recognition, frozen in a moment of wonder and indecision. The portrayal's revolutionary aspect concerns the representation of St Matthew as being just the same kind of person as those he is at the table with. The two boys immersed in counting remain blind to the scene, thus forsaking the possibility of deliverance, but St Matthew sees the light, the figures of Christ and St Peter, and so can turn to the will of God. The larger significance of Caravaggio is manifest just in this one picture. Although St Matthew is specifically being called upon, any one, no matter how fallen, craven, imperfect or depraved, can turn towards redemption. Partly as a result of Caravaggio's tendency towards erotic depictions of figures such as St John the Baptist, and although certain religious clerics supported him, the Catholic Church took rather less than kindly to his work. The assertion of the basic humanity of the central figures in the Christian drama challenged the Church's then basic attitude towards the laity, that they should unquestioningly worship the communion of saints. Hounded by the Church, Caravaggio was forced to flee Rome, ending up in Malta where he died prematurely in 1610 at the age of 36.

Consider, by contrast, our attitudes towards pastiches and forgeries.[6] A pastiche is a work made up of elements copied from another work or in deliberate imitation of the style of another artist. If you wander near the British Museum or the edges of London's Hyde Park on a Saturday afternoon you'll often come across stalls selling scenes in the styles of Monet, Van Gogh or Dalí, or cartoon-like pictures in the style of Lichtenstein. In many cases the canvases are not direct copies but stylistic and compositional imitations of different artists. Whilst we may admire the skill, virtuosity and veracity of the imitation, just as we may revel in the accuracy of a good mimic, we do not think such works have anything like the same value as the works produced by the original artist. The right explanation can't just be in terms of the imaginative experience offered by the original works as opposed to the pastiches. One of the pastiches might offer an experience as complex and vivid as an original. It could even be that a pastiche offers a more imaginatively rewarding experience than one of the poorer works produced by the original artist. Yet we would, and should, still value an original work much more highly. This might seem somewhat puzzling. Surely if we are evaluating two objects, the one which offers the more rewarding experience ought to be valued more highly? But this is to overlook the constitutive nature of the achievement involved. In the case of a pastiche little wit, ingenuity or imagination is required. All that is needed is a certain technical gift combined with the capacity to see how a certain artistic effect was achieved.

To knock out a 'Van Gogh' scene one only has to start from the striking use of blazes of blue, orange, green and yellow, and use broad, dynamic brushstrokes. But though the end result may look like a Van Gogh, a mere pastiche is neither the individual expression of an artistic vision nor the working towards the development or resolution of artistic problems in any of the ways one of the originals is. In Van Gogh's work from Arles we can see his concern for arriving at a very individual realisation of aesthetic and stylistic coherence. The blazes of colour expose us to the sun's piercing light, the baked orange earth and the intense blue-black sea of the South of France. The scratching, slashing, stroking brush mimics the movements of natural forms calligraphically so that the gnarled olive trees and the weathered limestone express a pattern seen in the landscape, something which would have been lost if he had used more traditional tonal shading. Van Gogh worked to develop his particular style to represent the landscape as he conceived of it, evoking the stifling air, the heat, the space, the distance, through vivid colour, brush marking and gouging. So a significant part of the reason why we value the intense colours and calligraphic contortions of Van Gogh is because we can see how the work expresses his vision of Arles as well as aspects of landscapes elsewhere. The most expressionistic of his works visually convey how he saw and responded to the ancient olive groves, the gnarled, clawing tree roots, the stratified, cavernous limestone hills and the tumultuous, windswept clouds. So we value original Van Goghs both because they constitute the development of a fresh, original, formal style and because, through his stylistic development, he expresses in a nuanced, bold way how he understands and reacts to the landscape around him. It is important to realise that it is not just a question of how the landscape may be perceived. Rather, his work expresses a particular way he conceives of and values the landscape. If this were not so then though we would still value his work for the development of certain formal techniques, there would be no significant relation between Van Gogh's use of colour and strokes, the means of representation and the landscape. The colours would still be vibrant, the style calligraphic and his work of aesthetic value. But the significance of the work, in terms of expressing how he conceives of the landscape in a particular way, would be lost. We would not be able to see Van Gogh in the landscape around us. So though we might say of a pastiche that it shows great use of colour or that it is an immensely skilled imitation, and we might greatly enjoy looking at it, we certainly would not claim that it is good or great art. It was Van Gogh who forged the development of this particular style, and the individual artistic vision expressed through that style is his, whereas that of the pastiche is entirely derived. Thus it is the originals that constitute the achievement.

Exactly the same line of thought applies to forgeries, since forgeries are pastiches which someone attempts to pass off as if they were originals. The most infamous forger in the last century was Van Meegeren, who produced a series of fake Vermeers that were taken to be and sold as originals. Although the quality of the works he produced was variable, the most famous picture attributed to Van Meegeren, *Christ and the Disciples at Emmaus* (1936–7), is certainly a masterpiece of its kind. Previously a very minor painter in Holland and in dire financial straits, Van Meegeren moved to the South of France in the 1930s to embark on his career as a forger. He painted over genuine seventeenth-century canvases, to prevent obvious dating, and experimented with various techniques to achieve the hardness of surface that is the mark of old oil paintings, including hand grinding his colours, and varnishing, distressing and engriming his finished works. He successfully sold a number of his forged works, including *The Woman Taken in Adultery* (1941–2), attributed to Vermeer, to Goering. Arrested for collaborating with the Third Reich in 1945, he suffered six weeks in incarceration before he confessed that the Vermeer was a forgery and proudly proclaimed he had forged five other Vermeers and two paintings attributed to Pieter de Hooghs. In 1946 the Coremans Commission was set up to examine his claims and in 1947 reported that all the paintings examined were by Van Meegeren. He then received a sentence of one year's imprisonment for forgery, as opposed to collaboration, though he died several months later.

For a time there did remain some dispute over whether the *Disciples at Emmaus* really was a forgery as opposed to a genuine

Vermeer, even though the scientific evidence was fairly conclusive. Interestingly, from our perspective, the work embodies a strikingly dated conception of what a Vermeer should be. The work is much heavier, the structure more simplified, the facial characterisation overly exaggerated, with enhanced cheek bones, heavy lidded eyes and thick protruding lips. However, for the sake of argument, let us imagine that one just could not tell from looking at and examining the canvas whether or not the work is a Vermeer or a Van Meegeren. Would it matter? Yes. If the work is a Vermeer then it constitutes a certain kind of artistic and imaginative achievement, if it's a Van Meegeren then, no matter how good, it is only technical mimicry. There is all the difference in the world between a painting that genuinely reveals qualities of mind to us and one which blindly apes their outward show.

Artistic achievements

There are many disagreements over just what particular kinds of valuable experiences art seeks to realise. Is an art work good because our experiences with it yield pleasure, emotional engagement, delight in the beautiful, personal understanding or social insight? These conflicting views all share the basic assumption that a work is valuable in so far as it affords a valuable experience. From David Hume through to contemporary philosophers such as Malcolm Budd, the idea that artistic value can be wholly captured in terms of the experiences works afford is a common one.[7] Much that is crucial to artistic value is bound up with the value of our experiences. But it can't quite be the whole story. As we've seen, a copy or pastiche of an artist's work might be just as imaginatively rewarding as the original and yet it is of far lesser worth. There are also further reasons which show why this thought is deeply mistaken. To see this, however, we must first of all understand the received view more clearly.

A crude way of interpreting the claim is to think of art works as valuable solely as a means to some end. So one might think that a work is good only to the extent that it enables us to feel pleasure, achieve personal insight or challenge social norms. This simplistic assumption is a non-starter. Consider, for example, money. Money as such is only valued for the experiences it makes possible but it plays no part in shaping them – its relationship to them is external. The £10 you pay to go to a Matisse exhibition plays no role in shaping or constituting the nature of the experiences it enables you to have. To take another example, consider certain kinds of drugs. A drug can induce a particularly pleasurable state of mind by virtue of its causal powers interacting with your physiological system. But how you arrive at the state of pleasure, by taking the drug, bears no internal relation to why the state is desirable. Yet we don't just value art works in this way. It may be true that both looking at Holbein's *Ambassadors* (1533), see pp. 94–5, and taking Prozac help to relieve someone from their woes and afford a sense of pleasure and relief. But the feeling caused by Prozac is not a function of his or her mental engagement with anything and is independent of the will. By contrast, in the case of *The Ambassadors* the experience is a direct result of his or her engagement with the work. So the nature of the experience afforded by good art is not wholly specifiable independently of the nature of the work. However, there are things we value in terms of the ends realised, where the means partly constitute and are internal to the ends involved. The pleasures afforded by coffee drinking, smoking, good conversation or sport are not wholly specifiable independently of the nature of the objects or activities involved.[8] Just think, for example, how one goes about explaining the interest of sport to those who don't get it. One might start by saying that such things give one pleasure, but rapidly one must appeal to how and why pleasure arises in ways intimately bound to the nature of the activity. It is impossible to specify the kinds of pleasures involved in watching football, say, without describing how the game gives rise to the confrontation of combating teams, the kind of individual skills that can be deployed, the tactical guile often required, and how a pass can be elegant and beautiful. So too it would seem with art generally. So valuing art in terms of the experiences afforded can, it might be thought, do justice to how and why we attend to and appreciate the specific features of works in a way which is not crudely utilitarian.

Now let us return to Malraux's imaginary museum. Imagine that in the centre of the museum is a large, sealed room which no one can enter. Unlike every other room in the museum, this room does not contain copies of great works but contains originals. The works by Michelangelo, Leonardo, Caravaggio, Poussin, Vermeer, Picasso and Matisse that it contains are ones which no one has ever seen, of which there are no copies and there are no descriptions by the respective artists. Furthermore, let us imagine that no one will ever see them since the room was constructed in such a way that should it be opened the works will be destroyed. Nigel Warburton has suggested that a similar thought experiment shows that such works could not have any value.[9] If no one could experience them, then they could not afford anyone any valuable experiences. If a work can't afford valuable experiences then it can't be valuable as art. But this is the wrong inference to make. It is not that the works in the room aren't valuable. Rather, it is a grave misfortune that there are great works we're not in a position to appreciate.

The idea that what is valuable is reducible to the pleasure or value of experiences afforded is deeply suspect. Many pleasant experiences, ranging from delight in hearing the good news of a friend to admiring the insights embodied in a painting, depend on a prior belief that something worthwhile has happened or been achieved. And isn't it the good thing, rather than the experience it affords, that we fundamentally value? We also commonly recognise that certain works are good, though they may do nothing for us. For some the work of the seventeenth-century French painter Nicholas Poussin does very little. Poussin's work tend to address noble, serious and often biblical scenes, captured in highly idealised forms. He also developed an interest in landscapes and his later works tend towards the highly allegorical. His artistic development towards austere classicism, moving away from the influence of Titian, was particularly important and his emphasis on the importance of pictorial design and formal types, as opposed to the primacy of colour, had a lasting influence on French painting. Yet even those who find Poussin unaffecting recognise that Poussin was a great artist. Consider *The Adoration of the Golden Calf* (1634), see pp. 26–7.

It concerns the story from Exodus in the Old Testament when, with Moses long absent, the Israelites began to lose faith in their God. Moses's brother Aaron commanded them to smelt all their gold, sculpt it into the shape of a calf and worship the idol. Poussin's group of revelling dancers pulls one from the right middle ground of the canvas to the left foreground in a way which conveys the swaggering sense of ecstasy and increasing loss of self-control of the crowd worshipping their false god. The impression is heightened by the sight of Moses and Joshua in the background descending from Mount Sinai, enhancing the sense of just how far the Israelites have fallen away. The general use of colour is reminiscent of Titian: the oranges, reds and blues help to bring the pictorial composition together, and the portrayal of Aaron all in white, carried through to two of the central dancers swaying round the calf, picks him out as the central figure inspiring the frenzied adoration. Despite the sense of movement, the figures are captured in a frozen moment, with exaggerated gestures both conveying the sense of individual ecstasy and reinforcing the structural composition of the picture. Although more elaborate than much of his later work, and despite the complex depiction of emotions through the stance, expression, gestures and interrelations amongst the figures, the picture fails to move some people. It isn't necessarily because they fail to appreciate Poussin's work or find it pleasing, it is just that their experience of looking at it isn't a particularly rewarding one. There are many other paintings, including ones we would recognise to be of lesser worth, they would rather spend time with. None the less, we can recognise a work is a great painting despite the fact that it might not happen to move us. The nature of his artistic development, achievement and lasting influence all testify to just how good an artist Poussin was. Similarly, listening to opera or Bach's Cantatas fails to move some, yet we wouldn't dispute their greatness as art. So how we explain the value of a work in such cases can't just be a matter of the rewarding nature of the experiences afforded. For we can and do recognise works as good or great even where the experience they give rise to leaves us cold.

We can make the same point another way. Clearly misfortunes can be suffered or great things achieved even though we don't experience them. The point is quite a general one. If friends gossip maliciously behind my back or secretly break promises, then surely

Nicolas Poussin, *The Adoration of the Golden Calf* (1633–4). Courtesy of The National Gallery, London

I am the victim of a wrongdoing even though I don't consciously suffer in any way. If I give money to Oxfam, which helps to save the lives of some who would otherwise starve, then my action is a good one even though I may not be aware of what good if any it does. What is valuable in our lives significantly depends upon our realising or losing things we value; we do not value them merely because they yield pleasurable or rewarding experiences nor repudiate them because they fail to do so. The same holds true with respect to art. If no one knew about the room of originals in our imaginary museum, everyone just thought it a block of solid marble say, it would still be a misfortune that the works therein could never be seen by anyone, even though no one would be conscious of any loss. The scenario is not really as far fetched as all that. Many apparently great works have been lost to us forever, through the passing of time, historical accident or puritanical zeal and we are aware of works that have only just survived, whether whole or in fragments. The writings and sketches of Jan Bisschop, a seventeenth-century Dutch lawyer, are invaluable today precisely because he travelled widely in Europe and recorded many works now lost to us. The late fifteenth-/early sixteenth-century Venetian painter Giorgione stands at the forefront of Renaissance art even though very few of his paintings survived. He was the first painter primarily concerned with the evocation of feeling rather than the depiction of subject matter – so much so that some of his contemporaries were not sure of the subjects of some of his paintings. His influence on Titian, amongst others, was crucial. We also know that Michelangelo attempted to destroy his second *Pietà*, a sculpture of Mary holding the crucified Christ in her arms, which was being carved for his own tomb. So it is not unreasonable to assume that there were or could have been works which no one bar the artist themselves ever saw and which have been destroyed. If an artist creates a work which consists in the development of a unique style or which manifests individual artistic vision, then it constitutes an artistic achievement, and the work is of value, irrespective of whether anyone gets to see it or not. Hence its destruction would be a loss.

Many people might remain uneasy with this train of thought. Surely, you might think, what motivates the claim is the thought that if someone were to experience the works in the sealed room they *would* give rise to imaginatively rewarding experiences. All that has really been shown is that works can be good even though no one actually experiences them. Fair enough. But what makes works good or bad is their capacity to afford fruitful or impoverished experiences. A work is good in so far as were we to look at it we would find doing so deeply pleasurable and fulfilling. The recognition of a work's value despite the lack of a rewarding experience with it, like the reaction of some to Poussin, can be explained in terms of the recognition that the painting will give rise to worthwhile experiences in others. Perhaps the very same reasons that Poussin does nothing for some, where their tastes and dispositions are romantically inclined, suggest that it will delight those for whom classicism chimes with their attitudes, outlook and tastes.

Yet though this is a more sophisticated version of the received view, it remains inadequate. Any view which reduces the value of *all* art to the disposition to afford us rewarding experiences still can't capture how and why we value certain kinds of works. Consider cubism. Cubism proper developed around 1907–14 and is commonly held to be one of the definitive moments in Western art. Primarily developed by Picasso and Braque, cubism marked a turning away from the assumption that art should imitate or conform to our perception of the natural world by rejecting, amongst other things, the use of traditional perspective. Foregrounding the flat two-dimensionality of the canvas, objects were depicted in terms of their mass, solidity, shape and volume from a myriad of radically fragmented perspectives. Initially the representations of geometric structure from multiple viewpoints went hand in hand with minimal colouring such as ochres and greys, though as cubism developed it became more vivid and elaborate, and incorporated elements of collage. For cubism's contemporaries, and some art lovers exposed to cubism now, many cubist works don't tend to please the eye or delight the soul. In purely visual terms, the very two-dimensionality, lack of colour and jarring viewpoints of many cubist works render them visually dull and difficult. Yet though the visual experience of some such works may be relatively anaemic, these works are to be highly valued, for their interest lies more in the intellectual, artistic feat achieved. The artistic vision and courage required to break free from traditional modes of depiction is admirable and it is the very manner of doing so which is impressive. In simultaneously showing distinct, fractured aspects of the objects depicted, cubism gave birth to a radically new means of representation, thereby creating a new world of possibilities for the development of art in the twentieth century. Hence one of the dominant artistic concerns for the rest of the century was to be the drive towards visual abstraction. Thus in the case of cubism we see just why it is that we sometimes do and should devote our time and energy to looking at works which are valuable over and above the visually rewarding nature of the experience they give rise to.

A related flaw with any solely experience-based account of artistic value lies in its inability to acknowledge that certain works which are disposed to proffer us rewarding experiences ought not to be valued, at least not all that highly anyway. As we saw earlier, pastiches such as Van Meegeren's *Disciples at Emmaus* may well be visually rewarding. Yet their lack of originality, artistic individuality or distinctive qualities of mind explains why they are of minor worth in comparison to other truly artistic works which may give rise to the same kind of experience. Imagine another room in our imaginary museum which displays two canvases which are visually indistinguishable – in every respect they look exactly the same. Hence the possible experiences any viewer may have of them are exactly alike. Yet one work was created a hundred years before the other, giving rise to new artistic possibilities, presaging some of the main developments in art in the years to come and radically distinct from the art that had gone before it, whilst the later work is merely an artistic recreation of that which had preceded it (whether copied or independently arrived at). The differences in the relations between the respective works and the works of both the past and the future fundamentally affect their nature and value. One of the works constitutes an achievement that is in contact with, contributes to and is partly responsible for the development of art, whilst the other is merely parasitic upon and freewheels above the art of times past. To contribute to the artistic conversation of humanity both constitutes and reflects an achievement of high value, whilst merely recreating a fragment of conversation shorn of its original context, at least where there are no further artistic innovations, is utterly derivative. Our experiences with both works may be pleasant enough, but only one of them is of any great value.

Lastly, certain strands in contemporary art, which can be traced back to the early twentieth century, emphasise the performative aspect of a work at the expense of the experience afforded the viewer. Marcel Duchamp, often taken to be the father of conceptual art, famously submitted for an exhibition a French urinal turned upside down, signed R. Mutt and entitled *Fountain* (1917), see p. 131, and his *In Advance of a Broken Arm* (1915) consisted of a snow shovel bought over the counter from an ordinary hardware store. In the 1960s and 1970s the Italian arte povera movement exhibited objects made from 'worthless' materials such as soil and leaves whilst the Anglo-American Art and Language movement often exhibited straight text. Robert Rauschenberg even went as far as erasing a pencil drawing by another artist, Willem de Kooning, and exhibiting it as *Erased de Kooning Drawing* (1953). Much more recently Cornelia Parker's *The Distance: The Kiss with Added String* (2003) wrapped a mile of string round Rodin's *The Kiss* (1901–4), which was cut by a protesting gallery goer and then restored by Parker. How we should make sense of conceptual art is, as we'll see in chapter 3, a complex matter. But the above may be conceived of as attempts to make works where experience of the object is, if possible, beside the point. This *might* be somewhat strained. The Rauschenberg seems to work by priming the spectator to try and see what is left after the act of vandalism; the Parker by seeing Rodin's romantic couple as bound by romantic passion and illusions; Duchamp's works by prompting us to see ordinary objects in terms of art appreciation. But their value isn't wholly reducible to whatever experiences are afforded. Part of what is being drawn attention to is the underlying expressive gesture itself, via the presentation of the object, and it is towards the gesture itself, whether it's funny, ironic, contemptuous or commentating on society and the art world, that our meditations are drawn in considering their value.

Any conception of artistic value which places the entire burden on the viewer's experience, whether it be of a vulgar or sophisticated kind, cannot but be misguided. It is either a trivial commonplace, since valuing certain experiences with works highly depends on the prior recognition of artistic achievement, or it is manifestly false, because the nature and value of some artistic achievements can't be wholly reduced to the value of the experiences we are disposed to have towards them. Many fundamental artistic achievements and our experiences with art works are to be valued independently of the pleasure or rewarding experience caused.

The triumph of artistic imagination

If we think about artistic creation and appreciation, the fundamental nature of some works concerns the artist's imaginative expression. This is not to deny that artists set out to create works in order to get viewers to respond in certain ways or have certain kinds of experiences. But the intention to convey certain experiences to viewers is sometimes secondary to the intention to express the artistic imagination creatively. Conceiving of art in this way has strong affinities with Romanticism, that glorious tidal wave of protest that crashed against the Enlightenment. As an artistic movement it embraced artists as diverse as Goya, Blake, Turner, Delacroix and Gericault through to Byron, Shelley, Wordsworth and Coleridge. In philosophical terms it was arguably inspired by the work of Giambattista Vico and Hegel's critique of Kant, ranging from Schlegel, Schelling and Schiller through, much later on, to the work of Bergson and Collingwood. Romanticism often took all 'true' human activity as giving licence to the imagination, thereby enabling self-expression, whether of the individual or of the community. In doing so the imaginative play of the creative process itself was what gave rise to individual creation rather than conformity to universal, classical rules or ideals. And often art was taken to be the highest or purest form of such self-expression.

R. G. Collingwood, perhaps one of the most sophisticated and most misunderstood of expressivists about art, held that through the artist's expression art proper draws into consciousness our own thoughts, feelings and attitudes. Hence 'art is the community's medicine for the worst disease of the mind, the corruption of consciousness'.[10] His theory is often criticised for presenting art works as if they are mental items constructed in the artist's head, which need no physical embodiment, or as falsely limiting all art to the expression of emotion. Yet his theory needn't be so construed. Rather he can be seen as emphasising the imaginative creation on the part of the artist resulting in the work and the imaginative participation required by the audience to engage with and grasp aright what is being expressed through it.[11] Nor need his theory be limited to the expression of emotion but, rather, it can be taken to incorporate the direction of our inchoate thoughts, feelings and attitudes in engaging with and meditating upon the work.[12] Construing the claims in this way enables us to see how expression in at least some works plays a significant role.

It is tempting to assume that any imaginative artistic expression should be identified with an act of communication. But this is wrong. Consider actions generally for the moment. Think, for example, of people watching their favourite sporting team. Whether it be at an actual match, in a bar or watching alone at home on television, at crucial periods in a game people tend to gesticulate in anticipation or horror, cheer in exhortation, shout in anger or mutter in disgust. Often such actions are performed in order to communicate – the supporters at the match want to convey their sense of urgency to the team or people at the bar may want to show their disgust to others in the crowd. But they may, and often do, express themselves in this manner without any thought for what others think or how they may respond. Similarly the person alone at home doesn't express what he is thinking and feeling in order to communicate anything – since he knows full well that talking or gesticulating at the television communicates nothing to anyone. Actions we perform through which we intend to express our feelings, thoughts and attitudes need not have any communicative intent or thought for how others may respond. At least some works should be understood as the embodiment of just this kind of action.

Now, why think that some art is like this? Well, there are particular features of both artistic creation and appreciation that only make sense if we conceive of a work as, primarily, an act of imaginative expression. An artist may intend to create a certain kind of experience in his viewers, but this need not be so. The creation of artistic sketches, often constituted by the rough characterisation of colour, simplified delineation of structure or reworking of pictorial composition, is usually intended not for viewers to experience but for working out the basis of a possible work, for attempting to find particular solutions for a finished picture or for practising and developing the artist's technique, skills and interests.[13]

Take the case of Rodin, who left thousands of drawings behind. He didn't make many sculptures from his sketches; rather he drew many of them as studies in their own right either from life models or from sculptures. No doubt some part of the motivation was to help him realise the kind of animating principles he was striving for in his sculpture and, as in his drawings after Michelangelo, to grasp the differences between his own developing style and that of others. Part of the motivation also stemmed from the role drawing played for Rodin in perfecting his ability to capture sensuous feeling and emotions from the look of a thing. But, even though Rodin considered sketches and drawing to be of minor importance in comparison to sculpture, many of them none the less show an imaginative artistic mind at work. By the late 1880s and early 1890s Rodin had begun to develop a new method of 'instantaneous drawing'.[14] Unlike standard academic drawing of the time, Rodin's drawing started from contour heightened by wash, drawing from the model's unstable pose without taking his eyes off her, resulting in many correction lines, heightening the sense of movement or animation. An additional effect of such incisive contour drawing, through foregrounding mass and volume with minimal shading, is to convey a sense of the subject's individuality rather than con-formity to classical type. His use of translucent wash flattened the surface depth, with the implied volume marked out in sharp delineations. This enabled his drawings, many from moving dancers and models, to capture the sense of movement and rotation of the body. In such drawings we have an emphasis on composi-tional and design elements, some of which are a striking deviation from classical nude studies, in order to capture a sense of animation, shape and sensuousness. The specifically artistic innovative devel-opments in Rodin's line drawing enabled him to characterize the lines of gestures and actions in a more athletic, impulsive, vigorous manner, one which enhances the expression of animated form, movement and feeling. Many of these sketches were not made or intended for viewing, yet they involve intentional artistic expression. The artistic development, innovation and imaginative realisation of Rodin's artistic concerns in these sketches are what explain why they are so valuable. And the case of Rodin's sketches, far from being peculiar, is a standard one. From Rubens to Constable to Picasso, sketches and works artists did not intend to be appreciated by viewers express their artistic concerns and interests in ways which we value highly – and in some cases more so than some of the works they did intend to be seen. The work of naïve artists, such as the unschooled Alfred Wallis who greatly affected Ben Nicholson and the St Ives school, art brut, a term Jean Dubuffet coined for work produced by those outside the art world, and many private works produced by artists just couldn't be properly explained except in terms of the imaginative expression of artistic interests and concerns.

Even when we consider works created to be viewed or appreciated, we cannot always capture their value just in terms of the experiences afforded. I remember going to a Mondrian exhibition in the 1990s at what is now Tate Britain. My main reason for going was out of a sense of curiosity. I'd seen many Mondrian reproductions, all from his middle to late period, of geometric, abstract works with variations on the theme of rectangular shapes and colour (nearly all of which were red, yellow, blue, black, white or grey). I just couldn't understand what all the fuss was about. I knew that the Dutch painter was held to be one of the most important figures in the development of abstract art and, having gone through various phases of naturalism and symbolism, had slowly arrived at his more abstract style from 1914 on. I had no doubt that the formal qualities of his abstract canvases would be pleasing to look at. But not much more so than the kind of graphic design one might find in the Conran shop. So I was interested to see if there was anything more to Mondrian's work than just a sense of good visual abstraction. This is not to underestimate the beauty or achievements involved in good graphic design, but it shouldn't be confused with good or great art. The exhibition was something of a revelation. It was laid out chronologically and having passed through some of his striking and very beautiful earlier, more traditional work, I reached two series of canvases that, although concerned with the same subject matter, were increasingly abstract. The first series, his *Compositions* of 1912–13, depicted a flowering tree in increasingly fragmented and abstract terms. Here we start to glimpse Mondrian's developing concern with geometric patterns and hard lines, both horizontal and vertical, to get at the underlying structure of the naturalistic world of appearances. But the second series, the *Pier and Ocean* drawings leading up to his *Composition: 1916*, show both the nature of Mondrian's artistic development and what underlies his drive for geometric abstraction.

At the beginning of the series, one can see the pier in the canvas, delineated by vertical lines projecting depth, with the vertical and horizontal lines characterising the sea radiating outwards. But as the series progresses, the projection of depth increasingly diminishes, the crossing non-symmetrical straight lines lose any apparent representational function and at the end one can barely see any object depicted in the canvas. Then in the more abstracted *Composition No. 10, 1915* and later works in the same series one confronts canvases resonating with the same fractured geometric structure, refined into a somewhat cleaner grid system, yet still with the same open-ended, non-symmetric lines. It was here that I came to grasp the nature of Mondrian's artistic project. In the development of his art, Mondrian was interested in

Piet Mondrian, 1872–1944 *Composition No. 10 in Black and White, 1915 Oil on canvas*, 85 × 108 cm, Stichting Kröller-Müller © 2004 Mondrian/Holtzman Trust c/o hcr@hcrinternational.com

capturing what he took to be the underlying reality of things. The visual world is one of mere appearances which belies a deeper, underlying structure. When we look at the world, we cannot help but see landscapes, buildings, people and their shifting relations. The world of our visual experience is made up of discrete, particular objects, detailed surfaces, textures, relations of depth, distance and volume. But the underlying structure of the universe is not given in such details nor straightforwardly apprehended in our ordinary visual experience. Rather what underlie the world of visual appearance and enable us to experience it at all are certain structural, geometric and universal properties. What Mondrian was striving after in the drive towards abstraction was a kind of representation of the underlying formal properties that structure the world, and which enable us to experience it. Not only could one see that Mondrian's abstract work was motivated by this concern but importantly it chimes with Mondrian's commitment to theosophy, a mystical belief in the divine order of the universe underlying the material world. The crucial point here is that, unless one is concerned with what Mondrian was striving to capture and express in his artistic development, one will fail to understand and properly appreciate his art. A mere concern just with the experiences Mondrian's work may happen to give rise to would occlude the very nature of his abstract work.[15] The point is not just a conceptual one but has practical implications. It follows that though comparative or thematic exhibitions are interesting, none the less a crucial means of coming to understand the nature of an artist's work and what he expresses in it is exposure to an artist's chronological development and a grasp of what he was responding to. The recent trend away from chronological and historically comparative exhibitions can suggest fertile relations between different works and artists, but it would be problematic were they to supplant them, for a most informative means of coming to appreciate the nature of an artist's work would be lost. It also means that the once much celebrated 'death of the author', the idea that one can appreciate and understand works without reference to what artists took themselves to be expressing through their work, cannot be right.[16] The death of the author has hardly led to a dearth of criticism concerned with artists' own self-understandings. But in such cases the swathe of criticism that blithely ignores what artists strove to achieve, and instead focuses solely on the possible experiences any viewer could have with the work they created, is deeply misguided if not corrupt.

A different way of making the same point is to consider how we appreciate good religious, morally didactic or politically propagandistic art works. There has been a long tradition of looking at works in terms of their meanings, where the meaning is not reducible to the experiences to which the work gives rise. The value of such works, and the ways in which we appreciate them, all outstrip the nature of the experience afforded. For part of the reason we value them, where we do, arises from the understanding expressed through the work.

To take a classical example, Michelangelo's first *Pietà* (1499), see p. 43, carved when he was just 24, is one of the most beautiful and moving sculptures in the history of art. Commissioned around 1498 in Rome by Cardinal Groslaye, for the Chapel of the Kings of France in St Peter's Basilica, the sculpture is a work of staggering genius. Traditionally a Pietà, literally meaning pity, represents Mary in middle age holding the body of Christ, her dead son, depicted in a dark, gruesome manner, heavily emphasising the bloody marks from his crucifixion. The theme developed in fourteenth-century northern Europe, stemming from Germany, and popularly emphasised the tragic and horrific aspects of the scene. The emphasis on the grotesque was compounded by a certain compositional awkwardness – since Mary's holding of the fully grown Jesus commonly looked unstable. But Michelangelo's *Pietà* radically reshaped both the contemporary understanding of the Pietà and the principles of sculpture. Mary is represented as a very young woman, looking down upon the son she holds in her lap. In order for the pose to look natural, Michelangelo distorted and enlarged Mary's body from the waist down using the folds of cloth masking her legs to give the visual illusion of proportion. All the grotesque signs of violence on Christ's body have been done away with, the stigmata marked only by slightly visible indentations, and he lies as if asleep in her arms. Not only is Christ shown in a state of peace but Mary herself is beautiful and serene, looking down on her son's body with a mixture of awe, compassion, love and sorrow. Mary's pose echoes that traditionally used to represent the Annunciation, when she accepts, from the angel Gabriel, God's command that she be the mother of Christ. Traditionally Mary is represented facing Gabriel with one arm outstretched signalling initial reluctance, whilst the other is raised to show openness to the wishes of God, and her head is bowed in a sign of voluntary submission. The echoing of this very pose in the *Pietà*, unlike every other that went before it, suggests that years before when she chose to submit to God's wishes, she knew and understood the sacrifice that would be fulfilled by her son and thus the sacrifice that she herself was being asked to make. The sculpture does not just embody the awe, love, compassion and pity of Mary for her son. The greatness of Michelangelo's *Pietà* also lies in its expression of a particularly profound understanding of Mary's own sacrifice, which naturally gives rise to similar sentiments in us towards her. Thus it cannot just be the value of the experience afforded that we value, it must also be the understanding Michelangelo distinctively expresses through the work.

It is not just classical religious art that shows us a work's value isn't always wholly reducible to the value of the experience afforded to the spectator. Much art, of a propagandistic, moralistic or socially progressive bent, is designed to express attitudes and convictions whose values outstrip the experience. William Hogarth's *A Rake's Progress* (1735) and *Marriage à la Mode* (1743), both series of etchings, represent descent into vice and its concomitant 'rewards'. The neo-classical French painter Jacques-Louis David

Michelangelo Buonarroti, *Pietà* (1498–99), Basilica of St Peter, Vatican © 2004 Photo, SCALA, Florence

was closely identified with the French Revolution, becoming a deputy at one point, and his paintings eulogised figures such as Marat and later Napoleon. But even the historical paintings, such as *The Death of Socrates* (1787) and *Brutus and His Dead Sons* (1789), cannot be understood apart from their expression of stoic civic ideals of duty, honesty, courage and self-sacrifice. The point of glorifying such virtues was not just to represent them as noble in and of themselves, but to strengthen the self-conception and resolve of those committed to the revolutionary cause. Francisco de Goya's etching series *The Disasters of War* (1810–14), in its horrific portrayal of the atrocities on both sides of the Franco-Spanish war, constitutes one of the most profound protests against the savage inhumanity of war. Something which found an echo in the visceral howl of revulsion expressed in Picasso's *Guernica* (1937), a reaction to the vicious bombing of the Basque capital during the Spanish civil war. 'Painting', Picasso claimed, 'is not done to decorate apartments, it is an instrument of war against brutality and darkness.'[17] Even Vladimir Tatlin's formal *Model for the Monument of the Third International* (1920), modelling what would have been the tallest building in the world as a skeletal, slanting tower of steel surrounding revolving glass buildings, cannot be fully appreciated unless one realises the dynamic interplay of plastic forms and structure are a glorification of the Russian revolution. Due to house the revolutionary government of the future, its projected scale and upward thrust proclaim not just the arrival of the revolution, but the mechanical unfolding of its inevitable progress into the future. The revolution was the future. Contemporary art too is shot through with works which seek to make a moral or social point. Judy Chicago's *The Dinner Party* (1978) consists of a large triangular table, with thirty-nine place settings consisting of ceramic plates and embroidered decoration representing particular women to be honoured.[18] The materials themselves, china painting and embroidery, are associated with women and are, like women themselves the piece implies, falsely relegated to a lowly creative status. The names of another 900 women are written on the marble tiles on which the table rests, and the communal, domesticated nature of the piece points up a sense of the celebration of the unrecognised history and achievements of women. Chicago's work chimed in with the rise in the 1980s of social protest art which ranged in subject matter from feminism, race, identity and environmental issues to AIDS awareness. But contemporary art has also been concerned with social and moral issues in more traditional ways. Peter Howson's *Croatian and Muslim* (1994) is a painting of a vicious rape scene from the war in Bosnia. It attracted a huge amount of controversy, partly because he'd been commissioned by the British Imperial War Museum and The Times Newspapers to go to Bosnia. The depicted scene was an imaginary event rather than detailing a particular scene Howson had actually witnessed – it was his response to the stories he'd heard from many rape victims he had encountered. Howson's choice to represent an imaginary scene, to symbolise the actual incidences he'd heard of, and its uncompromising nature, the thuggish brutality and mundane violence, signifies the bestiality of man at war. Even now works are often censored because of their significance and artists in turn respond to censorship in a variety of ways. In 2003, Pedro Morales, the chosen artistic representative of Venezuela at the 50th Venice Biennale, had his show closed down by his government's officials. It was deemed unacceptably political since sections of his interactive digital allegory through a series of rooms, *City Rooms* (2003), involved social commentary of a political, religious and sexual nature with elements of horror and violence. So he wrapped the entire Venezuelan Pavilion in a stream of Venezuelan flags sewn together and given to him by an association from his country called 'People of Culture', thereby blocking off the empty pavilion. A gesture of protest, the nature and significance of which can't be reduced to the experience afforded.

Romanticism emphasised the creative role of the artist and demanded that art be the finest imaginative expression of the human mind. Taken as a view of what all art must be, or the doctrine that art should only be valued in such terms, it loses sight of much that we appreciate art for. The excesses of Romanticism should not be allowed to cloak its insights. Held as a conception of what we value in some art, it contains an important truth. Originals matter where, given their relation to the artist, they constitute an imaginative achievement in a way in which forgeries and pastiches do not. Originality, and distinctive artistic expression, are often to be valued in ways which can't be captured by the sum of our experiences with a work. The artistry, expression of inner life, attitudes and meanings fundamental to appreciating many works aren't always exhausted by the value of the experiences afforded. Thus is some of the motivation for Romanticism vindicated. As a movement, it foregrounded expression by pulling away from the Enlightenment aspiration of conformity to universal ideals and classical conceptions of beauty. This leads us to the question: what, if any, is the nature and role of beauty in art?

Chapter Two | Beauty Resurrected

The death of beauty?

'The impulse of modern art is to destroy beauty.'[1] Thus, in 1948, did the American painter Barnett Newman identify one of the driving motivations of twentieth-century art. The pursuit of beauty was renounced, derided and left out in the cold.

This is not to say that particular artists and movements didn't still devote themselves, in new ways, to the evocation of beauty. Indeed the drive towards abstraction was taken by some to dovetail with its pursuit. As a young fauve (meaning 'wild beast'), Matisse, alongside other artists such as Derain, painted scenes with intense non-naturalistic colours. Throughout endless artistic mutations to his final cancer-ridden years, in which period he made abstract patterns from vividly coloured paper cut-outs, Matisse pursued beauty. Despite his formal ingenuity, Matisse's avowed lack of interest in expressing the troubles, horrors and self-doubts of the modern age set him against the artistic tenor of his age. It is a tribute to both his integrity and his genius that he was still recognised as a great artist; indeed Picasso saw Matisse as his only rival. Matisse's art did not seek to change the world or reject the art of the past. He aspired to create works that would sing with beauty. In his own lifetime Matisse lived through the machine age, the triumph of the city, the great depression, the end of empires, two world wars and political revolutions. Yet his work remained untouched by it all. Famously Matisse once wrote he dreamt of 'an art of balance, of purity and serenity, devoid of troubling or depressing subject-matter, an art which could be for every mental worker, for the business man as well as the man of letters, for example, a soothing, calming influence on the mind, something like a good armchair which provides relaxation from physical fatigue'.[2] The comparison is somewhat unfortunate. The idea of an easy, untroubling beauty akin to physical relief is open to cheap mockery, as is the apparent concern to alleviate the stresses of the bourgeoisie. But, as we will see, true beauty can be easy in the sense of being free from our practical concerns, interests and desires. It is no less demanding for all that and it is something to be cherished. As can be seen from his *Pink Nude* (1935), see p. 217, Matisse's work is indisputably modern in emphasising expression over naturalism and in its painterly concern with pictorial planes. None the less, Matisse articulates just what so much art of the past century took itself to be rejecting. His work embodies a traditional notion of art as beauty; timeless, self-sufficient, set apart from the world.

The plethora of artistic movements spawned in the dawn of the early twentieth century to its dwindling twilight, from expressionism, Dada, surrealism and abstractionism to pop art, conceptual art and various post-modern fragmentations, stand in complex relations to one another, sometimes antagonistic, sometimes complementary, but a significant strand concerns the cultivation of an anti-aesthetic sensibility. At best beauty and the pleasure it affords were deemed by many to be incidental to the value of art and, at worst, something to be positively eschewed. The reasons for this reaction against beauty were twofold. On the one hand, beauty was regarded as a trivial pleasure and thus irrelevant. The purpose of art, freed from the shackles of naturalism, was to change things. Art should sear, shock, unsettle, disturb, disconcert and enrage. It should awaken people from the dull slumbers of conventionality and confront them with the real world, themselves and the possibilities of change – something which modern society made them otherwise too desensitised to see. On the other hand, the very idea that beauty was something set apart from practical concerns, especially socio-political ones, was thought to be illusory. For what was found to be beautiful by particular groups of people was surely just an upshot of their background, class, education and environment. Hence André Breton, in exalting modern art's aim of unsettling bourgeois assumptions and values, condemned Matisse and Derain (whilst extolling the virtues of Picasso) for producing art which lacked any meaning, serving only to please and reinforce that which should be challenged; such artists 'have passed into a tiny arena: their gratitude to those who make them and keep them alive. A *Nude* by Derain, a new *Window* by Matisse – what surer testimony could there be to the truth of the contention that "not all the water in the sea would suffice to wash out one drop of intellectual blood"?'[3]

For Breton, artists like Matisse possessed neither intellectual blood nor backbone. Their preoccupation with the look of things, with mere painterly affairs, abrogated art's concern with inner reality. The only art worth bothering with, according to Breton, is that which challenges our self-conceptions and understanding of the world. The anti-aesthetic revolution in artistic practice foreshadowed a much later intellectual one. But to grasp the nature of the revolution we have to understand what was being revolted against.

The sensual, the beautiful and the good

In more academic and intellectual circles the assumed importance of beauty in art held sway for much longer. It's true that as early as 1896 Tolstoy had dismissed the idea that beauty, and any pleasure-based conception, could account for the value of art. Instead, for Tolstoy, good or great art should involve a kind of emotional, moral and spiritual communion. But Tolstoy was swimming against the dominant intellectual current. In 1913 Clive Bell, the high priest of formalism, did dismiss talk of beauty as useless. Rather, for Bell, good art gives rise to a distinct emotional state in us via its 'significant form' (an opaque notion if ever there was one). But Bell's formalism was an attempt to capture something like the traditional notion of beauty in a way which made sense of contemporary art's break with the past. And as late as the 1960s Clement Greenberg was still arguing for a kind of formalist analysis, where what mattered was the felt quality of our experience, and philosophers remained preoccupied with beauty, its properties and the conditions of appreciation. The lineage of such views can be traced back to Kant's magisterial *Critique of Judgement* written in 1790. Taking beauty as the central aesthetic judgement, Kant sought to resolve a fundamental problem. To claim that something is beautiful is a subjective matter, since it's based on the pleasure we feel in experiencing it. Yet when we claim something is beautiful, the judgement apparently lays claim to objectivity, since we expect people to agree with us. Kant's attempt to show how both these seemingly inconsistent assumptions can be reconciled, and thereby account for the nature of true beauty, exercised a profound grip on intellectual approaches to art for centuries to come.

The key to Kant's thought is the carving out of aesthetic judgements as radically distinct in kind from both judgements of goodness and the merely agreeable.[4] To judge something to be good or agreeable is to take an interest in it. Here in Leeds, on the ground floor of the University's Michael Sadler (Arts) building, there is a sculpture relief by Eric Gill. Originally commissioned by the city's patricians as a memorial to those who died in the First World War, Gill sculpted Christ driving the money changers out of the temple, with the fleeing financial traders depicted as contemporary industrial barons. Unsurprisingly the city fathers were furious, though the letter of the commission had been fulfilled so they were forced to accept it. A skilful but fairly derivative memorial, still standing in the city centre to this day, was commissioned in its place. Bent on having Gill's memorial destroyed, they only held back because the University stepped in to save it (though this was conditional on the University's being prohibited from putting it on public display). We could delight in the sculpture for many reasons: as something worth a lot of money to the University; as a memorial to the dead; as a condemnation of capitalism. Yet such pleasures are the result of judging the relief to be good in terms of some end – fiscal, sentimental or moral. Kant claimed that to appreciate it aesthetically we should not be interested in the ends to which it could be put but appreciate its form. We look at it as something patterned by purposiveness or design, but without further concern for the theoretical or practical ends to which it may answer. To delight in the sculpture as art is to take pleasure in it for its own sake.

The pleasures of the merely agreeable, by contrast, satisfy us just because we happen to be a certain way. People tend to like sweet things, soft textures and fairly light, bright colours whereas they tend to shy away from bitter tastes, harsh materials and dark, subdued tones. Of course, not only does what cause us sensual pleasure change as our tastes develop and modify, but since such pleasures are a function of our particular desires, interests and appetites, they will typically vary. I might get a certain pleasure from looking at works by Matisse just because I like the colours he uses, just as I like my coffee to be strong, quite bitter and sweetened with sugar (espresso only). But those particular colours might do nothing for someone else, just as they may prefer tea to coffee. It is not as if one of us would be right and the other mistaken in some way. Such preferences are utterly contingent. It could even be the case that everyone shared certain tastes. The French artist Yves Klein, who rose to prominence from the mid-1950s and who died in 1962 at the age of 34, patented a particular shade of blue in 1957. International Klein Blue, as it is called, is the most vivid and intense shade of ultramarine. Now everyone I know who has seen the colour likes it and it could be that everyone would do so. So the identical monchrome paintings he did of IKB without surface texture or interest might give pleasure to all. But, for Kant, this would show only that we happen to have a preference in common. It is a mere sensual pleasure that depends upon our contingent, empirical nature. Things could have been otherwise.

By contrast, that which is truly beautiful, or more broadly aesthetic, affords pleasure by engaging mental structures which we must all share in virtue of being rational embodied creatures. The details of Kant's account rest upon a grand philosophical architecture, the construction of which is breathtaking in its complexity and profundity. But as contentious as some of the underpinnings may be, and as elusive as some of the finishing touches are, the core thought may be put simply enough. What it is to be a rational creature, amongst other things, is to be capable of perceptions, thoughts, beliefs and imagining different possibilities. In order to do this we must be able to perceive and think of things by forming our experience in terms of concepts. I perceive the object I am writing on *as* a table, *as* constituted by a block of wood or *as* rectangular in shape. All human beings, as rational persons, necessarily have the capacity to perceive and think of experience in terms of concepts. Standardly, we're interested in what's in front of us; what an object is, or might tell us. The concepts implicit in perception or thought usually seek to capture an object's nature in relation to my interests. You must perceive it as having a certain shape if you are to perceive it as a distinct object at all; you need to know whether the object is really there, if you want to walk by; if it's a table, if you want to write on it. For Kant it is the imagination which enables us to give form to experience. Landscapes and art works which stimulate the free play of imagination, under certain conditions, give rise to an aesthetic judgement.[5]

Kant's truly aesthetic judgement must fulfil four conditions.[6] (1) It must be disinterested. In the case of aesthetic appreciation we're not interested in an object in terms of information, knowledge, satisfaction of sensual pleasure or desire. (2) It imputes universality in the sense that judging something to be beautiful implies that everyone else will find such pleasure in their contemplation of it. (3) The pleasure is derived from its form of finality: we're interested in the purposive form of our experience afforded by the object for its own sake; we're unconcerned with what theoretical or practical purpose it may have been made to serve or the ends it might fulfil. (4) The universality of the pleasure is not merely contingent but necessary since it is an upshot of the operations of the mind we all necessarily share. Kant attempts to resolve the problem of aesthetic judgement by holding that aesthetic judgement is subjective, because it involves the feeling of pleasure, whilst none the less making claim to necessary universal validity over all embodied, rational, judging subjects. To make a judgement of beauty is to command or expect agreement from others. The originality of Kant's attempted solution lies in the claim that taste has 'subjective universality.'

Kant's view is often represented as if he held to the view that only the formal qualities of a work count or that judgements of beauty are devoid of context, content or purpose.[7] This is true enough of Bell's notion of aesthetic appreciation. For Bell, it is the combinations of lines and colours alone which gives rise to the all important 'significant form' and representational content is utterly irrelevant:

> if a representative form has value, it is as form, not as representation. The representative element in a work of art may or may not be harmful; always it is irrelevant. For, to appreciate a work of art we need bring with us nothing from life, no knowledge of its ideas and affairs, no familiarity with its emotions. Art transports us from the world of man's activity to a world of aesthetic exaltation.[8]

But Kant himself distinguished between what he called free beauty and dependent beauty. Free beauty is indeed just a matter of something's formal interrelations, whether it be a landscape or marks on a canvas. Dependent beauty, however, is where the pleasure we take is aesthetic, since it is devoid of any sensual, practical or reasoned interest, but does depend upon attending to a work in terms of particular determinate concepts. No doubt some art works are freely beautiful, but most representational works, where they are beautiful, will be cases of dependent beauty.[9]

Consider Picasso's *Weeping Woman* (1937), see p. 56. The painting represents a woman's fingers slashing across her face, a tear drop acidly gouging her cheek. There are complex interrelations between the work's form and the ways in which that form coheres with, and represents, a particularly vicious form of grief. Appreciating the work involves delighting in its form as an aesthetically artful and apposite means of portraying such grief. The interrelations between the work's formal qualities and its content or what it represents are crucial. To understand it, one must not only have the concept grief, but grasp the ways in which it can be searing, vicious and possessive. Hence appreciating *Weeping Woman* is a case of dependent beauty. Kant's account recognises, in a way Bell's theory never did, the importance of form and content. And Kant's claim is that where one does possess the relevant concepts, and the proper pleasure is afforded, such a work is truly beautiful. Thus we may, or may not, happen to find similar things agreeable, but we ought to agree about what is beautiful. Judgements of beauty are necessarily universal.

How does Kant explain actual disagreement then? If someone says of Matisse's *Pink Nude* (1935), see p. 217, that it is truly beautiful and yet someone else denies this, what's going on? According

Pablo Picasso, *Weeping Woman* (1937) © Succession Picasso / DACS. Photograph © Tate, London 2003

to Kant, conflicting judgements are a function of confusing aesthetic pleasures with sensual and practical ones, comparing judgements of free beauty with judgements of dependent beauty or a failure to see the work in terms of the relevant concepts.[10] We can be mistaken, and no doubt often are, in believing we are making an aesthetic judgement when actually we're not since we may be judging something to be merely agreeable. We mistake one kind of pleasure for another. Furthermore, since our own motivations and the workings of our minds are often opaque to us we can never finally know whether the conditions for aesthetic judgement have been truly fulfilled or not. Hence we can't always settle disagreements because we often don't know whether we're prey to such a confusion in a particular case. But disagreement is far less common than we might think and it is often resolved in ways which suggest something is right about Kant's theory. Just think how we discuss our responses. Where there's apparent conflict we often ask each other why we're not responding in the same way. In the case of the *Pink Nude* someone may be underwhelmed because they find the woman unattractive, seeing the figure as an ill-proportioned representation. They feel dissatisfied since the painting doesn't seem to tell us anything. But such reasons suggest a failure of just the kind Kant identifies. If someone is concerned with whether or not the figure represented is attractive, then they're hardly interested in the work as such. What's driving the judgement is whether their particular sensual desires are spoken to or not. And, as we commonly recognise, beauty doesn't necessarily speak to desire just as desire isn't always geared towards the beautiful. If someone looks at the figure as a naturalistic representation of female form, then the disproportionately small size of the head, the elongated torso and impossibly stretched arms will seem like an ugly aberration. But this is to misconstrue what Matisse is doing in the picture, in which case one lacks the relevant understanding. And to be dissatisfied with a work for its want of a message is a disappointment borne of the failure to fulfil a practical interest. Hence we sometimes confuse the frustrations of our practical interests, or our lack of understanding, with a failure in the work. Conversely, we're familiar enough with recognising that particular works we once loved are not really that good, but spoke to particular passions or fashions or attitudes that once possessed us. In such cases our judgements were not fully disinterested. We often overestimate the worth of works because we confuse the pleasures of the senses, recognition and meaning with the pleasures of true beauty.

The virtues of aestheticism

Kant's theory is not only profoundly beautiful but attractive for several reasons. It shows us why the value of a work is not reducible to its content. A worrying tendency in contemporary art has been the emphasis on the meaning of a work at the expense of aesthetic virtues. A good example is the American artist Barbara Kruger. Kruger's work juxtaposes images and texts in a manner familiar from graphic design and advertising. The aim is to challenge the viewer with views on matters as diverse as marriage, abortion, commercialism and freedom. *Untitled (You are a captive audience)* (1992) is a photograph of a male hand placing a wedding ring upon the finger of a female hand overwritten by the words 'You are a captive audience'. It neatly captures a familiar feminist attitude towards marriage. But, it should be asked, in what way is this anything more than illustration? Illustrating thoughts, beliefs or attitudes can't be sufficient for making good art. Otherwise almost every depiction would qualify. Kant proffers a means by which we can distinguish mere illustrations from art works. What matters is the interpenetration of a work's content with the distinctively aesthetic experience it affords in shaping how we respond.

It is illuminating to contrast Kruger's aesthetically crude moralising with Goya's *The Third of May 1808, Execution of the Revolutionaries* (1814), see pp. 60–1.

Goya's concern is to confront us with and condemn the unadulterated harshness of war. The structural composition guides our visual attention from the faceless row of soldiers on the right, along their converging muskets, towards a brightly lit central figure. His posture is reminiscent of the crucifixion, and the lighting emphasises his vitality and individuality against the mass of ranked soldiers. Even Goya's use of paint shapes our visual and cognitive responses. If we look closely we see the roughly treated surface, the lightning stripe of the soldier's sword sheath in the foreground, the scraped, coagulated, dark splotches of crimson blood and the smeared facial features of the foremost prostrate figure, his individuality blotted out. Thus are we reminded of the swift harshness of merciless actions, the sharp precision of weapons of war, the look and texture of dried blood, and the blurred features of the disfigured we would rather not dwell on in detail. It's not a visual report or moralised illustration but a deeply horrifying work of art. The cruel obliteration of individual life strikes us to the quick. It is true that form is important to Kruger's work since the delivery of her message via the means of advertising and rhetoric is important to the meaning of her works. But this is insufficient to make it as good as art as Goya's work. What makes

Francesco Goya, *The Third of May 1808*
(1814). Derechos reservados © Museo
Nacional del Prado – Madrid

the difference? Goya's use of artistic means to shape and inter-penetrate the aesthetic aspects of the work with its content works at many levels. Mere illustrations and mediocre didacticism do no such thing or, at best, only superficially.

Kant's view also explains how we can value works that embrace views with which we disagree. Consider Masaccio's fresco Paradise Lost, containing the *Expulsion of Adam and Eve* (1426–7) in the Brancacci Chapel of the Santa Maria del Carmine in Florence. Masaccio was one of the originators of the Renaissance at the start of the fourteenth century and died tragically young at the age of 27. His greatest concern lay in the representation of three dimensions on the flat pictorial surface, leading him to master the newly devel-oped use of perspective, but his work has a profound expressive resonance and aesthetic grandeur. In the *Expulsion* we see Adam and Eve walking out from the Garden of Eden in despair at their banishment. Eve's uplifted, blank, open-mouthed face expresses utter loss. Her furthest arm slopes down to cover her genitals and her nearest arm is pulled across to cover her breasts in a posture of bodily shame and modesty. Closer yet to the viewer, his head and chest next to hers, Adam's head is buried in his hands with despair and shame at his own weakness. The triangular bodily planes point towards the genitals of both Adam and Eve, the source of their awareness and shame, with the angel above driving them onwards in unquestioning flight. Amongst other things, we have the embodiment of a severe religious suspicion of fleshly temp-tation, the commendation of shame at bodily awareness and the expulsion of mankind from a perfect heavenly state. For those unsympathetic to such a conception, such a work manifests atti-tudes thought to be fundamentally false and pernicious. Yet one needn't hold any of the beliefs or attitudes the work extols to appreciate it as art. This kind of sophisticated aestheticism draws a sharp distinction in principle between engaging with a work as art and evaluating it in terms of the truth or otherwise of the beliefs and attitudes represented. Considering Masaccio's work as a representational aid to devotion is one thing. But considered as art, we can appreciate the structural composition, its expressive features, the interpenetration of form and content, without any further concern for the beliefs represented. The truth or falsity, perniciousness or harmlessness of the attitudes conveyed are beside the point aesthetically speaking.[11]

Kant's account marks out art appreciation as a distinct kind of activity. Engaging with art works requires a special kind of attention to its aesthetic features. This distinguishes art proper from the functional artefacts of culture. The products of culture, for example those that are typically commercial and which aim to please, are evaluated in terms of their goals, such as the provision of diverting entertainment, or often possess moral ends, hence they are didactic in pushing some moral, social or political message. But being pleasing to the eye and absorbing, as many programmes and posters and much graphic design are, or didactically striving to communicate a message, as in much of advertising, propaganda and moralising illustrations, is insufficient for something to be good art. Where entertainment or the drive to communicate a message predominates, on the Kantian view, everyday culture cannot hope to rise to the level of art, for the purposes of mass culture artefacts are indifferent to the promotion of aesthetic features.[12] This is not to say that anything produced as culture cannot rise to the realm of genuine art. But where this is the case it will be a rare coincidence, since it will be despite operating within commercially imposed constraints that the artists concerned have been able to promote aesthetic features above all else. Art proper has as its autonomous goal the promotion of aesthetic values, to which all other considerations are subservient. Hence Kant's account makes a stark distinction between high art and culture by emphasising the distinctness of aesthetic experience and its pleasures.

I've spent some time characterising the apparent attractions of Kant's theory since, from the later part of the twentieth century to the present day, the tendency has been to dismiss it as a bewitching illusion. The very idea that judgements of beauty are necessarily universal is regarded as a romantic myth that has outlived its use. Furthermore the notion of disinterested appreciation central to Kant's theory, it's commonly assumed, has been shown to be impossible. Without it, the entire structure gives way and all we are left with are the poignant, evocative remnants of an edifice which bears witness to a once cherished but futile vision of a common human sensibility. We'll consider questions about the universality and justification of artistic judgements in the final chapter. But independently of those concerns, the case against Kant is threefold and can be summed up under the following headings: the cult of aesthetic appreciation; the delights of ugliness and the disgusting; meaning matters. Each individual objection is thought to show Kant's theory to be in error; taken together they are thought to be unanswerable. None the less, as we shall see, there is something worth salvaging from Kant's account of aesthetic appreciation.

The cult of aesthetic appreciation

It has been objected to Kant's notion of aesthetic appreciation that we are sometimes interested in the existence or nature of what we are looking at.[13] Hence aesthetic appreciation can't be disinterested. For example, it matters to us that Goya's *The Third of May*, see pp. 60–1, depicts something like what actually happened in the Spanish war. But this is unproblematic; the crucial thing is that our aesthetic appreciation cannot be reduced to that kind of interest. We aesthetically appreciate Goya's depiction in a way in which we would not appreciate a clumsy, ham-fisted representation of the same event. Similarly it might be thought that aesthetic appreciation can't be truly disinterested since we are interested in whether or not we derive pleasure from looking at it. This would be based on a crude misunderstanding of the way in which Kant uses the term. Disinterestedness does not mean we are detached or unconcerned with whether looking at a work affords us delight or not. It just means that our pleasure cannot be reduced to any sensual, practical or theoretical interest.

However, a much more forceful objection is often taken to strike at the core of Kant's notion of aesthetic appreciation. At the turn of the last century, Kant's notion of disinterestedness tended to be psychologised as a distinct mode of perceptual attending which could be switched on and off at will, though perhaps sometimes overridden by more immediate practical concerns. We may start to admire the branching pattern of blood as it runs from a cut finger but the pain involved may prevent our continuing to admire it for too long. The classic source for this is Edward Bullough, who introduced the term 'psychical distance' to capture the idea that aesthetic appreciation requires a certain psychological distance from one's own immediate concerns and interests. Perhaps the most philosophically sophisticated version of this kind of account is articulated by Jerome Stolnitz.[14] Admirers of this notion of aesthetic disinterestedness often looked to Gestalt psychology to support their claim. The most famous example of Gestalt perception is the duck rabbit picture:

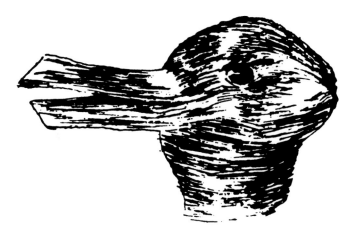

Gestalt duck-rabbit image

Looked at in one way we can see it as an outline of a rabbit and looked at in another as the outline of a duck. So too, it is thought, we can switch between aesthetic, practical and theoretical modes of interest.

This psychologised notion of disinterestedness marks out aesthetic appreciation from other forms of attention as taking up a distinctive kind of perceptual attitude. The basic idea is that the attitude we take up guides our perception in terms of the things we notice and how we respond to them. Normally our attitude is one of practical or theoretical interest. We are interested in what an object is, what knowledge we can infer from it or what we can or ought to do with it. But in the aesthetic case we have no further interest in it except in terms of whether attending to its pattern and structure affords us delight or not. We might look at a tree in the garden and be interested in it in terms of what species it is (theoretical interest) or whether it is blocking out the sun and should be cut back (practical interest). But we might just sit back and attend to the contours of the trunk and branches, their stratification, the way the leaves rustle and sway gently in the wind, the dappled shadows cast on the bough, the bent-arm-like crook of a branch as it stretches out. In this case we're disinterested since we look at the tree and, if we're lucky, so doing will afford us pleasure. Similarly we might look at Goya's *The Third of May* in terms of historical interest: does it represent an execution that actually happened; were the executions typically carried out in such a fashion? Alternatively our interest might be aesthetic, where we pay attention to the compositional structure which draws our eye towards the central figure in white or how the coagulating, smeared and quicksilver blood gleams and darkens.

The objection is this. The aesthetic attitude is characterised in terms of a distinctive motivation for attending to works. But it doesn't seem to pick out a distinctive kind of perceptual attention. We do approach works with different interests. Someone may go to see the Goya because they're interested in the history of the period, because they're interested in the kind of materials used or because they want to enjoy looking at it as a painting. But the difference is a matter not so much of distinct attitudes but of different motivations.[15] Hence someone might go to see the Goya out of historical interest and, as they look at it, start to appreciate it aesthetically. But as they start to appreciate it as a painting they don't thereby suddenly switch to some distinct mode of attending. So the notion of an aesthetic attitude is a myth. No doubt it proved useful, in reinforcing the primacy of art appreciation over and above the didactic, moralising or commercial pressures often brought to bear on art but it remains an illusion. At best we should just talk of a concern with the artistically constructed design features of a work.[16]

Although those who psychologised Kant's notion of disinterestedness seem vulnerable to this objection it is not clear that Kant himself is. Kant does not hold that aesthetic experience involves suddenly switching to some ineffable perceptual state radically distinct in kind from ordinary perception. Disinterestedness for Kant does not characterise a distinct psychological state of mind but, rather, the grounds of the response to the object in aesthetic judgement. In a proper aesthetic judgement, the pleasure cannot depend upon any particular interest in the work and must be a function of attending to its form. This may hold true even in the case of someone who is originally motivated to attend to a work for interested reasons. What disinterestedness consists in, for Kant, is attention which is free from or not constrained by theoretical or practical interests.

None the less there is reason to hold that it is a mark of our being disinterested that there may be a difference in the way we perceptually process and respond to objects when we're appreciating them aesthetically from when we're not. Imagine three trainee photo-journalists who, as an assignment, are told to go to a current Henri Cartier-Bresson exhibition. Cartier-Bresson was one of the founders of the Magnum photographic agency and is famous not only for his striking visual images but for the instantaneous impression of movement captured from many of his subjects. The students end up settling in front of one of his portraits of Alberto Giacometti and one of them says to the others:

I can see why we were told to come but what I don't get is why this
is all in an art gallery. The images are forceful, the sense of a specific
moment is vivid and he's a good photo-journalist. But why is this kind
of documentary photography supposed to be appreciated in some
weird aesthetic way? They're just images like any others, only more
striking, of events that happened. I look at them the same way I look
at all photos in newspapers. The pleasure I get is no different from the
pleasure I get from lots of other photographs which aren't put in art
galleries.

The second student doesn't start talking about some peculiar rarified response. He points to the Giacometti and says:

Look at the structure. Not just any image of him with his sculptures
would be as good. The sculpture is in the foreground, mottled, the
clay pressed deep with fingers and facing Giacometti. The artist
is facing the sculpture, each mirroring the other's posture, and his
left hand is reaching out touching the shoulder of the sculpture. This
brings them close together, so your eye sweeps round, as if one is
embracing the other in an act of creation and fatherly devotion.
It's like a visual allusion to Michelangelo's *Creation* where God
brings Adam to life. The effects of the light and shading also give
Giacometti's skin a mottled, worn and worked texture similar to the
sculpture's. Noticing that it's the sculptor facing one of his works isn't
enough. You have to look at the way in which the photograph is
composed, how it shapes, organizes and highlights certain features in
your experience of it, the way in which those elements are related to
one another within the visual structure of the whole image. If you can
see this in the image then you are looking at it aesthetically; you'll
notice how the hand is foregrounded, the mirroring stare and posture

of artist and sculpture. Once you start engaging with the visual relationships in the image you'll find yourself drawn in, looking for them in a way you haven't been, precisely because it's pleasurable and rewarding in a way most photographs aren't – because they lack these kinds of complex visual relations.

The third student then adds:

> Look I agree with your characterization of the photograph. I can see how the visual relations are structured, their interaction and how they shape the way I look at the picture. So I can take an aesthetic interest in it but it just doesn't do anything for me. I'm not disputing it's good, but all I get is the recognition without any real enjoyment.

The difference between the last two students lies in the fact that both of them take an aesthetic interest in the photograph but only the second student derives any delight from doing so. So taking an aesthetic interest in a work is necessary but not sufficient for aesthetic delight. Now according to Kant a truly aesthetic judgement is one which is not just disinterested, but universal, necessary, and the pleasure taken lies in the object's form for its own sake. The difference between the second and third students brings pressure to bear on the interrelatedness of these conditions. For the third student is not saying that the work is not beautiful, just that he doesn't derive any pleasure himself from looking at it. It seems common enough to think that something is truly beautiful without feeling any delight. A common enough case is the recognition that someone is beautiful, and you can see how and why this is so, yet looking at him or her doesn't really do very much for you. But because you can see that someone is beautiful you know why that may do something for others. On Kant's account this doesn't make sense: such judgements cannot be aesthetic but merely matters of taste concerning the agreeable. In the final chapter, through considering whether such delight in judgements of beauty or artistic value really must be universal, I will suggest otherwise. For, unlike Kant, I will suggest we should think of judgements of artistic value, including beauty, as partly being expressions of our character, and the nature of our characters can blamelessly differ.

None the less, the ways in which the first student and the other two originally look at the image differ in terms of the features they attend to, the visual relationships they are interested in and so on. Only in the latter two cases can we say they are looking at the picture aesthetically. Whether someone wants to call this kind of aesthetic appreciation disinterested or not is neither here nor there. What is important is that looking for visual relations in this way, and responding to them, is distinct from the mere visual recognition of what the image depicts. It marks out an aesthetic interest.

We can develop this thought more fully by considering the nature of ordinary object or image recognition. We tend to think of perception as a matter of conceptualising the raw information and sensations we are subject to via our distinct sense modalities. But even when a perceptual state is caused by what it represents, for example my seeing smoke is caused by the smoke from the fire, the information carried is less specific and more profuse than what we experience it as representing. Hence someone seeing smoke cannot form the belief that something is on fire unless they have the concept 'fire', nor can they discern the smoke as distinct unless they have visual processes which pick up on movement, depth and tonal variations. The role of perceptual experience is to provide the information required for our beliefs. But the raw perceptual information we are subject to must none the less be given form if it is to perform this role. This explains the evolved significance of perceptual formation, which in the case of seeing is driven by visual processes, schemas and categories.[17] In the ordinary case we are unconscious of perceptual formation and take it as a given, but in the case of an aesthetic interest there is something further involved in the experience. The way we attend to the image, the way we feel it crystallise, shape the interrelation of parts and suddenly foreground certain salient visual relations in the image as a whole, intimates to us in the experience the way in which we give form to experience. The image might do this by challenging, inverting, rendering more vivid, frustrating, or even oscillating between our standard processes and schemas for object recognition. Whether we gain any pleasure from attending to the object in these terms is a question of whether we delight in how the image forms, constructs, resolves, extends or renders more vivid our perceptual experience. From the more extreme cases, such as Picasso's fractured cubist period, to the more subtle cases, like Cartier-Bresson's photography, aesthetic appreciation draws on the ways in which we give form to experience. This is a much more attenuated form of aesthetic interest than that often articulated by defenders of the notion, but it is important to the appreciation of art, and natural landscapes, cityscapes or designed objects, to hold on to this notion. Much contemporary thought, through finding fault with Kant and the later psychological turn, has been falsely dismissive of the notion altogether. This is a mistake.

There is a further qualification that ought to be made. Kant's account of aesthetic judgement is commonly understood as being closely bound to experience. On standard interpretations of Kant, judging something to be beautiful, and aesthetic appreciation more generally, is closely tied to the form of an object as perceived in our experience of it.[18] This kind of thought often underlies worries some people have about conceptual art. For where experiencing a work adds nothing, or the material object is beside the point, then, the thought may be, nothing distinctively aesthetic is involved – and as such the work can only be bad art. Yet this is unfair both to conceptual art and to Kant. We often feel the aesthetic pull of certain ideas. The appeal of certain scientific proofs or formulas, $e = mc^2$ to take but one example, partly lies in their apparent beauty. For here we have an elegant, simple encapsulation in one formula of a highly complex, coherent and deeply explanatory physical law. Similarly the pull of certain religious conceptions of the world or philosophical ideas is often due to their elegance, explanatory complexity and coherence. In such cases it cannot be the intimation and nature of *perceptual* form that does the work. Rather, it is a matter of the conceptual form of the schemas, categories, beliefs and attitudes that constitute a particular conceptualisation of the world. The appeal of Christianity, for example, might partly be explained in terms of the way it seeks to reconcile the wickedness, fallibility and nobility of humankind, the foregrounding of love, forgiveness and mercy in light of that conception and the way in which it thus gives a form to the whole range of human experience. The form of such ideas may, in Kant's terms, be dependently beautiful. Kant's own conception of 'aesthetic ideas' suggests *a* way of understanding the aesthetic merits of conceptual art in less than traditional terms. For Kant himself suggests that an aesthetic idea is the representation of the imagination which stimulates ideas and mental patterns in ways which can't be wholly captured or reduced to one particular, determinate way of conceiving of things.[19] Thus Richard Long's *A Line Made by Walking* (1967), consisting of a photograph documenting his walk back and forth in a park to make a line in the grass, may provoke us to play with the idea of walking, separating ourselves off from the environment, marking the landscape or ways of being in the landscape. Simon Patterson's *The Great Bear* (1992), which consists of a map of the London Underground and replaces tube station names with the names of cultural figures from Karl Marx to Audrey Hepburn, may prompt our minds to play with ways of thinking of cultural space, of different individuals taking distinct routes through a common culture, the ways in which parts of the same culture hardly ever seem to connect up, the extent to which our navigation through culture may or may not be down to individual choice. Thus, despite the standard interpretations, Kant could perhaps be taken as recognising that aesthetic ideas may be appreciable as such – ideas we can take an aesthetic interest in. This is not just a matter of general importance; it also has particular interest in relation to contemporary artistic practice. Much of the derision directed at conceptual art is informed by the false assumption that something can only be beautiful in perceptual contemplation; this is a mistake. It might be that much conceptual art is banal, uninteresting to look at and intellectually adolescent. But in principle there is every reason to suppose that there could be aesthetically appealing, indeed beautiful works of conceptual art on Kant's account. Whether or not this is wholly adequate to the appeal of conceptual art is something we will look at more fully in the next chapter.

As we have seen, construing Kant's notion of disinterestedness as a distinct perceptual attitude is neither attractive, since it is too strong a requirement for aesthetic appreciation, nor faithful to

Kant. Whether we are disinterested or not should be understood in terms of the grounds of our response. None the less, it is worth holding on to a much weaker thought; namely that it is a mark of our being disinterested that we process and respond to works differently, in terms of the visual relations, schemas and forms, from those who are not. Furthermore, perhaps Kant's account of aesthetic ideas leaves room for a way of understanding and appreciating some conceptual art. Still, the idea that we can recognise works as beautiful without necessarily feeling pleasure ourselves puts pressure on the way in which disinterestedness is supposed to relate to the other conditions of aesthetic judgement. In particular it threatens the very universality of such judgements that Kant takes to be so fundamental.

Ugliness, the grotesque and the disgusting

Developments in twentieth-century art, alongside more historical precedents, suggest that there is also something fundamentally wrong with Kant's conception of aesthetic value. He starts by giving an analysis of judgements of beauty and effectively generalises this to incorporate the nature of aesthetic appreciation. The influence of this form of explanation cannot be underestimated and underwrites many different attempts to give informative characterisations of artistic value. Where the lower-level aesthetic features of a work, such as gracefulness, elegance, vibrancy, dynamism and so on, come together in harmonious unity and are complex, coherently structured, intense, then it is aesthetically appealing. The nature of aesthetic value is thus treated as a more generalized version of the appeal of the beautiful.[20] The core thought is that what we take delight in is itself delightful. Kant explicitly draws attention to the fact that where the subject matter concerned is itself ugly, none the less it can be depicted beautifully, hence an image of such things can itself be delightful though what it represents might not be.[21] Hence John Constable's statement that 'there is nothing ugly; I never saw an ugly thing in my life: for let the form of an object be what it may, – light, shade, and perspective will always make it beautiful'.[22] But ugliness, grotesquery, incoherence and the disgusting are as such held to be always aesthetically offensive. Moreover, according to Kant, 'one kind of ugliness alone is incapable of being represented conformably to nature without destroying all aesthetic delight, and consequently artistic beauty, namely, that which excites *disgust*'.[23]

Yet in visual art there is a long tradition of the rendering of grotesques, both real and imaginary, the disgusting, decayed and downright ugly. Not only was this tradition continued in the twentieth century, perhaps with unprecedented fervour, but there also emerged an artistic agenda concerned with pursuing the fractured, incoherent and positively disharmonious. It was as if ugliness and related aesthetic features, at least in certain contexts or depending upon certain aesthetic sensibilities, constituted an aesthetic virtue rather than a vice. Pre-Michelangelo, the Low Countries representations of the Pietà grotesquely emphasised the horrific nature of Christ's death; Hieronymus Bosch's *Garden of Earthly Delights* (1500) shows us many disgusting scenes, from torture through to the devouring of human bodies; Quentin Massys's *Grotesque Old Woman* (1520) displays a hideously wrinkled and ugly old woman for our delectation. In the twentieth century the distorted, corrupting and decaying figures from Francis Bacon's work spring to mind, as does the work of Joel-Peter Witkin, a photographer whose works solicit a compulsive interest in freakish, deformed and mutilated bodies, and that of the Chapman brothers, Jake and Dinos, whose mannequins of children are bound together with facial features distorted into sexual genetalia. And consider the 1928 Buñuel and Dalí film *Un Chien Andalou*. Several different parts are played by the same actor and actress, the scene outside arbitrarily changes from landscape one minute to cityscape the next, and the juxtaposition of surreal images, such as the grotesque slitting of an eyeball, and stark edits contribute to the film's narrative incoherence. It seems that we, or at least some people, derive aesthetic delight from the portrayal of distorted physiognomies, grotesquery and incoherence. Indeed, many works not only represent disgusting things or solicit repulsive emotions and thoughts but use repellant materials as well. Recent interest in what has come to be known as abject art, centring particularly around work by artists such as Cindy Sherman, Mike Kelley, Paul McCarthy, Kiki Smith and Janine Antoni amongst others, should also be considered in this kind of light. The preoccupation with materials resulting from bodily processes – fluids, such as vomit, menstrual blood or shit – and the concern with the base, disgusting or transgressive seem driven by a practical artistic attempt to investigate Kant's claim that disgust is something beyond the pale of an aesthetic response. Cindy Sherman's 'disgust' pictures from 1986–87 depict, amongst other things, items associated with female bodily identity, and various bodily parts, scattered amongst the dirt in her *Untitled 167* (1986) and *Untitled 175* (1987). *Untitled 172* (1987) depicts a table cluttered with filthy dishes, molten wax and, in the foreground, a plate glistening with worms. A work may be constituted from repugnant materials, depict perverse scenes and afford uneasy responses and yet we may appreciate it aesthetically. These kinds of cases look as if they fall outside the sphere of aesthetic appreciation on Kant's account, at least to the extent that they are ugly, disgusting or incoherent. Yet part of their aesthetic appeal lies precisely in such features.

Kant would no doubt claim that our interest in such things, whatever it may be, is not aesthetic. In some cases the artistic interest does lie outside the aesthetic arena. Consider the Dada movement. Turning its back on traditional figuration, it pursued radical techniques devoted to fracturing the viewer's experience. It's not as if the incoherence or brutishness becomes aesthetically valuable, since they are consciously anti-aesthetic, but they are being used for wider artistic purposes. In foregrounding the constructed nature of the work Dadaism challenged assumptions about the 'natural' and unchangeable nature of artistic practices and social structures. Dadaism was a reaction against the classical art tradition, in particular the post-World War I attempts to capture the 'universal' values of art, and a rejection of the avant-garde's prior glorification of war and machine aestheticism. Only given the background of classicism does Marcel Duchamp's *Fountain* (1917), see p. 131, an inverted urinal signed R. Mutt, make sense as a jokey refutation of the presumption that art must manifest some essential aesthetic property. Only in the light of a reasoned, aestheticised conception of art do the irrationalist, deconstructive and anti-aesthetic techniques of Dada make sense:

> The word Dada symbolizes the most primitive relation to the reality of the environment; with Dadaism a new reality comes into its own. Life appears as a simultaneous muddle of noises, colours and spiritual rhythms, which is taken unmodified into Dadaist art, with all the sensational screams and fevers of its reckless everyday psyche and with

all its brutal reality. This is the sharp dividing line separating Dadaism from all artistic directions up until now. Dadaism for the first time has ceased to take an aesthetic attitude toward life, and this it accomplishes by tearing all the slogans of ethics, culture and inwardness, which are merely cloaks for weak muscles, into their components.[24]

But though much Dadaist art is meant to be incoherent, it is generally about more intellectual concerns rather than tending towards an aesthetic appreciation of the ugly, disgusting or grotesque as such. So this can't be the full story.

Now, consider Shakespeare's lines from *Twelfth Night*:

O! what a deal of scorn looks beautiful
In the contempt and anger of his lip.[25]

The distorted, horrific features of scorn and contempt become beautiful when manifested in the features of one who is loved. What is normally harsh and repellent may, given a certain context or relations to other features, become pleasing. Devoid of the specific relations or context involved, we might not savour these features at all. So the grotesque, disgusting, ugly and incoherent may normally be aesthetically displeasing, yet, given certain relations in particular contexts, turn out to be delightful.[26]

It is important to distinguish the claim I am making from a related but weaker one. The weak claim holds that in certain cases features which are ugly in one context may be beautiful in another. The strong claim, that is being argued for here, is the idea that that which is ugly and thus usually displeasing may, in certain contexts, remain ugly whilst none the less becoming pleasing or delightful. Lucian Freud's nude paintings often represent their subjects' bodies as if they are slabs of meat. His series of Leigh Bowery from the mid-1980s, for example, draws attention to the mottled tones, contours and expanse of flesh. In one of them only Bowery's expansive back and the top of his domed head are visible so the viewer isn't even confronted with Bowery as a self-conscious subject. We are drawn towards the weighty substance, folds, excess of flesh, the inflections of shade, tone and the corporeal nature of the body. Yet something we standardly find quite disgusting, through the interplay of sheer volume, surface area, shades, tones and malleable contours of Bowery's flesh, is rendered aesthetically compelling. Jenny Saville is also worth considering in this light.

Her paintings often concentrate on large, fleshly female figures and possess some of the same virtues as Freud's work. In the mid-1990s she collaborated with the photographer Glenn Luchford on a series of self-portraits. They show her face and body in contorted postures pressed up against a pane of glass, doubly distorting the already bizarre bodily configurations. *Closed Contact #14* (1995/6), see p. 82, for example shows three quarters of the left side of her face, with her fingers pressed deeply into her flesh as if it were being pulled back. Right up against the glass the effect is to flatten facial features, pull them out of shape and emphasise the slashes of her fingers pulling across the face. It also affords a stark contrast in tone between the whiteness of the flesh against the glass and the dark crevices of her mouth, eye corner and nostrils. The strange shape, tones and structure are themselves fascinating. But the photograph works at many levels. At one level what does the work is the knowledge that this is the visual distortion of her face. The freakish physiognomy is jarring since it's at odds with what we expect to see as a human face, though we cannot but see it as such. So part of the interest lies in the oscillation between what, had it been a normal photograph, we imagine Saville would have looked like and the strange way in which she is presented to us. But we can also see it as a face which is almost human but not quite. It has something dark, primitive, almost alien about it. The jaw line is angular and protrudes at a much greater length than we'd expect in a human face. The prominent facial features are much more drawn out and give the impression of a face that slopes heavily forward. It is almost as if one were looking at a Neanderthal cousin, a forerunner or cousin of our species, definitely related but distinctly not one of us. We can also see it as a kind of quasi-expressionistic rendering of abstracted features of the face, a visual mapping of pain, melancholia or even death. But in all of these possible experiences, the centre of our visual experience is the surface of her face, the distortion or abstraction of form; malleable, deformed, remoulded and threatening. The queasy sense of disgust and repulsion arises from the sense, intrinsic to the visual experience, of confronting something which is essentially human and yet which threatens our categorical assumptions about how the living human face and its features should look. Here, that which is found to be disgusting and repellent is what grabs our aesthetic interest; is what drives the way in which we attend to the facial features and the interrelations of structure, tone and colour. Thus the disgusting, grotesque, ugly and incoherent, which are normally aesthetically offensive, can be turned into aesthetic virtues.

Recognising that delighting in the grotesque, ugly and disgusting can be aesthetically rewarding doesn't mean that what is grotesque, ugly and disgusting is a completely contingent matter. It is just that in atypical cases, where we can inhibit or modify standard conditions through interference or convention, we can come to delight in things we would normally find thoroughly unpleasant.

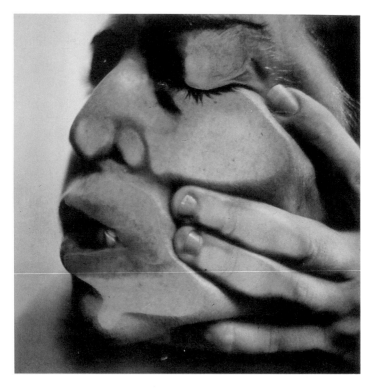

Jenny Saville and Glenn Luchford, *Closed Contact* # 14 (1995/6). Courtesy of Gagosian Gallery

We do the same with other affective states. Normally we think of fear as an intrinsically unpleasant thing to feel and are geared up to avoid it. But in non-standard conditions where there is no threat, from roller coasters to horror movies, or where the danger is thought to be a realisable test of our control, from motor racing to mountain climbing, many of us often actively seek out and enjoy the emotion. People actually vary over the degree to which they seek such things out, so to that extent there will be variation within the norms of desire. But such variation can be accounted for in terms of standard human nature, desires and dispositions; so too with the disgusting, grotesque and ugly. Different people will be more or less prepared to engage with such works. But those who do, at least where the works are good, will be aesthetically rewarded. For normally bad-making aesthetic features, in particular kinds of cases, can non-standardly turn out to be aesthetically good-making ones.

Some people might be tempted to push this line of thought one step further. Might it not be that, at least for people with certain kinds of aesthetic sensibilities, the disgusting, repellent and ugly are standardly good-making aesthetic features? Plato's *Republic* recounts the story of Leontion passing by the aftermath of a massacre thus:

> He noticed some corpses lying on the ground with the executioner standing by them. He wanted to go and look at them, and yet at the same time held himself back in disgust. For a time he struggled and covered his eyes, but at last his desire got the better of him and he ran up to the corpses, opening his eyes and saying to them, 'There you are, curse you, – *a lovely sight*! Have a real good look.'[27]

Leontion's delighting in the sight of the corpses suggests that it is the grotesque, horrific and disgusting features which are themselves delighted in. And everyday experience suggests this is hardly a rare phenomenon. People often gather at the scenes of accidents or slow down when driving by an accident scene for no other reason than to try and get a glimpse of the wreckage. Magazines, videos and programmes with lurid pictures of killings are commonly on sale and people are often fascinated by medical photographs of diseased bodies or cadavers. Nor is such an interest rare in art. Nero allegedly instituted a group of deformed and mutilated musicians to play for him; many representations of the Pietà are positively grotesque; some of Bosch's work is repellent; Grunewald's *Crucifixion* (1515) is stark, cruel and horrific. Ruskin condemned the art of the late Renaissance generally as being devoted to an aesthetic delight in brutal mockery, monstrosity and deformity. Hence his description of a sculpture at the base of the tower dedicated to St Mary the Beautiful in Venice: 'A head, – huge, inhuman, and monstrous, – leering in bestial degradation, too foul to be either pictured or described . . . in that head is embodied the type of evil spirit to which Venice was abandoned in the fourth period of her decline.'[28]

In the later twentieth century Andres Seranno's series of photographs entitled *The Morgue* (1992), Sue Fox's series of untitled works following the autopsy process (1996) and Richard Sawdon-Smith's *Symptom* series (1997) are all devoted to the colour, form and mortal contamination of human flesh. Damien Hirst's *A Thousand Years* (1990) consists of a putrefying cow's head containing maggots that develop into flies which again lay maggot eggs in a never ending cycle. Many of Francis Bacon's howling figures, some recognisably human, others distinctly alien, are concerned with the eternal corruption and visceral rottenness of bodily flesh and the soul. Perhaps it is not just that typically negative aesthetic features can on occasion become aesthetic virtues but that, at least for certain aesthetic sensibilities, such things are typically aesthetic virtues.

Perhaps some people subsist on an aesthetic diet mainly constituted from such works and seek out medical textbooks and the like for the same kind of reason Leontion was drawn towards the sight of the corpses. But of itself this does not show that the ugly, grotesque and disgusting can typically be aesthetic virtues. Rather what it shows is that the aesthetic delight felt by such characters is perverse. In the case of the works discussed above one can see how and why what is, by the standards of human nature, repellent can also be aesthetically attractive. But to devote one's entire sensibility to finding the disgusting, ugly and grotesque aesthetically pleasing as such is for one's human nature to have gone wrong. Granted we sometimes do delight in such features. In Yorkshire there is a tradition of gurning, competitions which involve seeing who can pull the most distorted and ugly faces possible. Similarly the pull of freak shows would be unintelligible if many didn't derive pleasure from gazing on the ugly, grotesque and deformed. But the point is that even here the cases are atypical. What we take an aesthetic interest and delight in may be far from delightful. But a compulsive fascination for and delight in the freakish is in a significant sense perverse.

This may be the right judgement to make regarding a strain of post-modern and nihilistic contemporary visual art. It is as if the recognition that such features can in certain contexts be aesthetically valuable has been confused with the mistaken assumption that such things are aesthetically valuable as such. No doubt part of this is caught up with attempts to confront and push back the boundaries of our ethical and social taboos. When this is well done, as in the case of Francis Bacon, Jenny Saville, Cindy Sherman or Grunewald say, the results can be aesthetically rewarding and challenge our comfortable assumptions about Christianity, normality, beauty and the ways in which we make sense of ourselves. But it is far from clear that such features themselves or attempts to push back our aesthetic, moral and social boundaries, at least for its own sake, are automatically a good thing. The corrosion of our natural human bonds may liberate us, but liberation from the truly beautiful, moral and socially good, unleashing the violent, ugly and brutal aspects of our animal natures, can be impoverishing. One of the marks of human civilisation is the sublimation of aspects of our animal natures towards what is humanly speaking valuable. Ruskin's condemnation of the late Renaissance does not involve disputing that, at least for certain sensibilities, the sculpture may be aesthetically rewarding. What he is really objecting to is that such works are 'evidences of a delight in the contemplation of bestial vice, and the expression of low sarcasm, which is, I believe, the most hopeless state into which the human mind can fall'.[29] With respect to contemporary art it may be that, as Robert Hughes suggests, part of the story involves the degeneration of modern art coupled with an obsession with the vagaries of fashion, commerce and artistic self-promotion.[30] None the less, part of the story also involves, contrary to Kant, the recognition that the disgusting, ugly and grotesque are themselves aesthetic qualities – ones which can have positive value.

Meaning matters

In the last few years, within both artistic and theoretical circles, interest in the notion of beauty and the aesthetic more generally has been reawakened. The American art critic Dave Hickey devoted himself to resurrecting the importance of beauty in art in the 1990s, while within the last five years or so there has suddenly been a rash of books on the subject and galleries are once more putting on exhibitions like the 1999 *Regarding Beauty* at the

Hirshorn in Washington.[31] Much of what is said in the name of this enthusiastic rediscovery of beauty and the aesthetic is confused. Elaine Scarry, for example, takes beauty, consisting in symmetry, to be necessarily associated with truth and thereby justice.[32] Yet beauty often isn't symmetrical – think of truly beautiful faces or landscapes as opposed to merely pretty ones – can divert from truth and be manifestly at odds with justice. None the less, much of the present interrogation of notions of beauty and the aesthetic is of interest. In particular Arthur Danto has recently suggested that we should distinguish cases where the beauty of a work is external to its meaning and those where it is internal. This is important to Danto since it is the embodied meaning of the work which matters – only where the beauty is internal are its aesthetic properties properly relevant to our evaluation of a work as art.[33]

Now the slogan 'meaning matters' captures the recognition that our appreciation of a work often depends upon knowledge of its context and its content. In both cases the role knowledge plays in our estimation of a work's worth seems incidental to its aesthetic qualities. Danto once wrote that 'to see something as art requires something that the eye cannot descry – an atmosphere of artistic theory, a knowledge of the history of art: an artworld'.[34] His classic example is Andy Warhol's facsimiles of Brillo boxes, of the kind found in everyday supermarkets in the 1960s, arranged in tidy piles. To all intents and purposes they look no different from the ordinary objects they mimic, yet we treat Warhol's boxes as art and not those found in the shops. The difference can't be explained in terms of the beauty of Warhol's objects, since the qualities they possess are more or less the same. We might then say that the beauty of Warhol's Brillo boxes, if indeed they possess any, is external to their nature and meaning as art. What makes the difference, Danto argues, is that in the 1960s we could look at objects presented to us as art in terms we could not have done before. The subject matter of Warhol's Brillo boxes, and much of his art more generally, was commercial popular culture. And in the presentation of the Brillo boxes as high art, objects apparently identical to ones in the shops, we have the idea that there is little difference between the ways we appreciate the products of fine art and mass culture. Warhol could present such a work as art because of its relations to other works; for example it shares certain commonalities with Duchamp's ready-mades and with the ways in which it could be viewed as such by informed members of the art world (whether that be curators, critics, theorists or the general art-going public). More prosaically, even the kinds of genre and categories we bring to bear in our appreciation make a difference. Famously, many artefacts once languishing in anthropological museums at the turn of the twentieth century came to be exhibited and viewed as art later on. In part this was due to Picasso's interest in anthropological objects and his subsequent use of primitive styles in seminal works such as *Les Demoiselles d'Avignon* (1907) and the development of cubism. Indeed, at one stage the Louvre and the anthropological museum in Paris fought over just which of them should be exhibiting particular artefacts. And at a much lower level it makes a difference whether or not we attend to a work as a sketch or the finished article, and whether it is supposed to be a naturalistic, expressionistic or impressionistic piece.[35]

A Kantian might balk at the charge that this presents a problem for his view. After all, Kant's notion of dependent beauty explicitly allows for the recognition that objects seen in terms of particular concepts and categories can be beautiful. It's just that the application of the appropriate concept doesn't determine whether an object is beautiful or not. Not all anthropological carvings or Greek vases will be beautiful but looking at some of them in terms of the kind of practical objects they are may give rise to aesthetic pleasure. All the objection shows, it might be thought, is that to appreciate the aesthetic nature of a work as art one must perceive it in terms of the appropriate categories. Even if Warhol's Brillo boxes were visually indistinguishable from the manufactured ones, none the less it is appropriate to view them as art in a way in which it is not regarding those on the supermarket shelves. Their appeal, if indeed it is aesthetic, is just a case of dependent beauty.

Taken another way – that the content and meaning of a work matters as such – it might be claimed on behalf of Kant that the objection is just question begging. As we saw in relation to Picasso's *Weeping Woman*, see p. 56, Kant can allow that the content of a work is crucial to its aesthetic value. But the crucial question concerns how this is so. Kant's claim is that where content matters we delight in the way in which the form of the work is an aesthetically apposite means of portraying what is represented. So the aesthetic value of a work is given by the interrelations between its formal aspect and its thematic content, unity, complexity, intensity and other such features. What we should do is keep conceptually distinct the fictional or historical status of a work, its content or meaning as such and its aesthetic aspect. A work is not better or worse as a work of art because it represents a historical or a fictional figure or predicts the future. A work isn't any better as art just because it is abstract, representational, subverts bourgeois values, extols the glories of human nature or condemns its depravities. What matters aesthetically speaking is whether we derive pleasure from attending to how artfully the content of a work, where it has any, is conveyed. So the content or meaning of a work is relevant to a work's aesthetic value, but only as an indirect side-effect. The message of a work as such is irrelevant to its aesthetic value. Its bearing emerges only where the content promotes or hinders its attainment of aesthetic virtues. Had Picasso been attempting to represent a certain kind of serene, beatific grief then *Weeping Woman* would be the lesser work for it, since the gouging of the face, the slashing of the fingers, the acidic tear drop are at odds with any attempt to convey serenity. The incongruity between what he would then have been attempting to represent and the means he used to do so would have marred the harmony and unity of the piece. But whether a work represents serene or vicious grief is as such neither an aesthetic virtue nor an aesthetic vice. It's how it's done that counts.

Having said all that, Kant's account does remain blind to the role meaning often plays in art. Consider Andres Serrano's *Piss Christ* (1987). It's a photograph of Christ on the Cross bathed in urine and backlit. Interestingly the visual appearance of the piece, far from being anti-aesthetic, is rather beautiful. But the point of the work not only requires knowledge of the medium involved, hence the title of the piece, but grasping the significance this has for the work's meaning. The beauty arising from the representation of the divine bathed in the profane brings home to us, *in our experience of the work*, that Christ was both divine and fallibly human in nature. The idea of which remains a deep mystery and profoundly beautiful. The pure aesthetic quality may be internal to the work but it is, here, subservient to the meaning of the piece conveyed through our experience of it. Although in such a case the medium, processes or manipulation of subject matter may possess aesthetic value, this is subservient to the way in which the work guides, shapes and affords us a particularly rich meaningful experience.

Andres Serrano, *Piss Christ* (1987). Courtesy of the Paula Cooper Gallery, New York

A different way to make the same point concerns works whose value we take to be diminished owing to their content. Both ordinary art lovers and professional critics alike use critical terms such as sentimental, callow, naïve, strident, simplistic, profound, insightful and imaginative. These kinds of evaluations are often directed at the work's content and how, given the ways in which that content is represented, we are prescribed to understand it. Some of Renoir's lesser portraits, for example, may display technical sophistication, complex coloration and a great unity of aesthetic coherence, harmony and balance. Yet our appreciation of them is often diminished by their cloying sentimentality. The naïve innocence of the red-cheeked young women and pretty children he so often painted betokens a superficial romanticisation of childhood. At their worst they are not far off the awful chocolate box pictures or birthday cards one often sees in gift shops. No matter what level of artistic virtuousity they attain, we think less of them because their representation of what they depict is shallow and naïve.

A sharp division between the purely aesthetic value of a work and the nature of the experience it affords, in terms of its emotional depth, insight or understanding, looks difficult to maintain. A work may be aesthetically appealing, artfully contrived and absorbing. Where a work is exceptionally absorbing and artful in its construction it may well be great art, for not all great art is profound in terms of its content or emotional resonance. But where a work's aesthetic virtues promote perceptions, attitudes or responses of great depth, we consider it to be a virtue of the work as art. Superficially Holbein's *Ambassadors* (1533), see pp. 94–95, is a superlative delineation of two ambassadors to the English court, surrounded by the accoutrements of their respective roles and attendant privileges.

As it happens, the two men are Jean de Dinteville, French ambassador to England in 1533, and the bishop of Lavaur, Georges de Selve, who acted as an ambassador on numerous occasions. But knowing this is incidental to grasping the essential meaning of the painting. They stand in front of a curtain on either side of a table, outer hands on hips, inner hands resting easily on the table, gazing confidently out at the viewer. Their stance is that of supremely self-assured men, bold, unafraid and easy in their sense of mastery. The table itself bears the clutter of the finest human achievements. The lute, flutes, celestial globe, portable sundial, hymn book, and various other navigational and geometric instruments betoken the vast realms of human knowledge, art and global territory conquered by Western culture since the Renaissance. The two men look slightly down at the viewer, indicating superiority, lack of fear and cognisance of the heights scaled in reaching such rarified realms. The substance and richness of their clothes also intimates the material rewards that accrue from such achievements. But there is a blotchy, egg-like smear running diagonally across the foreground of the picture. Looked at from straight on the viewer can't discern what it is. However, moving towards a different viewpoint, side on from the right, we see it crystallise into the most amazing representation of a large skull, a visual embodiment of the Book of Ecclesiastes' phrase 'vanity, vanity, all is vanity'. Even the greatest of human achievements will crumble into dust and the greatest of mortals will meet the same fate. From this perspective death looms large, casting its shadow over the unthinking pride and complacency of the ambassadors. Here, even the curtain in the background takes on a new significance: behind it lies the darkness that awaits us all, although, with their backs turned, the ambassadors fail to realise this. Viewed from one perspective, a representation of how the ambassadors conceive of themselves, they are seen as proud conquerors of all the world has to offer, with nothing to fear. Viewed from another, a representation of how things stand from the impersonal perspective of death, their pride is seen as arrogant hubris since their self-regard, status and achievements can only but be ephemeral in the face of their own mortality. This is not to say that Holbein's picture implies

Hans Holbein the Younger, *Jean de Dinteville and Georges de Selve (The Ambassadors)* (1533). Courtesy of The National Gallery, London

that there is no point in seeking to be wise or great. Rather, what is lacking in the ambassadors is a failure to contemplate life in the light of death, hence their unbridled vanity.

Notice that our understanding of the ambassadors is implied via pictorial means. The painting itself is in a familiar tradition which represents learned men with their instruments and books of learning. But over and above these elements we have the juxtaposition of the self-conception of the ambassadors with the impersonal viewpoint of death, embodied in the two distinct perspectives the picture makes use of. In order to make the right appraisal of the ambassadors as viewers, we must look at the painting from different viewpoints. Had Holbein not made use of such a device to convey the intimation of mortality, via the perspectivally distinct representation of the skull, then it would not have been as great a work as it is. Undoubtedly it would have remained a highly valuable piece, since his representation of the two men alone displays incredible mastery of painterly technique and aesthetic virtuosity. Yet the power of the painting lies in the light cast on the pretensions of the ambassadors, unknowingly undercut by the fact of their mortality. The painterly embodiment of this attitude towards the human condition, a deeply insightful and profound view on the aspirations even of the greatest of men, transfigures the work into truly great art.

We might be tempted to think that the embodiment of perceptions, attitudes or responses of great depth enhances a work's artistic value only in the case of strictly representational art. Yet nothing could be further from the truth. It is true that the twentieth century saw a significant movement in visual art away from the figurative towards formal, structural concerns, art's materiality and relations of colour, dimension and texture. But it doesn't follow that abstract art is only concerned with purely aesthetic virtues. Apparently contentless abstract art or sculpture is often not only highly expressive but concerned with our attitudes, responses and perceptions. In the first chapter we saw how Mondrian's drive towards abstraction was an attempt to model the underlying structure of the world. Hence, in one sense at least, even the most austerely abstract of works turns out to be representational. But consider a different kind of case, that of Mark Rothko. Rothko, along with Jackson Pollock, is one of the most celebrated amongst a group of American artists known as abstract expressionists who emerged in 1940s New York. From the end of that decade on, Rothko produced the work he is most renowned for, consisting of minor variations on the same theme. He produced large paintings with blocks and tiers of contrasting, complementing or subtly different colours, thinly layered over and over again until intense colour sensations resulted which respond subtly to different angles and shades of light. Unfortunately people often tend to descend into portentious hyperbole when talking about Rothko, alluding to his sublimity, profundity, evocation of the infinite, the unconscious and almost anything and everything one might think of. And at its worst Rothko's work is clumsy, repetitious and mundane, and its scale often manifests failed bluster rather than epic achievement. None the less, as blocks of colour fields, some of his work is beautiful and intense. But at its very best Rothko's work is more than just beautiful. Rothko strove to convey a sense of isolation, hopelessness and doubt which he despairingly took to be the spirit of his modern age. Perhaps he was only partially successful. Yet his paintings do sometimes produce, when up close, a sense of floating as if in some stretched out, receding and limitless space. The experience of being alone in an indeterminate world of shifting, receding colour conveys how we might see and respond to our place in the world as essentially solitary. Even work as abstract as Rothko's often has a point above and beyond a concern with purely aesthetic virtues – and where the point is worth making and conveyed well through the experience afforded, it is better as art for it.

The ways in which meaning matters bear on a related worry concerning Kant's sharp separation between high art and culture. For such a strict divide is out of step with the development of art as a cultural practice. Far from being independent of non-aesthetic purposes, art has typically been produced to serve a variety of purposes, whether its aims or forms of patronage be religious, public, private or commercial. The flattery of patrons, provision of propaganda and focus on material reward hardly prevented the religious art of the Renaissance, the courtly painting of Holbein or the portraiture of Joshua Reynolds from being great art. How fine a work is does not depend upon whether the primary purpose of creation is the promotion of artistically worked aesthetic features or the promotion of moral insight, religious devotion or flattery. Part of the story does depend upon how well the aesthetic features are worked and whether it rewards an aesthetic interest. But above and beyond that, what matters is whether our responses, the insight or understanding shown through engaging with the work, are worthwhile. Is it trite, banal, superficial or callow? If so, no matter how beautiful, then so much the worse for the work. Is it profound, interesting, suggestive, true to life or insightful? If so, the work is better for it as art. We should value beauty and the rewarding of aesthetic interest. But that cannot be the whole story of the value of art.

Chapter Three | Insight in Art

Art's craft

Samuel Johnson once said that it is a mark of a civilisation how it spends its leisure time. The early Victorian expansion of art galleries, by private philanthropists, associations and public institutions, was driven by the assumption that opening up art to all would educate, ennoble and civilise. Even in our sceptical age we spend large amounts of public and private money on art galleries, exhibitions and installations and people flock to many of them. Why? The pleasures beauty affords are not to be underestimated, but many other activities afford as much pleasure and involve less time, effort and money. So what motivates the high regard in which we hold good or great art? Looking at art tests us, stretches us, deepens our inner lives and cultivates insight into both ourselves and the world. Paul Auster's novel *Moon Palace* in part relates the struggles of a painter, Effing, to grasp how he fits into the world and understand his own nature. In a central scene he's painting out in the desert, alone, and is suddenly subject to an artistic epiphany:

> The true purpose of art was not to create beautiful objects, he discovered. It was a method of understanding, a way of penetrating the world and finding one's place in it, and whatever aesthetic qualities an individual canvas might have were almost an incidental by-product of the effort to engage oneself in this struggle, to enter into the thick of things.[1]

We've seen that an artist's attempts at self-expression, revelation and imaginative vision are important independently of and prior to our experience. But the point here is that looking at good or great works, which are the upshot of such artistic struggles, can enable us to explore ways of seeing the world and understanding ourselves. It is not the only one, true purpose of art to do so. Works can be good or great just in virtue of their beauty or artistic originality. But if that were all there were to art then it would remain puzzling as to why we value art so highly. The answer lies in the ways in which art works can cultivate insight, understanding and ways of seeing the world. The challenge is to show how such matters connect with a work's artistic value and the ways in which we can learn from art works.

The aesthetic tradition conceived of art as a practice radically distinct from other human concerns. In part this was no bad thing since it provided a buffer against the subsumption of art by crude utilitarian, commercial and moralising purposes. None the less, as we saw in relation to Kant, conceiving of artistic value as being exhausted by aesthetic value cannot but be radically mistaken. The ancient Greeks, by contrast, considered art to be a craft, tied to much else we value in other activities; it just realises, albeit particularly well, the evocation of responses, attitudes and ideas. Notoriously, Plato's estimation of art was scathingly negative. He thought that art proffered only the illusion of knowledge, appealed to our baser appetites and led us away from the light of reason. But Aristotle recognised that art could afford true insight and understanding. This is not to say that aesthetic virtues are of no significance whatsoever. Rather, the aesthetic aspect of a work only distinguishes the means in virtue of which art realises its goals. A history text, a piece of journalism, models, symbols and mundane photographs may impart information or knowledge. A philosophical work, psychological experiment or medical illustration can deepen our understanding of the human condition. But what is distinctive about art, where it is concerned with such aims, is the means by which it seeks to do so.

Now we should be careful not to be too hasty here. In the twentieth century many people assumed that art's value was a function of the viewers' responses or whatever it was that a work communicated. Hence the idea that a large part of artistic value resides in its cognitive virtues: the knowledge, insight and understanding conveyed by a work are taken to be at odds with the Romantic emphasis on artistic expression. This need not be so. As we saw in chapter 1, art works are often primarily the expression of the artist's imagination. Whatever is communicated or expressed to the viewer through the work, where this is the case, arises as a secondary matter which depends upon that imaginative expression. And not just any imaginative artistic expression should be identified with an act of communication. For example, someone may be devoted to revolutionising the use of new or traditional artistic materials, reworking the conventions of pictorial representation or modifying genre constraints. In such cases it may be that nothing of any great significance is expressed or communicated. Hence pieces can be good or great art prior to and independently of what viewers take the work to be communicating or how they happen to respond to it. Yet the Romantic impulse to conceive of art as imaginative expression need not deny that many artists set out to create works in order to get viewers to respond in certain ways or have certain kinds of experiences. It is just that the intention to convey certain experiences to viewers is secondary to the intention to express the artistic imagination creatively, so the act of imaginative artistic expression should not be identified with an act of communication. None the less, the imaginative expression of the artist enables the peculiarly powerful expression and communication of ideas, attitudes and responses. Given that we are naturally concerned with questions about how we should conceive of ourselves, our place in the world, our attitudes towards one another, it is unsurprising that much art is aimed at prescribing and promoting, through the artistically manipulated conventions, particular ways of seeing the world. We see in the canvas how we are to conceive of the characters, events, states of affairs and worlds represented, or imagine what it would be like to be such a character, or to have certain feelings, beliefs and attitudes. The distinctive expression of artistic imagination shapes the physical materials, conventions, genres, styles and forms which vivify, guide and prescribe our responses. Hence art works can enlighten us about how we may understand the world. The extent to which a work does so makes it better as art. Art can deepen or expand the horizons of our minds in ways we would not otherwise have realised. Travel may well broaden the mind, though whether it does so depends upon the mind and character of the person involved, but it is expensive and dangerous. By contrast, to travel through the imaginative lands evoked by art works enriches the soul at little cost even when its pleasures are hard won.

Illuminating the familiar

Consider Vincent van Gogh's *The Potato Eaters* (1885). When it was painted the details and features of everyday peasant life would have been familiar. Although it might be of historical interest to us now, that is not where the value of the painting lies. Van Gogh sought to evoke an imaginative understanding of the harsh living and working conditions the peasants were subject to. In part he achieved this through a particular labouring and abstraction of style that brings home the rough, coarse, brutal aspects of their lives:

> I personally am convinced I get better results by painting them in their roughness than by giving them a conventional charm . . . If a peasant picture smells of bacon, smoke, potato, steam – all right, that's not unhealthy . . . if the field has an odour of ripe corn or potatoes or of guano or manure – that's healthy, especially for city people. Such pictures may teach them something. But to be perfumed is not what a peasant picture needs.[2]

What the work teaches us does not lie so much in knowing about the conditions of the peasants. The picture is not a substitute for sociological information. If it were, then the point of looking at it would be lost as soon as one found a more detailed source of information concerning the conditions of the peasantry. What the picture seeks to teach us is that a particular imaginative understanding of the peasants' lives is appropriate: despite, or perhaps because of, their harsh conditions, their lives contain an earthbound simplicity and goodness which should be cherished. Van Gogh shows us this through representing the peasants unthinkingly sharing their meagre sustenance, the directions of their gazes and the group circle which displays their concern for one another. Van Gogh is open to criticism since his conception of the peasantry here errs on the side of an overly sentimental, quasi-religious reverence. The issue arises since we are being encouraged, via artistic means, to conceive of the peasantry as morally beautiful and good in virtue of their harsh conditions and relations to the soil. It is one thing to entertain this as a possible way of conceiving of people and quite another to consider it *the* appropriate attitude.

According to the Kantian influenced aesthetic tradition, this approach to Van Gogh's work is misplaced. Van Gogh talks of evoking the smell of bacon and guano. The point of the painting, the aestheticist will argue, is to utilise and evoke aesthetic qualities. Perhaps of all the artists we might have picked Van Gogh may be the least promising here, for in Van Gogh's work, the aestheticist will claim, we see the basic drive of the early modern movement made manifest: the primacy of the aesthetic. But even here we can show how the aestheticist is mistaken. A significant part of the reason why we value the intense colours and calligraphic contortions of Van Gogh is because we can see Arles, and aspects of landscapes elsewhere, as he represents them to us. Even the most expressionistic of his works show us how the ancient olive groves, the gnarled, clawing tree roots, the stratified, cavernous limestone hills, and the tumultuous, windswept clouds may look. The landscape is not used by Van Gogh as some springboard for his artistic fantasies. Rather, through the use of a developed, formalised style, he is striving to represent in a fresh, bold and nuanced way how the landscape may be understood. This is not merely a question of how the landscape may be perceived. Rather, his work expresses a particular way of conceiving of and valuing the landscape. If this were not so, then there would be no significant relation between Van Gogh's use of colour and strokes, the means of representation, and the landscape. True, the colours would still be vibrant, the style calligraphic, and his work aesthetically appealing. But the significance of the work, in terms of revealing how the landscape may be understood in a particular way, would be lost. We would not be able to see Van Gogh in the landscape around us. We might then say of Van Gogh that he was a great colourist or stylist, but not that he was a great artist.

The point is not just that the meaning of a work can be related to its artistic value. Referring to a work like Magritte's *The Use of Words I* (1928–9) would be enough to show us that. It's a visual depiction of a pipe with the words 'Ceci n'est pas une pipe' written underneath it, the point being that the spectator realises both that the thing represented is a pipe and yet, since it is a painting, that it is not. Nor should we confuse the claim with mere representationalism: the idea that visual art aims to mimic how things really appear. Rather, it is the way in which a work shapes how we look at what it represents, through the use of media, styles, genre constraints and individual working, that constitutes part its content. Our evaluation of the means of representation is often concerned with whether they 'fit' what they are being used to represent. How Van Gogh prescribes us to attend to the landscape may not only deepen our visual experience by foregrounding aspects of the natural world we previously hadn't noticed; it may reveal to us an understanding of the landscape as a place from which order can be forged, emotions given form and solace sought. If we cannot grasp how the landscape may thus be understood then the fault lies either with ourselves (perhaps we fail to pick up on aspects of the painting), or with Van Gogh (maybe he misrepresents how we could relate to natural landscapes).

The putative relations between what the work concerns and the way it shapes how we are to understand it, for example through the means of representation, afford art significance. Hence if we rightly say we cannot grasp what is represented in the manner prescribed, or that the work represents something inadequately, then the criticism is a telling one. This applies just as much to aesthetic features as it does to features more directly concerned with beliefs, attitudes and emotional responses. If the steam, guano and bacon had been evoked through a highly finished style, the rough, coarse, earthy nature of the foods would have been sanitised. More importantly, had the peasants' postures changed from those of people with arms outstretched and gazes directed towards one another to people hoarding their lot, distrustful, and uncaring of each other, then the whole nature of the work would have been radically different. Whether Van Gogh's conception and attitude in the representation is appropriate, intelligible and deep or glib, inchoate and misplaced applies equally to sensations and people. Given that the primary focus of *The Potato Eaters* is the peasants, their state and their attitudes towards one another, it is the prescribed understanding of them that is of primary significance.

It is far from the case that all good or great art seeks to prescribe a particular conception of its subject as true, correct or appropriate. Many works aim to provoke thoughts and reactions with respect to their subject matter, others to show us possible ways of perceiving or conceiving of their subject matter. Artistic aims are not always directed towards seeking to persuade us of the truth of something. But, as with much of Van Gogh's work, some works are directed towards doing so. There is a genuine question to be asked about how we can distinguish between works which aim to show us a possible way of apprehending their subjects and works which aim to persuade us that we should conceive of them as represented. We may experience what it would be like to perceive peasants as noble partly in virtue of their poverty and relations to the soil. But how can we tell that a work aims to convince us that a conception is the correct or appropriate one? How, we might ask, can a visual image *prescribe* how we are to understand or perceive its subject? There are often features concerning the image and the way in which it is presented to us which clue us in. The kind of title a work is given, the genre in which it's painted, the apparent nature of the symbolism, the representativeness or otherwise of the figures portrayed. But no one feature is always present and perhaps in some cases there may be next to none at all. But this is no different from the case of literary fiction. Often there are many clues in a text which prompt us to take it as fictional. But in some cases, devoid of background information about an author's intentions, there may be no way of telling. So too in the image case. What makes it prescriptive is a function of how the artist actually intended the work to be understood – whether as a possible way of conceiving of things or as a prescription as to how we should perceive things aright. In some cases, knowing which it is will require background information concerning the artist's attitudes and intentions with respect to the work. And not only are there clues in Van Gogh's work, as discussed above, but we know independently that Van Gogh did indeed want to persuade us that a particular way of apprehending the peasants and landscapes he represented was the right way to do so.

Certain strands of thought, strains of which can be found in the works of Adorno and Brecht or artistic movements like Dada, suggest that art works may be valuable *only* where they challenge our pre-existing beliefs, attitudes and values. As a characterisation of the thought of Adorno and Brecht this is overly simplistic, since their revolutionary modernism was driven by attachments to what they took to be the best elements of European art and culture. None the less, their views can be seen as precursors to the historical avant-garde thought that good art *must* be radically challenging.[3] Such a view is both too liberal and too narrow. It's too liberal since there can be many works that directly confront our beliefs, responses and attitudes but remain essentially worthless, for our views, attitudes and responses can be glibly challenged. It's too narrow since many great works don't radically challenge us.[4] For every Michelangelo, Carravaggio, Picasso or Bacon that is at extreme odds with our own attitudes, beliefs and responses, there are dozens of works by Holbein, Reynolds, Goya, Vermeer, Constable, Turner, Rodin, Van Gogh and modern artists which are significantly similar to what we already think and feel.

Take Bruce Nauman's *Good Boy Bad Boy* (1985). It consists of two colour video monitors showing two presentably dressed actors, one fairly young black male and one middle-aged white female, reciting the same series of a hundred phrases such as 'I was a good boy. You were a good boy. We were good boys. That was good . . . I was a bad boy . . .' through to 'I am alive! You are alive! This is life! . . . I play. You play. This is play! . . .' At the start the phrases are articulated in flat tones but as the series progresses they become much more varied in tone, emphasis and urgency.

The speed at which the actors are talking also varies, hence the looped video monitors gradually come to be out of sequence. With the increased variation, it is as if the actors are trying to persuade us of something, their sincerity perhaps, and the lack of synchronicity begins to make it seem as if they are responding to one another. By the end the actors are shrieking in ferocious hatred. Most of us are familiar with the idea that sexual and racial issues can distort and divide society. Nauman's piece foregrounds how the meanings and expressivity of the very same phrases seems to vary radically depending on inflection, who they're spoken by and what they seem to be in response to. When the woman angrily states 'You *have* work' it as if the black man should be grateful for having a job at all or when the man states '*This* is work' it as if he is saying that, unlike her, he has to suffer in his job in order to survive. The work gradually reveals to us the problematic nature of communication, even in the most straightforward of phrases, since what is being communicated depends at a deep level on variations in identity. In one sense we may not learn anything new as such. But Nauman's piece reminds us, forcefully, of the ways in which even the simplest of messages can be inflected with and vary according to issues of identity.

To be sure, works may modify thoughts and deepen responses by drawing our attention to features we often barely notice or by drawing on the implications of shared assumptions. But this is to illuminate and enrich our assumptions rather than challenge them. Goya's *Disasters of War* series (1810–14), for example, is a powerful condemnation of the futility, evils and destruction of war. The dismembered carcasses, the explicit cruelty and pervasive venality represented in the series offer up a searing indictment of war and despair at the baser nature of man. The abruptness of the prints is achieved by the clear treatment of volume, the use of dark back-grounds and the stark whiteness of figures and flesh.

Consider *What More Can We Do?*. Here two French soldiers are prising open the legs of a naked Spanish man into a V shape, whilst a third is cutting at the mid-point of his crotch. There are few background features so nothing else occupies our attention; what there is serves only to reinforce the act of cruelty being perpetrated. The curve of the main diagonal from the background tree through to the naked man's body draws our attention to the brutal downward thrust of the sword. The naked figure is almost a natural outgrowth of the tree so that far from being represented as a traditional martyr like figure, dying an ennobled death, set apart from the natural world, he, and by extension all the figures, are represented as just as much a part of the natural world and order of things as organic plants. Nature is vicious, without rhyme, reason or higher purpose – and human nature is just as brutish, baseless and blind as the rest of the natural world. The horror of war is not something many of us aren't aware of. We know it involves pain, cruelty and the wanton destruction of life. In one sense Goya's series doesn't really tell us anything we didn't know already. Yet the series does foreground, in a vivid, explicit and harsh way, what we normally shy away from. It forces us to concentrate on, to dwell on, the bloodshed, bestiality and annihilation of war. In doing so it also compels us to consider the drives that eternally impel us to repeat the cycle of violence and destruction. By making us attend to features of war we normally turn away from, Goya's series vivifies impressions of war many of us already dimly have. By foregrounding its violence in peculiarly vivid and striking ways, it compels us to contemplate aspects of our nature which lead to the perpetuation of human tragedy. Hence, even if Plato is right to complain that much art appeals to our ignorance and baseness, it cannot be true that all art is bound to remain at that level. As we have seen, works can start by drawing our attention to things we already glibly take for granted and, through our engagement with them, come to show or remind us of the nature of ourselves, humanity and how we ought to respond to them. Notice that this also helps us to explain why we return again and again to great art works, for the aesthetic aspect of such works would often be hollow and unaffecting if they were not so tightly intertwined with a deep concern for exploring and showing us human nature.

Francesco Goya, *Disasters of War, pl. 33 – 'What More Can We Do?'*. Courtesy of The Metropolitan Museum of Art, Purchase, Rogers Fund and Jacob H. Schiff Bequest, 1922. [22.60.25 (33)]. All rights reserved, The Metropolitan Museum of Art

The triviality of art?

I remember when I first became interested in philosophy haphazardly coming across Plato's infamous attack on art in *The Republic*. It is ferocious, scathing and disturbingly compelling. It unsettled me then and has continued to exercise me as the years have gone on. His arguments remain the most elegant and profound challenge to the conception of art I have been sketching. Part of his wrath focuses on art's alleged tendency to cultivate base desires or falsely glorify immoral characters, a matter to which we will return in the next chapter. What matters here is the challenge he presents to those who assume that we can learn something from art. It is true that Plato has a rather esoteric conception of knowledge; it consists in acquaintance with abstract forms of which the objects in the material world are merely imperfect copies. Artists, because they are engaged in representations of material things, only copy imperfect material copies of the forms themselves. None the less, considered apart from his peculiar metaphysics, the thrust of his challenge loses none of its edge. In Book X he condemns representational art generally, in particular painting and poetry, on the grounds that we can learn nothing from art – it serves only to mislead and distort. Without relying on Plato's metaphysics, we might say that those who possess true knowledge do so from direct experience, reason or deference to authoritative testimony. Artists as such, on the other hand, have no such knowledge. They are intellectual dilettantes who imitate what they see or feel without true understanding:

'The maker of an implement, therefore, has a correct belief about its merits and defects, but he is obliged to get this by associating with and listening to someone who *knows*. And the person with the relevant knowledge is the user.'

'That is so.'

'What about the artist and his representations? Has he the user's direct experience of the things he paints to enable him to know whether or not his pictures are good or right? Or has he the correct opinion that springs from enforced acquaintance with and obedience to someone who knows what he ought to paint?'

'He has neither.'

'So the artist has neither knowledge nor correct opinion about the goodness or badness of the things he represents.'

'Apparently not.'

'So the poet too, as artist, will be beautifully ill-informed about the subjects of his poetry.'

'Completely.'

'None the less he'll go on writing poetry, in spite of not knowing whether he produces what is good or bad: and what he will represent will be anything that appeals to the taste of the ignorant multitude.'

'What else can he do?'

'Well,' I concluded, 'we seem to be pretty well agreed that the artist knows little or nothing about the subjects he represents and that the art of representation is something that has no serious value . . .'[5]

Plato holds that art cannot convey any insight. Unlike science, history, philosophy, technology or proper practical activities, there is no object or kind of knowledge particular to art. Anything we may happen to 'learn' from art will be banal, distortive or the restatement of something we knew already. Even in the coincidental cases where a work does 'tell' us something, it cannot be the work that affords us knowledge, for knowledge, unlike mere prejudice, must conform to the requirements of truth, reason and experience. Yet art is hardly subject to the constraints of reason and truth and bears no significant relation to direct experience.[6] Art represents the appearance of everything and the nature of nothing.

Take Edvard Munch's expressionist *The Scream* (1893). In the foreground we are presented with a lone, skeletal figure, standing on a pier. The jetty juts out diagonally from the background far left, projecting away from two black figures promenading together. This pulls the foreground figure towards the viewer and away from any sense of contact with the background figures. The background consists in vibrant, stratified lines of varying thickness, prominently coloured red and with a decreasing use of yellow, white and blue. The sea and surrounding land mass echo the dynamics of the sky but are given a much darker, more rounded feel. Whilst the lines of the sky, water and land mass go across the picture, in the foreground right, just behind the solitary figure, the line cuts down towards the edge of the pier, physically confirming the isolation of the central figure. The person is of indeterminate sex and stands clasping the sides of the face, the shape of the hands echoing the elongated, skeletal shape of the face. Notice that the shape of the gaping mouth is not stretched widthways, as it would be in the expression of anger, but forms an impossibly long spherical shape which is itself emphasised by the facial structure and hands. Thus the picture conveys the sense of a keening wail of horror rather than a shriek or howl of rage. What, Plato might ask, do we learn from such an art work? It's a trivial commonplace that people can feel lonely. The extent to which the picture illustrates anything more interesting concerns a sense of anguish and fear, that may be part of the human condition, at being cut off, detached and isolated from the world. But surely this is either something we knew already, else it would hardly strike a chord, or we do not yet know it. And if it is not something we know then the picture itself can't provide grounds for thinking this is part of the human condition as opposed to the romantic flight of fancy of a melancholic.

Edvard Munch, *The Scream*, (1893), colour oil on canvas © Munch Museum/Munch – Ellingsen Group, BONO, Oslo, DACS London 2004. Photograph J. Lathion © National Gallery, Norway 1999

A tempting response to Plato's challenge is to claim that art provides a particular kind of knowledge or understanding. The cliché that a picture is worth ten thousand words conveys the idea that we can grasp much in a picture that we can't articulate in words. So perhaps we should bear in mind a distinction between propositional and non-propositional knowledge. Propositional knowledge is knowledge *that* something is the case, of the kind involved in history, philosophy, science and psychology. It concerns matters such as that an event happened, why human beings might feel a certain way or how reason and emotions are linked. But, we might think, such abstract reason cannot tell us, at least in any rich way, about how it feels to have certain perceptions, responses, emotions and attitudes. This kind of non-propositional knowledge is akin to knowing how to perceive, respond or act and knowing what it is like to be a certain way. On such a view, art works could afford us imaginative acquaintance with perceptions, responses and attitudes that more formalised cognitive activities concerned with propositional knowledge cannot.[7] This kind of non-propositional knowledge is a function of experience – what the sensation of anguish is like, what feeling horrified at one's isolation from the world might be like, what it may be like to see oneself in terms of utter detachment from the world. Now affording such knowledge can hardly be distinctive of art if it is a function of experience generally. But we needn't hold that the knowledge afforded by art must be distinctive, just that art is particularly good at conveying such knowledge. If a particular kind of knowledge is grounded in the having of an experience, because the phenomenal aspects of an experience are basic, irreducible and non-propositionally articulable, then it looks as if we have a straightforward link to knowledge from experiencing art works.

The experience afforded by a work may convey to me what having an experience of an expressed emotion, feeling or attitude is *really* like even though I may not myself have felt it before.

In philosophical circles, Frank Jackson famously articulated a picture of experience by using the example of Mary.[8] She is a captive scientist who has lived and worked all her life in a black and white room where everything (herself included) is black and white. She comes to be the leading scientist on colour, colour vision and related brain states through diligent hard work and using her television screen to communicate with the outside world, read and have her experimental results conveyed to her. And yet she doesn't know what it's like to see colour (and will never do so unless she escapes her room). What seems to be missing are irreducible phenomenal properties constitutive of seeing colour. And it is knowledge of the phenomenal properties that is required to know what a new experience we have not had before is *really* like. Hence no matter how much Mary knows about colour she will never know, until she experiences it, what it is actually like to see colour. If experience has an irreducible phenomenal aspect that can only be known by actually experiencing the relevant states (or closely enough related states), then works can afford us knowledge by getting us to experience such states, or closely related ones, for ourselves. And this holds not merely for brute sensations but for much more complex states such as emotions, for example horror, desires, for example to be with other people, and attitudes, such as existential anguish. Such knowledge, knowing what it would be like to feel such things as opposed to merely knowing about them, would be far from trivial or obviously known already.

The nature of this response is on the right lines but the claims made are overly strong. Part of what goes on when we identify with art works is that they express feelings and attitudes psychologically close to us. But it doesn't follow from this that some kind of special knowledge is involved. Furthermore, the thought that the phenomenal properties of experience (even just with respect to sensations) are basic and irreducible is highly controversial. In part this is because the idea that there is something to experience above and beyond what can be propositionally articulated, albeit in highly complex ways, threatens to render our relations to the physical world deeply mysterious. For that reason alone it is better to consider a more minimal basis for asserting the experiential grounding claim.

Here's a more minimal basis for the experiential grounding. It is not that experience involves certain extra-special subjective entities which we otherwise would not have knowledge of but, rather, that experience gives rise to certain capacities or abilities. Mary does not lack some factual knowledge but, rather, lacks the know-how to recognise colour just by seeing it. Consider an ordinary case of someone learning from experience, say someone who has never played pool before. By grasping the underlying principles of the game they can come to a theoretical understanding of the game. But they may lack practical understanding in the sense of not being able to play it. What they lack are the abilities to line the balls up, predict velocity and angles, co-ordinate the movement of their arms smoothly to push the cue through the ball and so on. So they lack the capacity to play pool unless they have had enough similarly related experiences before. Understanding an experience, then, may be cashed out in terms of the ability to put oneself in or recognise states representative of the relevant kind of experience. And exercising this ability is just to adopt the perspective of experiencer. If I have new enough experiences I may come to have new abilities – to recognise sights, sounds and smells I had not recognised before, to make finer discriminations amongst them and to remember or imagine experiences I hadn't done before. Having these abilities doesn't involve a peculiar kind of knowledge but does depend upon experience – it is a matter not of knowing that such and such is the case but of knowing how to remember, imagine, discriminate amongst and recognise experiences.

A related way of making the point is to see that we often take up different perspectives on the same experience. Imagine you've read various art books and seen many reproductions of Matisse paintings. You know that he is one of the great twentieth-century artists because of his bold use of colour, formal and structural concerns and imaginative reworking of older artistic traditions. There's an exhibition of his on at the Royal Academy and you go two days running. The first day you look in a formal, academic manner at those features of the paintings held to be of art-historical significance, take note of his artistic development, attend to the use of flattened perspective, duly note the bold colours and expressive brushstrokes. The second day you return just for fun. You go back to the same paintings and look at the same features. However, this time you don't look at them as instances of significant art historical features but, rather, just as bold sweeping brushstrokes, vivid colours, foreshortened canvases. The first day was worthy but dull, the second vivid and alive. It is not that there was some ineffable aspect to your experience on the second day that was missing on the first. Rather you just took up a different perspective on the experience. On the first day you were concerned with the works in terms of academic interest and on the second in terms of how you responded to them. There is no additional fact that you came to know on the second day, it is just that the different perspective you took up on your experience afforded you a new way of knowing what you knew already: Matisse was a great artist. But in order for you to take up different perspectives on the work of Matisse you must first have the experience.

We do not need to claim that there is some special ineffable feeling possessed by experience over and above what can be propositionally articulated. All that is being claimed is that there are different avenues to knowledge and understanding. Munch's *Scream* may afford the same kind of understanding of existential anguish, the horror of being alone, the feeling of radical displacement from others and the world, that principled reason may give. Reading Sartre's philosophical tome *Being and Nothingness* may yield the same understanding. Yet good art works constitute a particularly valuable way of conveying such an understanding, since they engage us in particularly stimulating and moving ways. Munch's *Scream* gets us to identify with the central existential figure, to feel the grip of isolation and anguish, and gets us to respond to such a vision of the world. Sartre's *Being and Nothingness* lays that vision out for the intellect. Hence works can get us to grasp certain truths, insights or possibilities, and make us realise their import in psychologically immediate ways, in ways pure reason rarely does. So we need not hold that only art conveys a distinctive kind of knowledge nor that experiencing art works involves ineffable properties. We only need the recognition that artistry enables psychologically vivid experiences which can convey putative insights particularly well in a non-abstract affective fashion. If the artistic means utilised are poor, clumsy or impoverished, then a work has failed to realise the affective understanding we value in much great art. In such cases we are unlikely to care about or take much interest in whatever insight is implicit in our experience of the work.

Truth in art

Even given this defence, there remain two further challenges to be met. First, how can we distinguish between works where the insight afforded is extraneous to the work rather than intimately tied to its artistry? Second, how can it be that we value works embodying conflicting insights? In other words, how relevant is truth compared to other virtues associated with understanding?

The first question must be addressed since works can provoke thoughtful responses and yet be lacklustre as art. Tracy Emin's *My Bed* (1998/9), for example, consists of her unmade bed, on and around which are strewn used condoms, soiled underwear, cigarette ends, empty vodka bottles and a pregnancy test kit. Emin is an artistic creature of the 1990s, was collected and promoted by Charles Saatchi, and enjoyed a spectacular rise. The confessional nature of her work tended to concentrate on her sexual history and emotional life. Perhaps the visual dynamics of the objects in *My Bed* are not particularly interesting nor is it clear what's so interesting about this aspect of her life. But one could make a case for the work in terms of its provocation of responses that are of some interest. The bottles, dishevelled sheets, condoms and pregnancy kit suggest a careless night of alcohol-fuelled sexual activity. In its earlier incarnations, a noose hung above the bed, threatening something underlying the detritus of apparently carefree pleasures. So it could be that looking at the work brings to mind thoughts about the hidden costs of hedonism, the ways in which power, cynicism or futility can underlie apparently innocent pleasures. Such thoughts are of genuine human interest and significance. Yet the connection between the ways we are required to engage visually with the work and the thoughts that may be provoked is attenuated. There is little about the objects' arrangement, other than their juxtaposition, that takes us any further in developing our responses. All that guides our visual attention is the recognition of incongruity. So the work does no more than prompt the thoughts of the viewer rather than shape and develop them in our experience of looking at the work. Hence it is a relatively superficial piece. The juxtaposition is interesting but easy enough; doing something with it is the hard part.

Much more extreme cases can be found amongst the didactic works of the British Empire, Soviet Socialist Realism and the Third Reich. Many involve a high level of artistic draughtsmanship and the attitudes represented may provoke thoughtful responses. Yet in many instances, the initially prompted attitude remains undeveloped in any artistically relevant fashion. Hence the viewer is left to reflect on the nature and ramifications of their immediate response independently of the work. Such works are poor because we expect art not merely to prompt but to guide and deepen our responses. This is no different from recognising that terrible novels can provoke interesting thoughts and responses though they remain terrible novels. Reading a Mills and Boon romance may occasion us to think about the nature of romantic love, its illusory nature, the possessiveness of desire and its all-encompassing nature. But the thoughts themselves are merely occasioned by the work rather than developed in any interesting way by our engagement with it.

A different way of making the same point is this. We could add more objects to Emin's *My Bed*: a crucifix; a pornographic magazine; a clock mechanism. Adding such objects might prompt us to have further thoughts about the nature of sexuality, death, our animal nature, redemption, mortality and time. But adding such objects would not automatically make it a better work of art merely because they prompt yet more interesting thoughts. In this case, what's crucial is whether the way the objects are placed, their visual relationships, penetrate our engagement with the work and thus guide our thoughts as we attend to them.

Posing the problem in this manner itself suggests the answer to our first question. What matters is whether the means of representation penetrate and shape our grasp of the thoughts and attitudes conveyed through the representation. Where they do so, our responses are intimately tied to the experience as shaped by engagement with the work. In which case the putative insights are internal to the work as art. Where this is not the case, they are extraneous. Returning to Munch's *Scream*, see p. 115, we can see how the composition of the picture emphasises the central figure's isolation. For example, the diagonal of the jetty on the left projects the figure towards the viewer; its isolation is emphasised by the more vertical carving out of the landmass directly to the right and the sense of depth is exaggerated by being set against the horizontal stratification of the landscape behind. Here the means of representation penetrate and shape our experience with the work in ways which emphasise the isolation, angst and horror portrayed.

The second question may be posed in the form of an objection. If we valued insight in art then it would be puzzling as to why we rate highly works we take to reveal a flawed understanding of the world. We may admire Francis Bacon's portrayal of humanity as rotten, corrupted and diseased, value his work highly as art, and yet think such a picture profoundly mistaken. But this seems to sit ill at ease with the claim that insight matters. Take Caspar David Friedrich's *The Wanderer above the Sea of Mists* (1818).

The Friedrich represents a conception of man's relation to the world that conflicts with the vision embodied in Munch's *The Scream*. Friedrich presents us with a solitary figure, back turned,

standing atop a jutting rock outcrop. He's looking out across an endless stretch of mountain tops below, cloaked in hazy, wispy cloud cover. Towards the horizon, where he's gazing, the ridges converge and another mountain top rises far into the distance. Again we have a sense of the individual set apart from both the world of others and nature itself. But the mood and attitude is radically distinct from the Munch. The man bestrides the rocks, right hand proximate to his hip with walking stick in hand, suggesting a sense of mastery. His pose is contemplative, a man solitary yet not alone, as he looks out, just as we do, over the serene view before him. The expansive space defined by the cloud tops brushing the ridges below and the infinite reaches of the sky above sets him apart from the natural world below, whilst not quite being of the heavens above. Far from conceiving of man's isolation as a condition of existential angst, Friedrich's painting intimates a splendid spiritual detachment. Although Munch's and Friedrich's pictures reveal conflicting visions of humanity's condition and place in the world, both are truly great works.

It is tempting to sidestep the problem with the retort that truth in art is always irrelevant.[9] What matters most is whether the understanding prescribed by a work is interesting and complex, and expands our imaginative horizons. Art works are concerned with developing our responsiveness, a matter which concerns the vivifying of imaginative possibilities. Whether such possibilities are true or not is neither here nor there, since that's a matter for whichever area of enquiry by which the envisaged possibilities are to be properly assessed. There is much to be said for this view, and

Caspar David Friedrich, *The Wanderer above the Sea of Mists* (1818). Courtesy of Hamburger Kunsthalle/bpk, Berlin; photo Elke Walford

in many cases this is all works aim at. But such a move concedes too much, since the aim of some works is internally linked to truth. Assessing works in terms of their insight, profundity, complexity, interest, coherence, consistency, depth or intelligibility, or their sentimentality, callowness, banality or naivety, involves a cluster of notions that are mutually interdependent, amongst which is the notion of truth. Works can indeed be profound yet mistaken or true to life yet banal; insights can be partial. But this doesn't show truth is always irrelevant. All it shows is that there are many intellectual and affective virtues proper to art, only one of which is truth.[10] Which of the affective and intellectual virtues are relevant to assessing a particular work, and in what respects, will depend upon the kind of work involved, the genre worked within and the intentions of the artist. In many cases truth will *not* be relevant since what matters is the interest and intelligibility of the vision laid out before us or the psychological closeness and depth of the feelings evoked. In some cases it will be, and where it is the ways in which this is so may differ. Perhaps Munch's *Scream* and Friedrich's *The Wanderer* should be construed as conveying what particular psychological attitudes to oneself and others are like, rather than recommending they be ones we should take up. But it makes sense to ask of Picasso's *Weeping Woman* whether grief can be that possessive and vicious, to praise Van Dyck for capturing the weak sensuousness, melancholy and refinement of Charles I in his triple portrait or to qualify one's praise of Van Gogh's *Potato Eaters* because it conveys a rather partial and naïve, if attractive, conception of human nature. Could grief admit of such viciousness? Was the weakness of Charles I bound up with his sensuality? Are the poor who till the soil more nobly virtuous than those alienated from it? To assess such questions we have to oscillate between paying attention to the ways in which the works represent the implied links or characteristics and how we conceptualise, experience or understand them to be ourselves. The mistake made by most people who subscribe to the notion that truth matters in art is to overemphasise the extent to which it does so, as if *the* most important factor in evaluating a work concerned whether it was true to life in some fundamental respect. But, as with novels or philosophical works, truth may sometimes matter but much else besides is just as fundamental. How good is the artistry? How well do the visual interrelations penetrate and shape our experience with the work? Do they convey feelings, emotions and attitudes in striking and interesting ways? Is what is conveyed worth taking seriously? Is it an intelligible way of perceiving or conceiving of its subject matter? Any art that stands up to this kind of critical examination is a good work indeed.

The challenge of the avant-garde and conceptual art

A striking anomaly in the picture just sketched concerns the place of art produced by the historical avant-garde and conceptual artists. If what matters is the ways in which the form and content of a work shape our experience of it, thereby guiding our thoughts, feelings and attitudes, then it looks as if conceptual art must be of little or no artistic value whatsoever. This is based on the assumption that the point of conceptual art lies not in any experience afforded by a work but in the recognition of a given idea. No doubt something like this thought lies behind why many people dismiss conceptual art as worthless. It is not enough to claim that conceptual art can change the way people think about things, thus affording a valuable experience of some kind, for the notion of experience here is too broad. In one sense a work of philosophy, science or mathematics may change how we think about things. But in philosophical, scientific or mathematical texts elements of style, rhetorical technique and artistry are downplayed as much as possible. What distinguishes art works from such texts is the means used to guide and shape how we look at what is represented, the artistic style, pictorial techniques and genre conventions which are used to cultivate certain feelings, thoughts and responses as we engage with it. But in conceptual art it looks as if, where there is an object at all, we are merely called to register the idea it points to. Where is the artistry in that?

To answer this challenge we have to think a little more carefully about the nature of conceptual art.

Although the term itself didn't come into common artistic parlance until the 1960s, perhaps the best-known conceptual art piece is Marcel Duchamp's *Fountain* (1917), see p. 129. It consisted of an ordinary French urinal, inverted, signed R. Mutt and was entered as sculpture for an exhibition in New York in 1917. Though rejected for the exhibition, it is Duchamp's most famous work and is just one example of his ready-mades: pieces which involved taking ordinary objects and juxtaposing, modifying or displaying them in provocative ways. He mounted a bicycle wheel on a kitchen stool, displayed a bottle rack bought from a Parisian shop and a snow shovel bought over the counter from a hardware store, and painted a goatee on a reproduction of the *Mona Lisa* inscribing it *L.H.O.O.Q.* (1941–2). Duchamp's work, as a precursor for the development of conceptual art, held sway over an increasingly dominant strand in twentieth-century art. It is worth noting that his work even then was hardly so anomalous. Many artists at

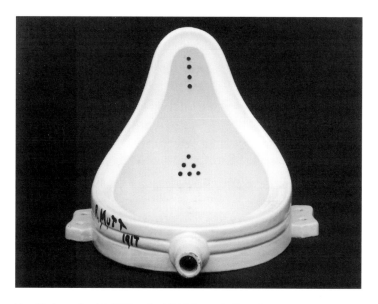

Marcel Duchamp, *Fountain* (1917), replica 1964 © Succession Marcel Duchamp/ADAGP, Paris and DACS, London 2004. Photograph © Tate, London 2003

one time or another did similar things; for example, Picasso took a bicycle saddle, placed it face on and topped it with handle bars to make *Bull's Head* (1943). The juxtaposition of two mundane bicycle parts works because when we look at it we can indeed see it, albeit schematically, as a representation of a bull's head. But such concerns were taken to a much more extreme limit by the Dada movement, which emerged in 1915 as a radical reaction against traditional conceptions of art. Artists like Hans Arp, Francis Picabia and Man Ray, along with Duchamp himself, emphasised the random, the provocative gesture, the use of ordinary materials in collages, montage and ready-mades. Dadaism itself helped to give birth to surrealism in the 1920s, sharing with it an emphasis on the anti-rational or 'chance' nature of artistic creation, assembled constructions and apparently arbitrary juxtaposition of objects. The influence of such attitudes waned somewhat with the death of surrealism but started to emerge again in the 1950s. Jasper Johns painted representations of two-dimensional objects like the American flag and made sculptures of ordinary objects like beer cans and brushes. Robert Rauschenberg incorporated three-dimensional objects into his paintings, used silk screen processes and developed an interest in experimental media. The development of the pop art movement in the 1960s, with artists like Andy Warhol, Peter Blake, Richard Hamilton, Roy Lichtenstein and Claes Oldenburg, saw a renewal of interest in mass culture objects, media and concerns. This developed, in the late 1960s and 1970s, into an explosion of artistic interest in conceptual art. The Anglo-American Art and Language movement foregrounded language by painting or printing words on canvases, considered itself anti-visual and often political, and was concerned with reflexive questions about the nature of art works and the art world. The Italian arte povera movement used the most worthless materials such as earth, leaves and raw clay and the New York artist Les Levine, most well known as a pioneer of video and media art, once bought and ran an ordinary restaurant and declared that all the bills would be works of art. The content was determined by the customers and made out by the waiters. From the 1960s until the present day, the profusion of minimalist works, like Carl Andre's Equivalent VIII (1966–78), two bricks high, six across, and ten lengthwise, multi-media explorations, performance works, installation art and the presentation of ideas can all be traced through this lineage back to the ready-mades of Duchamp. The characteristics of these movements and phases are not all shared but there remains a cluster of features, some of which are possessed by them all to a greater or lesser extent. What makes the artistic lineage of conceptual art into a coherent story is the concern with ready-made or mundane objects, the primacy of ideas, the foregrounding of language, the use of non-conventional artistic media, reflexivity and the rejection of traditional conceptions of sensory aesthetic experience. If we bear in mind the variety of strands woven into the term conceptual art, then we can see the main ways in which such works can constitute good art.

Ironically enough, some pieces which are in part conceptual also involve sensory aesthetic appreciation. They may not conform to traditional notions of beauty, or may involve materials we are not used to approaching in aesthetic terms, but there is no denying that sometimes they yield aesthetic rewards. Take Yves Klein's 1950s monochrome series of ultramarine canvases which were exhibited as being for sale for different prices. Klein's attempts to deperson-alise colour or play with the commercial evaluation of art may be intriguing but what stands out about these paintings is the sheer luminosity and appeal of the colour itself – a shade he patented as International Klein Blue. His *Cosmogoniesseries*, made by exposing prepared paper to the rain, and his *Anthropométries* series (1960), made by smearing IKB on nude models who then imprinted themselves on to canvases, are radically unconventional methods for creating art but the results, in at least some cases, are strikingly beautiful. Similarly Anya Gallacio's *Intensities and Surfaces* (1996) possessed aesthetic appeal. It consisted of 34 tons of ice blocks, stacked into a large, 4 metre tall rectangle, placed on top of an electric blue light in Wapping pump station in London. Half a ton of rock salt was placed on the top, working its way down as the ice melted into translucent pools of water surrounding the object. The luminescent colour refracted through the ice, the colour reflected back from the wet, half frozen pools and the contrast between the surfaces themselves afforded a deeply sensuous experience. Although the idea of the dematerialising art object forms part of the concerns of Gallacio's work it was, as Tony Godfrey put it, 'essential to see the work: the sensory experience was far more important and interesting than the concept *per se*'.[11] And the appeal of Damien Hirst's *Away from the Flock* (1994), which consists of a sheep preserved whole in a cage of steel and glass containing formaldehyde, lies if anywhere in its beauty. The incredible sense of fine texture, structure and richness of the lamb's wool is so pure and, heightened by the conditions of preservation, it seems unreal.

However, in much conceptual art, sensory appreciation is either beside the point or irrelevant. To try to engage with Duchamp's *Fountain* in terms of its sensory aesthetic rewards is to miss the point. And in many conceptual works the material object, if there is one, is eminently disposable. At best it is a sign that serves only to suggest an idea. The American sculptor Sol Le Witt, who coined the term, once stated that for 'conceptual art the idea or concept is the most important aspect of the work. When an artist uses a conceptual form in art, it means that all of the planning and decisions are made beforehand and the execution is a perfunctory affair.'[12] So for many conceptual pieces sensory appeal is negligible. It is true that ideas themselves can be beautiful or aesthetically appealing. The simplicity of the formulae $e = mc^2$ appeals because of the rigour, complexity and depth of the ideas involved, the economy of expression of their relations and its explanatory value. But the ideas, concepts and abstractions picked out by conceptual art are often not aesthetically appealing in this way.

Take the work of Jenny Holzer. In the 1980s she became successful for a series of works on items of clothing, plaques, cinema billboards, electronic readouts and the like which consisted of simple slogans such as 'CHARISMA CAN BE FATAL'. Superficially the slogans are banal, but further consideration sometimes provokes interesting questions. In what ways is charisma supposed to be fatal exactly? And to whom? Think, for example, of the ways in which someone can come to be a victim of their own charisma, developing into a pastiche or parody of themselves. The slogans are meant to remind us of clichés, though often they are not quite those we might expect. Moreover, where the slogans are themselves displayed is often important to the nature of what she is doing. Her more political slogans, for example, have often been displayed on items of clothing, cinema hoardings and billboards. The point of so doing involves highlighting the ways in which forms of advertising, entertainment and style we normally consider to be harmless and personal may be highly politicised. Hence their positioning and form drive home the provocative nature of the gesture itself. But there is more to her work than this. The scale of her work became ever larger by the end of the 1980s when she exhibited on a large scale selections from *Truisms*, *Inflammatory Essays*, *The Living Series*, *Under a Rock*, *Laments* and *New Writing* (1989/90) at both the Guggenheim and the Venice Biennale. The large numbers of LED electronic readouts displaying her slogans ranged from 'YOU ARE A VICTIM OF THE RULES YOU LIVE BY' to 'WHEN SOMETHING TERRIBLE HAPPENS PEOPLE TEND TO WAKE UP'. These are not really candidates for intellectual beauty. Considered independently, by being just off from the sort of cliché we might expect, some of the slogans may provoke thought. Perhaps we are prompted to consider the ways in which we take things for granted until we are confronted with misfortune, how life itself seems more vivid in misfortune and how tragedy often prompts us to re-evaluate and see our lives as if awakened from a slumber. But this is hardly the case for all the slogans she cites. The real force of the piece lies in the way the slogans cited are piled up one upon another. They are not straight-forwardly being put before us as ideas to be contemplated. Rather, she foregrounds the stock of clichés in circulation in contemporary culture, their sheer volume, in a manner that undermines them. The truisms unravel before us under the weight of their own absurdity.

Conceptual pieces can also be good art because they stretch our visual and conceptual schemas. Sol Le Witt's *Two Open Modular Cubes/Half Off* (1972) consists in the construction of two cubes half joined together. As we look at it we can switch visually back and forth between different ways of dividing up the spaces and lines. It's not the case that all conceptual art does this or does so well. The conceptual artists who concentrated on language and ideas in this way in the sixties and seventies tended to present propositions, such as those culled from philosophers like Carnap or Austin, ripped out of context, as the Art and Language group was fond of doing. Others presented documentation tracing and questioning social developments, such as Dan Graham's *Homes for America* (1966–7), or presented objects or propositions which invited the spectator to question the nature of art, such as Keith Arnatt's *Trouser-Word Piece* (1972), which consisted of a photograph of himself with a bill board proclaiming 'I'M A REAL ARTIST'. But as a provocation to thought, manipulating both forms and an audience's artistic expectations, conceptual art often strives to make us question assumptions about our lives, culture and art itself.

The best way to appreciate some conceptual works is as a kind of anti-art. Consider Duchamp's Fountain, Rauschenberg's *Erased de Kooning* (1953), where he rubbed out a drawing given to him by de Kooning, Joseph Kosuth's *One and Three Chairs* (1965), consisting of an actual chair, a life-size photograph of it and a definition of the term 'chair', through to the pronouncements by various artists that a particular empty room, intellectual object, found object or even hidden object is a work of art. The purpose of such works is to subvert and jar with our ordinary conceptions of what constitutes art, what confers artistic status upon an object and our assumptions concerning how we should engage with art objects. The interest of the point diminishes rapidly with repetition, unless it is made with exceptional wit or complexity, which is not usually the case. But notice that even the particularly original and witty pieces, such as *Fountain*, only have a value in contrast to the standard conception of art. In other words this kind of conceptual art is parasitic upon the standard conception of art it seeks to subvert. So conceptual art of this ilk requires the standard assumptions about artistic value to be in place in order to have any value at all. Some such works are good. *Fountain* is both a clever and witty questioning of artistic authority and the art world. But there is little to be gained by the glib repetition *ad infinitum* of the questioning of arthood status in this way.

Perhaps the main motivation behind people's suspicion of conceptual art is the recognition that, at least in some such art, the material object is dispensable. As we saw in chapter 1, some conceptual art seeks to make works where experience of the object is, if possible, beside the point. But if the material object truly is dispensable, the worry goes, how can we really be dealing with a *work* of art? As I've already suggested, ideas themselves can be aesthetically appealing. The appeal of an equation such as $e = mc^2$ may be partly explained in terms of its elegance or simplicity, but not all conceptual art can be so tightly tied to traditional conceptions of beauty or the aesthetic.[13] Consider, as a test, the following hypothetical case. There is a courtyard that was the scene of a Nazi pogrom in the Second World War. An artist has the idea of visiting the courtyard unobserved at night to take up and replace its cobblestones, engraving on each one the name of one of the Jewish victims. Now she might only have the idea, she might sketch it, or she might even do it in such a way that the courtyard looks no different from how it appeared before. But independently of what she does with the idea, the idea itself has a certain kind of appeal. The thought of individually marking out each particular victim with a cobblestone, leaving an unobservable causal trace, gives form to the presumption that each individual matters. The victims may have left no mark upon the world themselves, we may not be able to notice their absence in any way, yet the annihilation of each and every one of them constituted its own particular tragedy. The bleak reticence of the idea is in part its strength. The appeal of the idea is closely related to that of other pieces such as Maya Lin's *Vietnam Veterans Memorial* (1982) in Washington DC. Two black granite walls meet at an angle of 125 degrees and slope down to nothing at either end. Approached from one side the memorial is invisible, since the top of the walls starts at ground level, going down to another level, with the names of more than 58,000 men and women missing in action engraved upon it. The design of the memorial is aimed at bringing out 'the realisation of loss and a cathartic healing process . . . Brought to a sharper awareness of such loss, it is up to each individual to come to terms with this loss. For death is in the end a private matter and the area contained within this memorial is a quiet place meant for personal reflection and private reckoning.'[14] In our hypothetical case, no doubt some properties would be added were it to be materially realised. For example, how we would look at and perceive the courtyard concerned may well be affected in terms of what we pay attention to and how we respond to features of it. But the appeal of the idea isn't reducible to properties bound up with our experience of the courtyard. That's why we can grasp the appeal of the idea without seeing anything at all. This is not an uncommon phenomenon. In philosophy people often advert to thought experiments as a way of testing intuitions, teasing out conceptual distinctions or implications. Imagine a world where you seemed to experience everything just as you do in this one, but in that world you're plugged into a machine which creates those experiences for you rather than the world actually being as you experience it. From Descartes to *The Matrix*, variations on this kind of thought experiment are profoundly thought provoking, suggestive, illuminating and affecting. In straight philosophy, science or cultural thought, the profundity of an idea, the sudden throwing into order and structure of disparate phenomena or the sudden inversion of standard ways of thinking about problems have an appeal which can't be reduced to their aesthetic, narrative or material properties. So too with some conceptual art. The insight, cognitive inversion, illumination and affect which is the upshot of the form of an idea in consciousness, independently of its realisation in a material object, can be appreciated and valued as art. It's true that presenting such ideas to us for appreciation as art doesn't involve materials or artistry specific to art alone. But not all that we value in art is specific to art. Art is a cultural practice which tends to realise particular things we value very well and that often includes things which other practices realise too. The same can be said for philosophy. What ties even the appreciation of a conceptual piece to other artistic works is the imaginative expression of the artist as given form in the idea itself, hence we can appreciate the idea by entertaining the form of the idea in our minds even though there may be no material, perceivable object involved. Infamously Collingwood held that the art work proper is the mental object in an artist's consciousness, so any material object is merely a means for the audience to re-create the same mental object in theirs. He has been rightly criticised for such a view.[15] Many material properties of art works partly constitute them. But there can be art, good art at that, which just is constituted by the form of the idea in consciousness – if anything is, that truly is conceptual art.

The art of discrimination

The preceding thoughts bring us on to a much underappreciated way in which good art can deepen and refine our mental life. In considering how art cultivates understanding, at least in philosophical and critical circles, the focus has tended to be on the content of our responses to art works.[16] As we've seen, the nature of the perceptions, feelings and attitudes evoked, and how they are done so, is fundamental to our evaluation of art works. But we should not let this eclipse a distinct way in which art relates to understanding. Good art works can develop our capacities for discrimination and appreciation.

To see how this is so we must first consider the nature of experience itself. Appreciating and understanding the nature of an experience generally, 'what it is like', admits of degrees and depends upon the capacities to attend, take different perspectives on and discriminate amongst elements of the experience and how they interrelate. Appreciation involves estimating the nature, quality and value of an experience and understanding is to be taken as grasping the meaning of an experience.

Consider perception. When we see, taste, hear or feel things we are subjected to the appearances of an object: how it seems. The appearances are relative to the sense modality, such as vision, in which an object is perceived, the conditions of perception, such as lighting conditions, and the perceiver's point(s) of view, for example from where I see the object. What an object appears as depends upon (1) the selective attention of the perceiver to the object and (2) the discriminative capacities exercised by the perceiver. What it is for an object to appear as something is for it to appear in experience the way objects, events or states of affairs of a certain kind typically do. On the basis of appearances we can and do have non-inferential perceptual knowledge. In other words, we don't just make inferences or reason about what we perceive but we gain knowledge from the way things manifestly appear to us in perception. Two everyday cases help to bring out the contrast:

(a) You are in a heated office. In the first scenario you look out of the window and see that the sun is dull, it's icy and the ther-mometer on the building opposite says −1 degrees centigrade. So you infer that it's cold. In the second scenario you go outside for a cigarette only to feel icy wind and shiver with cold. In the first scenario the cold is not perceptually manifest; you're warm and it's possible that you see the weather conditions and thermometer as they are and yet it be relatively warm outside (the thermometer could be wrong). In the second scenario, assuming there is nothing wrong with you, what is perceived is the way things are.

(b) You are at a party. In the first scenario you note that after someone else has spoken out of turn your friend, who is normally
very lively and engaged on the matters in hand, is abnormally
quiet and reticent. You infer that she is frustrated. In the
second scenario she reacts by rolling her eyes, grimacing and
exaggeratedly shrugging her shoulders. You see that she is
expressing frustration. It is important here to note two points.
In the first scenario you may see her actions as being expressive
of anger but this is not the same as her expressing anger. In the
second scenario you see her expressing anger but it is not
perceptually manifest that she is angry (since she may express
anger in order to annoy the person who spoke out of turn
without herself actually being angry).

What it is that is manifestly known depends not just on the
appearances that the object or event perceived has but also upon
the selective attention, perspectives and discriminative capacities
exercised with regard to it. We may attend differentially to the
movement, shape, colour or size of an object, its relations to other
nearby objects, how certain properties or parts of the object
stand in relation to each other and so on. An object or event can
also be perceived from different perspectives which will give
rise to contrasting differences in the apparent interrelations
of appearances. Furthermore, we can also be more or less discriminate regarding the appearance of an object in different ways. For
example, if someone goes to wine tasting classes they can be taught
to discriminate between different kinds of wines, flavours and
vineyards of origin, something which, above a certain basic level,
someone lacking comparative experience would be unable to do.
So our understanding of an experience, what we can know from

appearances, and our appreciation of an experience, our estimation of the nature and quality of an experience, depend upon our capacities for attending, taking up different perspectives and discrimination. The greater these capacities, the more we will understand and appreciate an experience – as vintners will testify.

In order to expand our capacities to attend, take up different perspectives upon and discriminate amongst experiences, we must be subject to a variety of experiences. Consider wine tasting or coffee drinking. We would not trust the discriminative capacities (upon which taste depends) and thus judgement of someone who had only ever drunk Lambrusco or instant coffee, for they lack the relevant experience required to develop and refine their discrimination. They would thus be unable to pick out many of the relevant differences between richly bitter, finely roasted coffee beans and burnt acrid coffee beans or between a saccharine, metallic, shallow wine and a slightly oaky, medium-bodied wine. Thus both understanding and appreciation of an experience require comparative experience amongst the relevant kind. Furthermore certain ways of attending and taking up perspectives on an experience depend upon different experiences not just of the same kind but of relevantly contrasting kinds. Consider architecture. If the only buildings around were ultra-minimalist, hard edged, clean lined and functional then though I may be able to distinguish between good and bad examples of minimalism I would lack the relevant comparative experience to (1) attend to them as clutter free, shorn of decorative embellishment and distinctively modern and (2) view them from the perspective of one who has been numbed, overwhelmed and suffocated by the complex geometry, insistent gaudy coloration and intricate, individualising stone work or gilding of other styles of architecture (different elements of which can be found in architecture of the Gothic, Renaissance and Baroque periods). Hence I may even be unable to appreciate what may be appealing and valuable about such architecture without the relevant comparative experience. It follows that coming to a fuller understanding and deeper appreciation of a kind of experience, to the extent that kind admits of attending to different aspects, taking up different perspectives and exercising different and finer discriminative capacities, requires comparative experience both within the relevant kind and of relevantly contrasting kinds.

Grasping this general truth about experience enables us to see that good art often cultivates and rewards our capacities for discriminating between and appreciating elements of experience. A supreme master in this respect is Chardin. His oeuvre consists mainly of still life studies, from inanimate objects to intimate portraits of eighteenth-century Parisian bourgeois domestic life. His work is devoid of social comment and significance; there is no message about the human condition nor attitude of praise, blame or ambivalence directed towards the scenes he portrays. His concern with the content of what he represents is descriptive, pure and painterly. Chardin's work is devoted to visual attention and discrimination. His paintings tend to reveal themselves very gradually. Take his *Boy Playing Cards* (1740), displayed in the Uffizi. Done before he'd reached the height of his powers, none the less its pictorial composition is typical of the concerns he was to develop for the rest of his life.[17] At an initial glance we are drawn to the side-on face of the young boy, since we are naturally inclined to register faces first and foremost. But then our visual attention switches down to his collar, an illumined white designed to stand out and draw our attention away from the face. In doing so this brings his left arm, laid across the table, into our visual field. His cuff is illuminated in the same way as his collar, so our visual attention is naturally brought down and across once more. This then brings the whole visual relationship between the boy's hands, the cards he is holding and those on the table into distinct view. Here there are four points of illumination: (i) the shirt sleeve cuff; (ii) the cards in the boy's hand set further back; (iii) the cards standing in rows on the table on the left parallel with the cuff; and (iv) in the foreground in a straight line from the cards in the hand, the bright, white back of a card disposed of in the open table drawer. So here we have a diamond shape emphasised by the four points of illumination, giving added depth to the picture and shaping our visual attention. All the points of illumination are themselves contrasted with finer details surrounding them, of the face, hands and cards respectively, which shade off into darker colours and loss of detail before one meets the next point of illumination. It's a sophisticated and complex play with our visual attention using multiple points of illumination and contrasting distinct detailing. Chardin's painting highlights the importance of illumination to our visual organisation, how it shapes the formal patterns, structures and details that we notice in our experience. But what is important about the Chardin is that it stretches our visual attention, shaping and extending our capacity to look at the visual field presented to us by the world in this kind of way. The very expression of the boy in the painting, mutely engrossed as he looks down at his cards, mirrors the visual absorption that Chardin's work yields to the viewer.

Impressionism and cubism, in their rather different ways, are concerned not so much with visual discrimination as such but, rather, with visual flexibility. As is well known, the impressionists, like many before and after them, were initially met with cries of incomprehension, accusations of artistic degeneracy and inability. It took a while for people to realise what it was they were supposed to be looking for in the paintings. Much is often made of how the impressionists were trying to uncover the notion of an innocent eye, representing the flux of experience prior to its categorisation by the mind. But the most interesting thing about impressionism is the way in which people came to see how the brightly coloured strokes, flecks and daubings of paint could be seen as crystallising into concrete images. Indeed, this occurred to such an extent that people were wont to describe natural scenes themselves in such terms. Not only did impressionism succeed in stretching how we can look at images but it brought about a radical shift in the way nature itself could be looked at. Cubism was likewise concerned with visual adaptability but its focus was the representation of three-dimensional objects on the two-dimensional surface of the canvas. The particular visual attraction of cubism lies in the oscillation between the fractured planes which highlight the artificiality of the two-dimensional surface whilst none the less succeeding in representing from different angles three-dimensional objects. Whilst the Chardin draws out our capacities for visual attention and discernment, these works stretch and modify the very ways in which we perceive.

Another visual concern, the discernment and expressivity of patterns, can be seen in the work of Jackson Pollock. *Summertime* (1948) conveys the airy freedom of summer via the expressivity of increasingly liberated movement.

Unlike most of Pollock's works from this period, the overlay of dripped paint, with yellow and blue colour patches, is on bare canvas rather than a labyrinth of encrusted paint. Hence, when contrasted with other Pollocks, its appearance is one of lightness. The colour patches are attached to the main leitmotif of a thin,

Jackson Pollock, *Summertime: Number 9A* (1948) © ARS, NY and DACS, London 2004. Photograph © Tate, London 2003

black figure-like form that's serially represented. The series of figures moves from a rather static posture on the far left through to the increasingly expansive and frenzied movements on the far right, as if engaged in a vital celebratory dance. The surrounding paint drips, as the figure progresses, grow in number, are ever thinner and more energetic as if the paint itself were a cascade of sweat showering off the twirling figure. The underlying figures are not unlike the cut out figures from his *Rhythmical Dance* (1948) and bring to mind Matisse's *Dance* (1910). The way in which the abstract drippings, patches and outlines coalesce into the repeated pattern of a figure, conveying a sense of movement and gestural expressivity, is an immense visual achievement given the highly abstract nature of the work. More generally, particular cases aside, good landscapes, cityscapes, photography, still lives, often cultivate our potential perceptual capacities and thus, indirectly at least, deepen our discrimination with respect to visual experiences of such objects themselves.

As with the discrimination developed through wine or coffee drinking, in some cases we might have to be fairly discriminate already to get the effect, whilst in others the knowledge and discrimination required to appreciate the work is more minimal. Chardin's *Boy Playing Cards*, for example, requires more from the viewer in this respect than Pollock's *Summertime*. No doubt there is some level beyond which we judge that the discrimination or knowledge required from us is too great for the returns, given the other things in our lives we value and wish to pursue. Where that level is will vary from individual to individual, as it does with respect to the lengths people are prepared to go to go to for good coffee or wine. But it doesn't mean the differences aren't there or that further rewards aren't to be had.

Art stretches, extends and revolutionises the ways we come to see the world. It is one of the most powerful means of cultivating our perceptual capacities. And this is not to mention the ways in which art may do so with respect to expressive gestures, facial character, symbolic imagery, allegory, similes, metaphor and the like. Pollock's *Summertime* shows how we can see the increasingly free dance of a figure as an analogy for the life and vitality that bursts forth in summer. Van Gogh's *Potato Eaters* visually engages us in terms of how we might see the gestures and facial expressions of people as responding reciprocally to one another. Impressionism showed the world how nature could come to be seen as patches of light, shade and colour coalescing into discernible structures. Far from mirroring nature, art helps to make the visual world for us. Patiently looking at and responding to such pictures makes us more discerning perceivers. It deepens and enriches our mental life. A world without good art would be myopic indeed.

Chapter Four | Art and Morality

Moralisers against art

In the late 1980s Senator Alfonse D'Amato stood up in the US Congress and ripped up a reproduction of Andres Serrano's *Piss Christ* (1987). This sparked a long-running feud over the awarding of grants for artistic projects considered by many to be obscene. In the UK in 1998 police from the West Midlands raided the home of a Birmingham fine art student, confiscated photographs of pictures by Robert Mapplethorpe and confiscated the book itself from the University of Central England's student library. Both the institution and the student were threatened with possible prosecution on the grounds of obscenity, though no prosecution was forthcoming. In 1997 the Sensation exhibition at the Royal Academy, subsequently transferred in 1999 to the Brooklyn Museum, caused a great furore. A large-scale portrait by Marcus Harvey of Myra Hindley (1995), sentenced to life in the 1960s for murdering children, was considered so offensive that it was defaced by ink and eggs thrown by angry members of the public. In Brooklyn controversy focused on Chris Ofili's *The Holy Virgin Mary* (1996) which, in its depiction of an African Madonna, used collage cut outs of bare bottoms from pornographic magazines in its decorative patterning. The then Mayor of New York, Rudy Giuliani, publicly declaimed it as blasphemous. In March 2001 the Saatchi Gallery's 'I am a Camera' exhibition was raided by Scotland Yard's obscene publications unit. The police's consternation focused on two images by the photographer Tierney Gearon, depicting her six-year-old daughter and four-year-old son. Her partly naked son urinates in the snow in one and, in the other, they are both looking at the camera wearing nothing but theatrical masks. The photographs themselves were part of a series of fifteen representing her personal family life. The fine art book associated with the exhibition was also considered to be in possible breach of the Children's Protection Act. Again no action was taken by the Crown Prosecution Service. In 2002 the US Department of Justice covered in drapes two semi-nude art deco statues that had stood in their Hall since the 1930s.

There is nothing new about attempts to censor works deemed offensive or obscene. In the Victorian era it was standard practice to cover the sexual genitalia of statues with fig leaves and the like. John Ruskin's puritanical nature got the better of him when he destroyed Turner's sexually explicit sketches and he condemned William Mulready's nudes as vulgar and abominable on the grounds that they were 'more degraded and bestial than the worst grotesques of the Byzantine or even Indian image makers'.[1] This is somewhat ironic given the praise heaped on works by Alma-Tadema, Frederick Leighton and others who specialised in exotic nudes set in neo-classical contexts. No doubt the erotic Roman mosaics the Victorians had been shocked to discover on the walls of bedrooms at Pompeii alleviated their sense of impropriety. None the less, nudity as such was taken to be provocative and offensive unless ameliorated by other concerns or sanitised by classical backdrops. In Europe the story is a similar one. Both Gustav Klimt and Egon Schiele to name but two ran into trouble over their depictions of female sexuality. Schiele was arrested on 13 April 1912, and tried on 7 May in Lower Austria. Although he was acquitted of corrupting minors, the judge symbolically burnt some of his drawings and imposed a fine. The sixteenth-century renowned Mannerist painter Giulio Romano made a series of pornographic prints, on which Pietro Aretino's *I Modi* sonnets were based, which were destroyed by the Vatican (only bastardised copies remain extant). Nor has moralistic censoriousness been confined to representations of sex and sexuality. The Third Reich held an infamous exhibition in 1937 of Degenerate Art as an example of the moral baseness and perversion of twentieth-century modernism. Caravaggio was almost excommunicated by the Church, dying in exile in Malta, for having the audacity to repre-sent Christ and saintly religious figures in naturalistic, human terms. And at the very birth of the philosophical consideration of the arts, Plato denounced most art as base, cultivating desires that should be suppressed and potent with the dangers of moral infection.

There is a cluster of attitudes underlying these kinds of judgements and views. Each one can be held independently of the others, but many people tend not only to run them together but to assume that they lend each other mutual support. The first is the notion that what is truly pornographic can never be art (at least not good art). The second view is that to the extent that the moral character of a work is defective, where it has one and it is related to its artistic nature, then its value as art is automatically lessened. The third is that to the extent a work is deeply obscene or morally perverse this constitutes grounds for censorship. I will argue that all three assumptions are fundamentally wrong. In essence they seek to domesticate, falsely, the nature and value of great art.

The erotic and the pornographic

It is an intellectual commonplace that what is pornographic cannot be artistic. The erotic can reach the heights of great art but the pornographic can only be bad art (if it is art at all). The following discussion of Schiele is not untypical in this regard:

> It is true that Schiele makes erotic drawings of adolescent girls, or paints them in watercolour, and it is also true that the girls let their nudity show. But although his works express the troubled beginnings of sexuality, their exceptional artistic quality saves them from the sin of pornography.[2]

Sometimes this is held to be true just by definition. The pornographic solely aims at sexual arousal whilst the erotic can have other goals including artistic ones.[3] This is nothing but moralistic prejudice masked by intellectual sophistry.

Nudes are not necessarily erotic or pornographic; they can be sexually explicit without being arousing or sensuous. The erotic needn't involve sexual explicitness. Titian's *Venus and Adonis*, Corregio's *Io*, Degas's portraits of ballet dancers, Robert Mapplethorpe's flower studies, for example, are all devoid of sexual explicitness though they solicit sensuous thoughts, feelings and associations which aim to be arousing. Hence there are many things that are erotic but not pornographic. But that which is pornographic is erotic. The pornographic is a sub-species of the erotic or erotica – it seeks to realise the aim that all erotic works do but via distinctive means: sexually explicit representation. So we have no reason to suppose that what is possible with respect to the erotic generally is precluded regarding a sub-category of the erotic – namely the pornographic. It is true that most pornographic representations possess no artistic merit or intention. However the same is true of most watercolours, from those painted by children at school to those painted for birthday cards, but we don't thereby assume that watercolours as such can't aspire to the dizzy heights of art. One just has to look at watercolours by Turner, Nolde or Klee to see this is palpable nonsense. Yet the same rule hardly seems to apply to people's assumptions about the pornographic. Celebrated ancient Greek Dionysiac images from cups and vases show orgiastic scenes of buggery, fellatio and group sex. Indian temples and monuments, such as the tenth-century one at Khajuraho and the thirteenth-century one at Konarak, have façades adorned by numerous reliefs with multiple figures in myriad explicit sexual positions. Works by the later Picasso, many studies by Egon Schiele and Gustav Klimt, sketches by Rodin, much of Aubrey Beardsley's work, prints by Hokusai and Utamaro, illustrations to the Kama Sutra, to name but a few, all conform to the typical characterisation of pornography, and possess artistic intent and no little merit. Indeed, the sexual candour of much ancient Greek, Graeco-Roman, Roman and medieval Indian art may suggest that the paucity of pornographic works within the Christian-influenced civilisations is an anomaly rather than the norm. Yet pointing to such works does little to convince most that the pornographic can constitute great art.

Part of the reluctance to concede the point depends on the assumption that pornographic sexual explicitness is inherently formulaic and fantastical and, as such, precludes artistic expressivity. But why should we grant that sexual explicitness in the service of arousal could never be expressive? Explicitness as such cannot be the problem. Lucian Freud's often highly explicit portraits of his nude subjects are highly expressive – the way the mottled flesh tones, contrasting textures of different parts of the body and differing proportions are conveyed prescribes a fascination with and understanding of what it is to apprehend another just as a body. Presumably the thought is that Freud as an artist has a choice as to whether or not to be explicit. Only if there is a horizon of possible choices available to a creator can the choice of what to represent and the level of detail chosen to represent it become significant. It is thought that in the case of pornography there is no such choice. Yet though there is little choice about whether or not to be sexually explicit in pornography, it does not follow that there are no expressively significant choices available. Choices remain concerning what should be rendered explicit and the degree of explicitness involved. More significantly there are multifarious choices concerning how the explicitness may be treated and conveyed. A host of possibilities remain: concerning, for example, which actions are to be represented, the angle of portrayal, the perspective used, which if any character's viewpoint is privileged, the kind of lighting evoked, what responses are portrayed, how the bodily movements are represented, for example whether they are aggressive or serene, what the facial expressions are, what parts are in or out of focus or what coloration is used. All such choices could in principle be put to expressive use in an artistically interesting and significant manner. Different choices with respect to the features of the very same act may prescribe different ways of understanding what is being represented and how one is supposed to find it arousing. Hence sexual explicitness in the service of arousal does not in principle preclude expressivity. It can't follow from the fact that certain things are required to constitute the pornographic that no room is thereby allowed for artistic expression. We don't think that this holds in the case of religious icons, which must depict a saint or holy personage in the service of religious devotion, since what is prescribed still leaves a wealth of choices open to the artist concerning the details and manner of treatment that can be put to expressive use. So too in the case of the pornographic.

Consider, for example, many of Rodin's pornographic nude drawings, such as *Naked Woman Reclining with Legs Apart, Hands on Her Sex* or *Naked Woman with Legs Apart* (1900), his many drawings of lesbians and female nudes masturbating and his drawings that accompanied Octave Mirabeau's pornographic novel *Le Jardin des Supplices*. They are formulaic in virtue of explicitly representing female models singly or otherwise in various standard sexual poses and acts. But they are delineated via Rodin's newly developing method of 'instantaneous drawing'. Unlike standard academic drawing of the time, Rodin started from mere contour heightened by wash, drawing from the model's unstable pose without taking his eyes off her, resulting in many correction lines, heightening the sense of movement or animation. An additional effect of such incisive contour drawing, through foregrounding mass and volume with minimal shading, is to convey a sense of the subject's individuality rather than conformity to classical type. The manner of representation Rodin developed in his line drawing was far from formulaic and served not only to convey but solicit sexual arousal from the viewer. The explicit focus on the models' genitals, sexual acts and sensuous stimulation is enhanced by Rodin's emphasis on the sense of movement and rotation of the body. In such drawings we have an emphasis on compositional and design elements, some of which are a striking deviation from classical nude studies, in order to evoke sexual stimulation by sexually explicit means – evoking sensuousness, fascination and arousal. The artistically innovative developments in Rodin's line drawing enabled him to characterise the lines of action, sexual embraces and actions in a more athletic, impulsive, vigorous manner which enhances the evocation of sexual arousal. It is perhaps no surprise that Rodin's sexual drawings were in great demand when compared to the formal, static and, by comparison, somewhat languid sexual fare that preceded him. Alternatively, consider the prints from the Japanese Ukiyo-e school by artists such as Hokusai and Utamaro. The Ukiyo-e school specialised in scenes from the courtly prostitute quarter depicting, amongst other scenes, prostitutes, bath-house girls, couples and even women with animals in varying degrees of sexual explicitness. In some cases explicit or enlarged sexual detailing is fairly graphic, conveying the ferociousness or subsumption of self in sexual arousal. The subjects of the Ukiyo-e school, their expressive pictorial structures and use of flat decorative colour in the compositions are formulaic. None the less, the formulaic elements are artistically deployed in a manner that serves not only to convey but, in many cases, solicit sexual arousal.

Perhaps it is the fantastical nature of the pornographic which is supposed to be artistically indifferent, since, it might be thought, fantasy cannot but fail to be true to life in any interesting sense.

Hence, according to Roger Scruton, the distinction between erotic art and pornography is 'that between representation, which is addressed to the creative imagination and bound by a principle of truth, and substitution, which is addressed to the sexual fantasy and bound only by the requirement of gratificatory power. The latter must always offend against the proprieties of art, while the former may remain obedient to them.'[4] But if this is the thought then it is overly narrow and prescriptive about what good art should be in the business of doing. Gustav Klimt's private drawings are a good case in point. We can get an idea of the nature of Klimt's drawings by looking at his *Danae* (1907–8), see p. 158, which represents a naked woman, curled foetus-like in a state of somnambulant arousal, with a shower of gold hugging her rear. In his private drawings the female subjects are represented in even more explicit poses where they are revealing, prostrating, offering or caressing themselves before the viewer. The sole concern is with the women subsumed in sexual arousal directed towards soliciting arousal from the viewer. The scenes represented are formulaic – absorbed female masturbation, passionately or languidly embracing females and the like. There is no context, background or allusion to any further meaning or significance, just the isolated outlines of figures with little by way of detailed modelling of their bodies. The represented subjects' passivity, provocativeness or autonomy is represented solely in terms of sexuality – self-absorbed in the sexual act, eyes averted or appealing to the viewers' gaze. The sole focus of interest is on the sexual aspect of the female body: its sensual, aroused and arousing nature. Although the formulaic elements of pornography are manifest, in so far as sexual explicitness and the fantastical representation of women are in the service of sexual arousal, none the less the works are artistic. Formal artistic techniques are deployed in a highly imaginative manner in order explicitly to emphasise sexual parts, features, actions and states – including the use of extreme close-up views, foreshortening, exaggerated perspective, distortions of posture and proportion, shifts in framing and heightened contrasts between right angles and curves of the body. The effect not only is beautiful, in terms of the grace of line drawing and structural composition, but serves to draw attention to sexual features such as the genitals, breasts, buttocks and open legs. The artistry gives form to our awareness of the states of sexual absorption, sensual pleasure or languid sexuality represented.

The Klimt nude studies are inherently fantastical in so far as they portray rather idealised, blank and even somnambulant subjects, and our interest in them is directed entirely towards their sexual features and aspect. But when art works are dismissed as merely fantastical this is because they are construed as a flight away from reality – they remain unconstrained by considerations of believability, plausibility or truth to life. But Klimt's explicit portraits of intimate sexual arousal do not obviously fail to be 'true to life'. As a study in sexual self-absorption, the line drawings capture certain kinds of sensual states rather well. And they do so in virtue of Klimt's imaginative, artistic treatment of the sexually explicit, formulaic and fantastical elements that constitute the pornographic. Thus even if works should always be evaluated in terms of whether they are true to life or not, it does not follow that pornographic works can't constitute good art on these terms. Conversely if we denied that Klimt's drawings were 'true to life', in virtue of their fantastical nature, it still would not follow that they're not good art. For 'truth to life' is not the only criterion of artistic evaluation and, moreover, it is not always applicable.

Gustav Klimt, *Danae* (1907–8), Private Collection © Bridgeman Art Library

There is a cluster of general criteria we apply in evaluating art works which concern the quality of the imaginative experience afforded. And there are many kinds of works, such as Goya's *Saturn Devouring His Son* (1820), where considerations of 'truth to life' are hardly applicable. Much non-pornographic fantastical work, from the Pre-Raphaelites, Chagall, Odilin Redon, Miro, Magritte, Max Ernst, Klee and M. C. Escher to Dalí, fantastical in one way or another, affords striking, complex and coherent imaginative experiences and is valued highly as art. But such works are not meant to stand in close relations to the actual world. Thus they should not be evaluated on such a basis. Even if Klimt's drawings are fantastical this is irrelevant to the quality of the imaginative experience afforded.

Even showing that pornographic works can manifest great artistic skill and expressivity is not quite enough however. For one might think, as Kenneth Clark once suggested, that we cannot appreciate something both as art and as pornography at one and the same time.[5] This is the deepest reason for objecting to the idea that the pornographic can aspire to the condition of great art. There is something to the notion that the coarseness of sexual arousal, its crudity, strength, the kind of objectifying interest taken in the object of arousal, threatens to obliterate wholesale attention to a work's artistic aspects. In the heat of sexual arousal, attention to the peculiarities of artistic style, fascination and play with artistic materials, imagery and pictorial composition might wither and fade. This is true of most pornography, but then most pornography has little that is artistically interesting. When we consider pornographic works that are truly artistic, it turns out to be false.

Part of the objection relies on a notion of a pornographic interest that is crude and ill-conceived. Typically it is thought to involve something like an objectifying interest which precludes the represented person's subjectivity (their viewpoint, interests and desires).[6] But there are many works which solicit an interest which is objectifying in just this way and are appreciable on this basis as art. Just consider the work of Corregio, Rubens, the Pre-Raphaelites, Rodin, Eric Gill, the nudes of Courbet and Renoir through to the more recent fetishistic work of Allen Jones. And some of these works, Corregio's *Jupiter and Antiope* (1521–2), Gervex's *Rolla* (1878), Courbet's *Le Sommeil* (1866), Degas's erotic sketches, depict explicit nudes where the subject's consciousness is precluded entirely. The viewer's attention is directed towards their body parts to solicit an objectifying interest which gives rise to sensuous thoughts and arousal. Our attention is drawn to the tones and contours of flesh, and the sexual parts are framed by the structural compositions of the works. The eyes are closed and the subjects asleep so our attention is solicited only with respect to the physical nature of their bodies. Yet we wouldn't be tempted to say that we cannot appreciate such works as art.

It's also the case that the kind of objectifying interest usually identified seems to mark out a depersonalised one.[7] It's assumed that we are not interested in the subject, as a person, whom we take a pornographic interest in. Yet, at least in many cases, taking a pornographic interest can be essentially interested and personal. One way of naturally eliciting sensuous thoughts and arousal is to cultivate interest in someone's viewpoint, interests and desires with respect to sensuousness and arousal. Unsurprisingly this is something pornographic art often does. Torii Kiyonobu I's *Erotic Contest of Flowers: Scenes of Lovemaking* (1704–11), perhaps the finest erotic scroll created by the originator of the Torii school, consists of eleven (originally twelve) scenes of lovemaking. The vibrant colours, juxtaposition of postures, fluidity of line all enhance the sense of explicit sexual arousal. But the figures' focused direction of gaze, the gestures of responsiveness and curiosity also serve to enhance the sense of particular individuals, sexually aroused by and interested in each other as persons. Similarly, to return to the Japanese Ukiyo-e school, Utamaro's *Two Lesbians* (*c*. 1788) is pornographic in the same kind of way. It shows two women, nearly touching, attending to and anticipating each other's sexual arousal. The one on the right has a large dildo strapped to her, the one on the left is reaching out to caress the base of its top. Just as the viewer's attention is directed towards the fleshly signs of arousal, so too is that of the women represented. And this is enhanced by attention to the pictorial composition, the artistic enlargement of the genitalia, the diagonal planes of the woman's posture on the left towards the centre and the woman's posture on the right, again directing our gaze firmly down centre, towards the sexually explicit. The denial that such works are pornographic is driven by the idea that all good art civilises. Pornographic art threatens this assumption because it speaks directly to sexual instincts, desires and drives which often threaten to overwhelm our higher natures. That is why they are troubling. Attempting to domesticate them by pretending they do not is to avert one's gaze both from their artistry and from our own nature.[8]

A rather different kind of worry about pornographic art, which sometimes generalises into worries about art more generally, takes something like this recognition as its starting point. Consider Rodin's drawing from his models 'without taking his eyes off them'. To some the phrase might suggest a visual caress, but to others it may intimate a form of molestation, as if the ways of looking implicated here constitute something akin to fondling or groping the body. Rodin once declared that 'people say I think too much about women. But what is there more important to think about?' His well-documented renown for sexual relations with models and the ways in which some of his drawings are styled suggest that the very act of looking in such cases can be sexually charged and possessive. Now think back to the examples of pornographic works being adduced as good art above. It might well be asked whose sexuality, drives, desires and interests are 'we' concerned with here? The artistic stylisation and devotion towards sexual interest all seem to assume a heterosexual male viewer. In speaking to such a gendered gaze, the thought goes, such paintings perpetuate an asymmetry in sexual relations: women are to be considered as passively receptive to male desires whilst men actively seek out the objects of their desires, women, and mould them according to their will. The pleasures of looking involve a kind of visual molestation or possession by reducing the women represented to pliable, fungible sexual objects. In assuming such a viewer, pornographic paintings, and perhaps painting more generally, is to be condemned for aesthetically camouflaging morally pernicious pleasures.[9] Laura Mulvey's critique of Allen Jones's fetishistic representations of women suggests how the worry generalises:

> By revealing the way in which fetishistic images pervade, not just specialized publications, but the *whole of the mass media*, Allen Jones throws a new light on woman as spectacle. The message of fetishism concerns not woman, but the narcissistic wound she represents for man. Women are constantly confronted with their own image in one form or another, but what they see bears little relation or relevance to their own unconscious fantasies, their own hidden fears and desires. They are being turned all the time into objects of display, to be looked at and gazed at and stared at by men. Yet, in a real sense, women are not there at all. The parade has nothing to do with woman, and everything to do with man. The true exhibit is always the phallus. Women are simply the scenery on to which men project their narcissistic fantasies. The time has come for us to take over the show and exhibit our own fears and desires.[10]

We should be wary about overgeneralising too quickly. There are lots of art works, including many which represent the human body, which are not a function of or do not implicate sexual desire. Moreover, it doesn't follow from the fact that a work assumes a male heterosexual viewer that therefore the rewards to be derived from looking at and appreciating it as art are themselves gendered or accrue only to such a viewer. Consider an analogy to religious art works. It doesn't automatically follow from the fact that a work was made assuming a particular religious belief system that therefore its value as art can only be appreciated by those with the assumed religious beliefs. In both cases it may be that the underlying assumptions in question embodied in the work are either irrelevant to appreciating it as art or, where relevant, may be entertained. This is not to deny the force of the worry as such, just its generalisability.

Art historically it seems true that most pornographic works, and indeed many non-pornographic ones, do presuppose a male interest in a manner which is bound up with heterosexual desires. But it needn't be the case that all painting is or must be like this, hence there is nothing to preclude the creative development of more historically marginalised sexual interests and desires or to critique standard male heterosexual ones. Indeed, strands of the art world from the early 1970s on have set about doing just this, from Sylvia Sleigh's various male nudes in *Turkish Bath* (1973) to some of Cindy Sherman's series of untitled photographic self-portraits which make use of the erotic conventions of film stills. In a different vein, artists like Robert Mapplethorpe seek to enshrine the exaggeration of perfect form, tone and movement of the male body, in ways which speak to male homosexual desires, or play with female stereotypes as in his series of studies of the female body builder *Lisa Lyon* (1981–2). Where works are predicated upon sexual desires, of whichever sex and orientation, it may be that our gaze is invited in to see things as we may not have seen them before, or to entertain ways of looking predicated upon desires we may not happen to share. But it doesn't follow that such works cannot be appreciated unless we actually possess those desires.

None the less, many nudes and pornographic works do seek to speak to actual desires, which art historically have been predominantly male and heterosexual, and may do so in ways which are morally problematic. It can't be the case that all these works do so merely in virtue of speaking to desires, since sexual desire as such isn't morally problematic. So for such works to be morally problematic it must be in terms of some further account of the misapplication, distortion or form of the desire spoken to. In the characterisation above, what seems to do the work is the representation of the desired object, woman, as reducible to passive pliancy in conformity to the male viewer's gaze and thus desires. I suggested above that pornographic works need not be like this. Torii Kiyonobu I's *Erotic Contest of Flowers: Scenes of Lovemaking* (1704–11), for example, depends upon an essentially personalised interest in both the represented male and female viewpoints and desires. Gustave Courbet's *Woman with a Parrott* (1866) conveys a sense of the vitality, animation and singular interest of the represented female subject. If that is the case, then not all pornographic works are subject to the kind of criticism being considered. But undoubtedly many are not like this. Consider again the earlier description of Klimt's erotic sketches, with their somnambulant subjects, Allen Jones fetishistic women in corsets, high heels and exaggerated body proportions, or Degas's erotic sketches, in which there is little to no interest in the viewpoint, particular desires or even consciousness of the women represented. Now it is not clear that representing, looking at or considering others in terms of sexual desires which objectify in this way is *necessarily* morally problematic. However, that is a controversial matter. Let us just take it for granted that at least sometimes, where, say, there is a link to contempt, disdain or a failure to respect female autonomy, it certainly is. What it shows is that good art can be prurient or solicit morally dubious attitudes that should not be endorsed, not that such works can't be artistically successful. The difference between pornographic art works and ordinary pornography is that the former deploy artistry in imaginative and interesting ways and thus can be appreciated as pornographic art. Indeed, this enables some such works to reveal something to us about the nature of sensuality, desires and the human condition. In some cases, looking at such works, or responding to them, may be morally problematic. But to condemn pornographic pictures as necessarily bad art or unappreciable as art is nothing short of puritanical wishful thinking. Pornographic works can be great art indeed. Of course, we may want to allow this to be true whilst holding that the morally problematic nature of a pornographic work may constitute an artistic defect. But this depends upon the more general claim that a moral defect, where artistically relevant, thereby constitutes an artistic one. Whether we should subscribe to this general claim is a matter to which we must now turn. Is the moral character of a work at all relevant to its artistic value?

Moral questions

> A little sincerity is a dangerous thing, and a great deal of it is absolutely fatal. The true critic will, indeed, always be sincere in his devotion to the principle of beauty, but he will seek for beauty in every age and in each school, and will never suffer himself to be limited to any settled custom of thought, or stereotyped mode of looking at things . . . The critic should be able to recognise that the sphere of Art and the sphere of Ethics are absolutely distinct and separate. When they are confused, Chaos has come again . . . Art is out of the reach of morals, for her eyes are fixed upon things beautiful and immortal and ever-changing.[11]

Thus Gilbert speaks, a cipher for Oscar Wilde in his *The Critic as Artist*.

In the late nineteenth century Wilde was perhaps the most renowned spokesman for aestheticism. Alongside figures like Walter Pater he stood opposed to Ruskin's waning creed that truth and moral sentiment in art were all important. 'Ethical sympathy' he took to be 'an unpardonable mannerism' in any art. The clash between these views mirrors an age-old conflict. On one side there are those who consider the moral character of a work to have a bearing on its value as art, from Aristotle, St Thomas Aquinas, Hume, Ruskin and Tolstoy through to the feminist, post-colonial and socio-political criticism often favoured today. On the other there are those who are adamant that the one is entirely separate from the other, from Kant, Nietzsche, Wilde, Bell and Fry through to the kind of art criticism found in Greenberg, Fried and Sylvester. For the latter, as Nietzsche put it, 'the struggle against a purpose in art is always a struggle against the moral tendency in art – against its subordination to morality. Art for art's sake means, Let morality go to the Devil.'[12]

Aestheticism does have much to be said for it. It needn't subscribe to simplistic formalism or deny that the moral character of a work may indirectly affect its artistic value. Many works do not have a moral character but, where they do, the moral assessment of a work is in principle distinct from the artistic assessment.[13] By analogy we might allow that a picture frame can indirectly affect our appreciation of a painting. If the frame is too heavy to put up, too grandiose and rococo for us to be able to concentrate on looking at the intimate watercolour it surrounds, then the frame is getting in the way of appreciating the painting. But we wouldn't be tempted to say that the frame as such lessens the artistic value of the watercolour. So too the moral character of a work might get in the way of our appreciating a work. Perhaps one might find it hard to attend properly to the artistic aspects of a work if the materials used are deeply repulsive, partly constituted by a foetus say, or the attitude profoundly abhorrent, glorifying rape. But all that shows, for the aestheticist, is that we're not in a position to appreciate a work as art, not that our moral qualms are relevant to its artistic value. No artistic creed has ever made such a strong case for the importance of the quality of an artistic experience nor been at such pains to emphasise how great works can convey ideas, beliefs and attitudes one might find detestable. It is a great buffer against ignorance and crassness. Grünewald's *Crucifixion* (1515) may dwell too lovingly on Christ's pain, Titian's *Rape of Europa* (1559–60) eroticises an abduction for the purposes of sexual assault, Marinetti's futurism lovingly aestheticises the nature of war, Schiele's genitally fixated portraits of young girls are ferociously sexual and much of Bacon's work viscerally conducts a sensation of the diseased, rotten and corrupt nature of humanity. But all these works, over which one might have many moral qualms, are great works indeed. The violent reactions of moralisers who respond only to a picture's content can be tempered by aestheticism, so they learn to attend to the quality of a painting, the artistic mastery, its beauty, independently of the truth or falsity of its claims. But the truth of a doctrine does not follow from its utility. Aestheticism is false.

As we saw in chapter 3, common art critical appraisals of works as profound, subtle, interesting, insightful or trivial, sentimental, banal and callow can't always be made without reference to criteria such as intelligibility, coherence, explanatoriness or truth. Aestheticism's conceptual separation between the quality of an artistic experience and its content is problematic, for the quality of an artistic experience will sometimes depend upon whether what is conveyed is worth conveying. Hence, where a work has a moral character, assessing its artistic quality often gives rise to questions concerning its intelligibility or appropriateness.

Critics may qualify their praise, and viewers be subject to conflicting responses, where a work commends, extols or glorifies that which should be condemned.

But why think this must be right? Because of what many art works strive to achieve. As the creative expression of an artist's imagination and vision, many works aim not only to engage us but to get us to respond to them – perceptually , emotionally and intellectually. So it is internal to the purpose of many works, as art, that they aim to get us to respond in certain ways. The way the paint itself is shaped and coloured, the posing of the figures, the structural composition, the facial expressions, figurative gestures, allusions, allegories and metaphors we find in paintings are all there, in the way they are, in order to shape our responses in some way. So it is a mark of a work's success if it gets us to respond in the way that it is shaped to do. Sometimes failing to respond as solicited is a mark of a failing, lack of sensitivity or ignorance in ourselves, but often the failure is down to faults in the work. Perhaps the rendering of the figures is unconvincing; perhaps the intended sympathetic grin looks more like a grotesque grimace or the supposedly erotic, noble or admirable scene depicted is just downright horrifying. In all such cases a work fails in certain respects. For it fails to get the response it aims at, as art, owing not to a failing in the viewer but to a failing in the way the artistry, figure or scene is represented to us. Moreover, as we saw in the last chapter, part of a work's value is tied up with whether or not the experience afforded deepens our understanding. To the extent it does so, that is an added artistic virtue. In some cases this will be linked to the work's moral character as it is artistically represented.[14]

Compare, in this light, the *Roettgen Pietà*, see p. 170, and Michelangelo's first *Pietà* (1499), see chapter 1 p. 43.

The *Roettgen Pietà* (1350) is an unattributed wooden sculpture, around three feet high and one of the finest examples of the Pietà tradition from northern Europe. A Pietà is a representation of the grief-stricken Mary holding Christ's dead body on her lap. The point of the work was to engender empathic meditation and devotion on the part of the viewer. Traditionally Pietàs were placed in side chapels for veneration all year round but they were given particular prominence during the Holy Week of Easter, particularly Good Friday, for the contemplation of Christ's redemptive wounds. Mary's outsized face inclines to the viewer's left, her eyes directly on Christ's head, drawing the viewer from her gaze to her prostrate son. Her facial expression is one of blank,

Roettgen Pietà (1350). Courtesy of Rheinisches Landesmuseum, Bonn

mute horror, as seen in the brow, sunken eyes and stark cheek-bones, shot through with desperate sadness, emphasised by the down-turned lips and mouth. The rest of her body seems static, frozen as she holds out her son for our contemplation. Christ's figure is rigid, grotesquely distorted, his outsize head snapped back, looking heavenward, in a mask of death. Here, Christ's wounds are exaggerated in scale and rendering, the size, scoring, gashes and bloody coloration pouring out, drawing our attention to them. The overall composition of the piece is additionally striking in its echo of a mother struggling to hold her newborn child, and the distortions in scale of Christ's figure are not unlike the dispro-portioned figure of a baby. The horror of the piece is even more striking because of the jarring incongruity between the pose and harrowing grief. The point of the piece is to convey a particular attitude, and solicit a certain kind of response, towards the divine sacrifice. One is invited not merely to take up an attitude of devout piety but to dwell on the sheer sense of physical violence, the grotesque horror of the assault on Christ's body and Mary's searing sorrow. It is the sacrificial annihilation of Christ as victim which is given by far the greatest prominence. Mary's expression is itself a guide and mirror for the attitude the devout contemplator is to take up; one should be rent with anguish at the nature of the sacrifice required. Furthermore, unlike Mary who was born without the taint of original sin, we all shoulder the responsibility. Jesus is held out towards us not just for the benefits of contem-plation but as if to say, 'Look what you have done, what you are responsible for. You too are at fault for the death of my son.' Adam and Eve's revolt against God in the Garden of Eden severed the human condition from divine will. As such all mankind partakes in the original sin responsible for the rupture from God. Thus our very nature is at fault in requiring such a sacrifice from Christ. For without expiation humanity cannot be cleansed of the defilement of sin. It is only through Christ's sacrifice that divine grace is available to all and we can come to be forgiven. So it is that the *Roettgen Pietà* seeks the recognition of human guilt and an attitude of thankfulness at the violent mercy shown to we who are not worthy. There may be many for whom such a vengeful conception of human nature, no matter how great the artistry involved, qualifies their appreciation of this work, for conceiving of ourselves thus or responding as the work solicits us to do is not an intelligible option for them.

Michelangelo's first *Pietà*, by contrast, plays down the grotesquery and violence to the point of vanishing. Part of the reason for this work's greatness lies not just in its breathtaking beauty but in the way Michelangelo revolutionised the Pietà genre. But what is crucial is what that revolution served: a deep sense of Mary's beatific sacrifice. This marked a radical shift in the way Christ's sacrifice was represented. The much more naturalistic representation of Christ's body conveys a sense of peace and rest, his wounds are marked by barely visible points, and he is cradled by a youthful Mary who looks down on his body in resigned sadness. Mary's youthful face and pose echo the Annunciation, suggesting the acceptance of her sacrifice was embraced years before in the moment she acceded to God's wishes for her to bear his son. Notice that Mary's face, instead of directing us towards Christ's face, directs us towards the middle of his prone body. By doing so the viewer is encouraged to see Christ as cradled by his mother first and foremost (as opposed to the *Roettgen Pietà* which directs us to his deathly face). By enlarging the size of Mary's legs, disguised by the folded drapes, Michelangelo was able to show Christ's figure as being fully supported in her lap. Thus far from seeing Mary as thrusting Jesus awkwardly towards us in an accusatory fashion, we see it in terms of a wholly private, personal scene in which she contemplates and comforts her dead son's body. This is given added weight by her eyes being wholly downcast, closed off from the viewer. Jesus' figure, his curves of flesh, prominent ribs and slumped posture reminiscent of sleep, is wholly naturalistic and fully human. There is no impression of deep physical violence or grim, gruesome sacrifice but a sense of sorrowful serenity. The attitude conveyed, and responses solicited, towards Christ's sacrifice are markedly different. In dwelling on Mary's restrained, resigned sorrow and Christ's prostrate naturalistic form, it is the human psychological cost that is given greatest prominence. Again Mary's expression is a guide and mirror for the attitude the devout contemplator is to take up, but this time it is one of sorrowful resignation. Furthermore, rather than distancing the devout contemplator from Mary, as the *Roettgen Pietà* does, we are encouraged to identify ourselves fully with her. Jesus is to be mourned for as one mourns for any son, indeed as the Son of Man. Far from emphasising the bloody horror of the sacrifice, the work implies that it is no more than Jesus having returned to the Father from whence he came. None the less the marks of the crucifixion, subdued but still there, remind us that his death ushers in a new reconciliation with God. His and Mary's sacrifice makes available forgiveness for all for the human condition in which he has shared. Thus has our salvation been made possible. For this we should give thanks to Christ and Mary.

The moral character of these works could not be more radically distinct. The *Roettgen Pietà* prescribes an understanding of ourselves as defiled, contaminated and unworthy. Its conception of

Mary and Christ as radically distinct in nature from the viewer, the suprahuman nature of the violent sacrifice required, and our guilt in it, would seem to many aggressive, vengeful and cruel. The world the *Roettgen Pietà* opens up and invites us to inhabit, with its concomitant internalisation of guilt and self-mortification, is one that has passed for many. Its attitudes and self-understandings are not live options. Hence the responses and attitudes it is artistically designed to solicit from us seem alien and inhumane. As depraved and wicked as human nature can be, and we often do underestimate the dark depths of the human heart, a religious world-view according to which we are wholly debased in this way seems antipathetic. The point is not one about religious belief being beyond us. Rather it is that a particular medieval conception of Christianity and our place in the world seems to most of us, in Nietzsche's words, a 'crime against life'.[15] Looked at in this light, the work's savouring of the grotesquely violent details can seem morally problematic, since a picture of humanity which solicits our self-abasement in this manner seems only a notional possibility. For this reason we may find its artistically shaped moral character much harder to appreciate and thus we may evaluate it less highly as art than Michelangelo's *Pietà*. Michelangelo's work emphasises the fully human nature of both Mary and Jesus, the sacrifices required of them and the pain to be embraced in order to realise what is good. Such a conception seems more intelligible in a post-Renaissance or secular world, and one we may be more sympathetic to, hence we may appreciate it more highly. Although Christ's sacrifice is foregrounded, so too are the virtues of love, forgiveness and mercy. For many this world view is closer and more intelligible, hence it is psychologically more open to us to respond to the work as solicited. Thus the moral character of a work may affect its intelligibility, and in so doing be relevant to how we appreciate and evaluate a work.

Moralising art

On this basis it would seem that where the artistry of a work shapes its moral character, at least to the extent this is relevant to its intelligibility, then it is relevant to its value as art. We can entertain and accept all sorts of speculative, fantastical and mythological scenarios. But with respect to a work's moral character, we should ask ourselves whether the perceptions, responses and attitudes solicited are open to us. We should also ask ourselves whether we learn anything interesting, profound or insightful. In considering both questions we were able to see just why many appreciate Michelangelo's *Pietà* more highly than the *Roettgen Pietà*. So far so good. But recently certain philosophers have wanted to go much further. The underlying thought is that intelligibility as such isn't just what is at issue. Rather, where artistic means shape a work's moral character, a moral defect in the work constitutes an artistic vice and a moral virtue constitutes an aesthetic virtue.

Aristotle held that for a work to constitute tragedy it must have a certain moral character. The central figure must be morally admirable in order for us to sympathise with him and regret his downfall as tragic. Were we to judge him to be wholly undeserving of sympathy, to deserve his fate, we would consider his end not as tragic but just. Noël Carroll takes this consideration to show that at least sometimes a work's morally defective character counts against it artistically.[16] But the thought can be extended more generally. In Hume we find the following:

Where the ideas of morality and decency alter from one age to another, and where vicious manners are described, without being marked with the proper characters of blame and disapprobation, this must be allowed to disfigure the poem, and to be a real deformity. I cannot, nor is it proper I should, enter into such sentiments; and however I may excuse the poet, on account of the manners of his age, I can never relish the composition . . . where a man is confident of the rectitude of that moral standard by which he judges, he is justly jealous of it, and will not pervert the sentiments of his heart for a moment.[17]

In fact Hume's articulation of the position has probably been the most influential amongst contemporary philosophers arguing for the moralist claim. Berys Gaut, for example, has argued that where 'a work manifests ethically reprehensible attitudes, it is to that extent aesthetically defective, and if a work manifests ethically commendable attitudes, it is to that extent aesthetically meritorious.'[18] Works try to get us to respond in certain ways and, where the response makes essential reference to moral attitudes, whether they succeed depends upon conformity to the right ones.

A big worry is that this thought encourages critics to reach too quickly for moral denunciations at the expense of artistic sensitivity.[19] Moral provincialism myopically lends itself to the overly emphatic, generalised and judgemental in evaluation. It is important to recognise there are many different kinds of art works. Many have no moral character at all and those that do are often highly complex in terms of subject matter, genre, evoked responses, attitudes and their interrelations. John Ruskin, for example, is one whose criticism conforms to the moralist's stance and it does tend to flatten out the topography of the artistic landscape. In the *Stones of Venice* Ruskin charts the artistic decline of the Renaissaince in terms of declining moral temperament and the moral character of their art:

> the phases of transition in the moral temper of the falling Venetians, were from pride to infidelity, and from infidelity to the unscrupulous pursuit of pleasure. During the last years of the existence of the state, the minds both of the nobility and the people seem to have been set simply upon the attainment of the means of indulgence.

And, in the next section, he goes on to claim that

> the architecture raised at Venice during this period is among the worst and basest ever built by the hands of men, being especially distinguished by a spirit of brutal mockery and insolent jest, which, exhausting itself in the deformed and monstrous sculpture, can sometimes be hardly otherwise defined than as the perpetuation in stone of the ribaldries of drunkenness.[20]

The tendency of Ruskin to allow his own moral obsessions to betray his critical judgement, to see baseness, corruption and self-indulgence in the art of the late Renaissance, cannot be denied. More recently the critic Peter Fuller unfavourably compared Francis Bacon with Graham Sutherland on a similar basis:

> Bacon is an artist of persuasive power and undeniable ability, but he has used his expressive skills to denigrate and degrade. He presents one aspect of the human condition as necessary and universal truth. Bacon's work is currently more highly esteemed than that of Sutherland, but this may merely tell us something about the values of those who express such a preference. Bacon's skills command our

admiration, but his tendentious vision demands a moral response, and I believe, a refusal.[21]

Although we can appreciate why Fuller goes on to make the claim he does, his moral concerns are clouding his critical judgement, for it is hard to see how Sutherland could be the greater artist. But the fallibility of critics in allowing their moral concerns to weigh too heavily in their critical judgement shows nothing about the truth or falsity of the moralist's thesis. It only shows that critics can err. And note that moralist criticism need not be insensitive to differences in subject matter, genre constraints and the inter-relations of responses and attitudes. Moralists can recognise that a work can be great art for formal reasons alone. Where the work has a moral character, how it is assessed depends upon how we are to understand the genre, whether it be historical, mythological, portraiture or still life studies, and artistic concerns. And even though a work may be morally flawed it may still constitute good or great art – as Fuller acknowledges even with respect to Bacon. Such a worry doesn't yet touch the moralist's claim.

In addition to arguments concerning the appropriateness of responses and what we learn from works, Hume also offers another consideration sometimes taken to underwrite moral criticism. To start with Hume suggests an analogy between blameless differences in the kind of friends we may choose and those artists we tend to prefer: 'We choose our favourite author as we do our friend, from a conformity of humour and disposition.'[22] Owing to individual differences in character, or between distinct ages or cultures, we may vary in our evaluations of particular works. This is akin to the way in which we may blamelessly differ over the kinds of friends we choose to keep. None the less, 'where a man is confident of that moral standard by which he judges, he is justly jealous of it, and will not pervert the sentiments of his heart for a moment, in complaisance to any writer whatsoever'.[23] For this to be consistent with the friendship analogy it looks as if Hume assumes that a certain level of moral agreement in both cases is required for us to respond as sought. For me to pity my friend I must share certain core assumptions and values with her, for example that the slight she received was unjust. For me to respond with horror and acceptance to Francis Bacon's work I must assume, with Bacon, that the human condition is corrupt and that we should accept it as such. Where the moral assumptions are essential to a work, it supposedly follows that a certain level of agreement is required for the work to succeed. Where they are not shared, we supposedly cannot properly appreciate the work's other artistic aspects – just as where the relevant moral assumptions aren't shared with my friends I'm not in a position to appreciate their other qualities. Thus, it might be thought, Bacon's work is flawed because its success depends upon assumptions and responses which, morally speaking, many of us do not share and none of us should accept.

Let's start by assuming the analogy to friendship. As articulated, it seems far too moralistic.[24] We can and often do appreciate friends whose values are radically at odds with our own; in some cases this may be one of the very reasons we're drawn to being friends with them in the first place. Perhaps there must be some sort of shared interest or understanding but it doesn't follow that what is shared must be basic moral assumptions. We may be friends with someone who is witty, vivacious, likes particular kinds of movies, art or bars. It may be that our moral attitudes in many respects are radically at odds. She thinks manners a form of hypocrisy, I think them part and parcel of social intercourse; she thinks minor shoplifting is fun, I think it immoral and so on. Yet her attitudes in these moral respects do not preclude my appreciation of her finer qualities and responding to her with empathy and understanding. That may make it difficult for me to separate them out psychologically, so perhaps her other qualities have to be that much finer to disentangle them from the divergences in moral attitudes. But so too with art works. We can enjoy and appreciate many works whose moral assumptions are at radical odds with our own. If, like Bacon, the artistry is skilful and imaginative enough, we find our resistance to them can be overcome. Such works are artistic successes indeed.

The defender of the moralist thesis might resort to the point about genre constraints. Yet such an appeal does no good. What it is for something to be in a certain genre is carved out in terms of the characteristics of a particular artistic form, style or purpose. Even granting that all works can be so characterised, the general moralist thesis cannot apply across the board. In genres such as satire, a morally defective perspective can enhance rather than hinder the realisation of its purpose. The point of satire is to ridicule. One of the standard means employed is the gross exaggeration and distortion of recognisable features of the character or institution being ridiculed. A character may be exaggerated by concentrating wholly on her faults without recognition of her virtues or rendered absurd by concentrating on irrelevant yet easy to lampoon mannerisms. George Grosz's satirical drawings, which appeared in *Die Pleite* and *Der Bluteige Ernst* before 1933, when he fled Nazi Germany, are a case in point. His targets were the corruption of the Weimar Republic, the racketeers, businessmen, the remnants of the military and what he took to be a thoroughly diseased culture. In Grosz's caricatures absolutely everyone is on the make, sly, coarse, selfish, greedy and lecherous. Contemporary humanity is portrayed as inhabiting a modern Bosch-like garden of earthly delights where everyone manifests the most venial desires and appetites. As Grosz himself said, 'I made careful drawings, but I had no love of the people, either inside or out. I was arrogant enough to consider myself as a natural scientist, not as a painter or satirist. I thought about right and wrong but my conclusions were always unfavourable to all men equally.'[25] The exaggerated scenes in restaurants, of racketeers dining in luxury, in nightclubs, of men prowling for predatory prostitutes, and of slums, where everyone is trying to get one over on everyone else, betray a profound disgust and revulsion at humanity in general. Such a response is hardly wholly morally appropriate or adequate. Not all men and women are equally disgusting, self-serving, repulsively grubbing around or seeking to prey on others. Addison once suggested that ridicule 'is generally made use of to laugh men out of virtue and good sense by attacking everything that is solemn and serious, decent and praiseworthy in human life'.[26] But recognising the morally problematic aspects of satire should not puritanically blind us to how important and effective it can be. To achieve its aims, satire, caricature and ridicule are often unfair, morally distorted and vicious. The work of artists such as Hogarth, Rowlandson and Gillray are evidence enough of this. But such morally dubious distortions enable their works to debunk authority and challenge the unquestioning acceptance of attitudes, activities, institutions and cultures. Here we have a genre where a morally defective character can enhance rather than hinder the achievement of its artistic aims.

Furthermore, even considered as a claim limited to certain genres, the moralist's claim is dubious. The most limited version of the claim concerns the case of dramatic tragedy; a tragedy cannot succeed as such if we're to pity someone who's not morally admirable. Similar considerations often seem to apply to historical, mythological and biblical paintings. In many paintings pity or sorrow is sought for the central characters and the fate that befalls them. But one can feel pity for those one does not admire. We may feel compassion or sorrow for one who is tortured just in virtue of that fate befalling them, independently of whether we admire them or not. Perhaps true epic, historical or mythological paintings don't concern ordinary mortals and thus might fail to elicit admiration in the right way. We might feel compassion for anyone tortured but that's different from sorrow for the fate of one who is deeply admirable and yet brought low. So let's grant that the qualities of central figures in certain genre paintings must be exceptional, in order to elicit admiration for them in particular in the right way. David's *The Death of Socrates* (1787) and *The Murdered Marat in his Bath* (1793), Delacroix's *Heliodorus Expelled from the Temple* (1852–61), Puvis de Chavannes's *The Beheading of St John the Baptist* (1860s), Rubens's *Samson and Delilah* (1609–10), Caravaggio's *Crucifixion of St Peter* (1600–1) all fit nicely with this requirement. But even this is a million miles from the requirement that they be morally admirable. The motif of a *morally* admirable figure violating social taboos or attitudes, thus giving rise to their sorrowful fate, makes sense of many historical, biblical and mythological paintings. But it hardly fits works such as Van Dyck's *Samson and Delilah* (1619), which gives the impression of comic farce arising from the fallibility of mere mortals, Velazquez's *Triumph of Bacchus* (1628–9), where all are brought low by the god of wine, and Titian's *Danaë* (1554), where Danaë's openness to Jupiter is associated with prostitution through the shower of gold coins being collected, to name but three. The central figures of historical, epic, biblical, mythological or historical paintings are often, but need not be, of exceptional natures and, where they are, they need not be morally admirable.

Still, the moralist could wave aside genre considerations. The claim remains that, where artistically relevant, a moral defect is always an artistic vice and a morally commendable character an artistic virtue. It is true that the moral character of a work is often partly constitutive of a work's artistic value. Comparing Michelangelo's *Pietà* with the *Roettgen Pietà* looked amenable to this kind of claim. But the moralist stretches too quickly towards the general claim. For the moralist, if a work tries to get us to respond, morally speaking, as we ought not to, then the work's artistic value is marred. If that means that Grosz's satirical caricatures are lesser works for all that, so be it, and if Bacon's work is shot through with a jaundiced view of humanity, so much the worse for Bacon. Why, the moralist will ask, should we respond to works in ways we deem to be immoral (no matter how artfully constructed they are)? To show moralism is false we need only advert to two kinds of cases. The first, where a work's value is lessened in virtue of its morally admirable character, we shall look at directly. The second, a case where a work's value is enhanced owing to its immoral character, requires a section of its own.

Norman Rockwell is a famous American painter, though one would not find him mentioned in many dictionaries or encyclopaedias of art. By the end of 1930s he was a national institution in the USA. He specialised in homely portraits of ordinary folk, families, kids, scruffy pets, domestic scenes, which fitted perfectly with the iconography, attitudes and indulgent sentimentality of middle-stream America. Rockwell's well-known Four Freedoms series was inspired by a speech of Franklin D. Roosevelt's, articulating the basic freedoms all should have: freedom from fear, freedom from want, freedom of speech and freedom of worship. The sentiments and attitudes manifested are deeply admirable and the paintings are far from artistically poor. *Freedom from Fear* (1943), for example, has a strong pictorial composition. The line created by the standing father intersects with the horizontal line of the sleeping children's bed. The mother's hands and forearms, drawing up their sheets, form a diagonal line which is mirrored by the paper held in the father's hand. Her upper body, crooning over the sleeping children, forms a mid-plane between the upright father and the diagonal of her forearms. The style is unadulteratedly naturalistic, rendered with high technical skill. Yet for all that the painting's artistic value is fairly low. The visual interest is in the service of morally good sentiments which are cheaply won. The father is holding a paper whose headline indicates bombing by the Germans in London, and the contrast with the safety of the comfortable children is vulgar. Of course we want our children to be safe, not vulnerable to the destructive, blind rampages of war. There is nothing of interest to be won or learnt from looking at this kind of morally sound painting. Its moral character, appropriate as it may be, counts against rather than for its value as art.[27]

Immoral art

Francis Bacon, considered by many in the 1980s to be Britain's greatest living painter, first made an impact in 1945 with the exhibition of his *Three Studies for Figures at the Base of a Crucifixion* (1944), see pp. 186–8. The viewer is presented with three separate canvases, reminiscent of a triptych, each depicting a strangely anthropomorphic animal-like form. The figure on the left is crouching on a table, huddling itself in a bird-like manner, its vaguely human face a quarter on and turned away. The central figure is side on, the elongated neck stretching from the bulbous, ostrich-like body, bringing its face in full confrontation with the viewer. The threatening, repulsive, mouth of lips and teeth is somewhat agape, and where there should be eyes the face is bandaged. The mouth emerges directly from the neck rather than belonging to a distinct face. The third canvas represents a sharpened, cow-like body, its elongated neck bringing a viciously howling mouth into three quarter view. The neck opens up into rows of teeth, an ear placed behind the lower jaw juts out, the mouth stretches open in a scream, extended in a manner impossible for any human skull. These frightened, blind, raging figures are visceral in their impact, jolting one into sensations of fright, horror, isolation and angst. Their force derives from the fusion of bestial forms with anthropomorphising faces. We react to them as self-conscious creatures, their postures and expressions revealing feelings of petrified isolation, searing horror, pain and blind confusion. But the heads, though recognisably akin to human faces, are distinctly anything other than human. The painful emotions we feel in response to them are shot through with the recognition that these creatures both are and are not akin to ourselves. In a profound sense they both portray and threaten our conceptions of what it is like to be an embodied human being. For here are creatures, ugly, deformed, who suffer deeply in their self-conscious condition, and yet are radically removed from something we would recognisably call human.

It is tempting to think of Bacon's work as being in a lineage familiar from the work of Edvard Munch and German

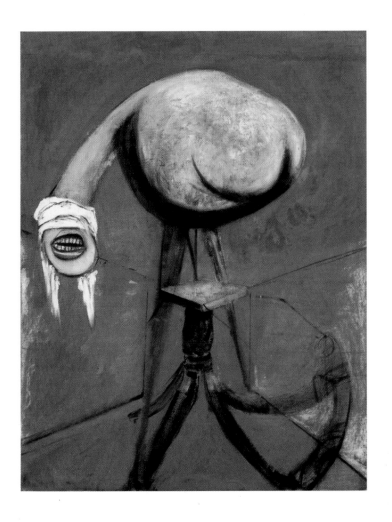

Francis Bacon, *Three Studies for Figures at the Base of a Crucifixion* (*c*.1944) © Tate, London 2003

expressionism. Distorted figures, vivid colours, themes of isolation, horror and angst chime with the expressionist impulse to convey heightened inner states and sympathise with those represented. Yet Bacon always disavowed such an attribution and considered himself to be a realist, albeit of a very particular kind. In what sense did Bacon consider himself a realist? The iconography of Bacon's works is familiar. Isolated, often single figures, howling, despairing, as in his *Study for the Head of a Screaming Pope* (1952), are evoked with smeared paint, twisted, smudged and blurred faces. The corrupted, distorted, distinguishing fleshly features carnivorously emerge from embodied structures. His use of religious imagery, particularly crucifixion motifs, and vicious forms reminiscent of the savage furies of Greek legends, all heighten the visceral sensation that clamps on to the viewer's nervous system. The pictorial space sets up a sense of isolation, as if the viewer watches their plight, distanced, through glass pane rather than being invited in to share their plight. It is no accident that some of Bacon's richest source material consisted of books on oral disease, repulsive medical conditions, photographs of human bodies and animal locomotion. The clinical gaze one sees displayed in medical texts of skin diseases is generalised by Bacon to the entire treatment of the human form and condition. Mankind is seen as animated meat, decayed flesh, driven by rage and pain, devoid of higher emotions, finer feelings or any sense of belonging. It is a cold, distanced, aestheticised eye on a corrupted world of brutish decay, suffering and isolation. It is difficult to think of another painter whose view of the human condition is so intensely bleak, bereft and base. Expressionism invites pity for its romanticised conception of the human condition. Bacon's work shows a world of embodied pain we are to observe, feel and accept.

I take it that we should not accept Bacon's conception of humanity. The physicality of the paint, the whorls, smears, fungibility of the faces, the distortions of the figures, the intense colours are all in the service of a denial of life: ordinary life made up of the higher aspirations, finer feelings and social relations which make it worth living. No one doubts that in our darker moments life can seem as Bacon paints it. But it is not so unremittingly, as a permanent condition from which there is no escape. At a stretch Bacon's disgust, repulsion and acceptance might make sense against a background of religious belief which promised a heavenly world to come. But Bacon goes out of his way to preclude any such possibility. His recurring use of crucifixion motifs and papal figures is no accident. Perhaps the most famous is his *Study after Velazquez's Portrait of Pope Innocent X* (1953). Here we have a seated figurehead of the Catholic Church, *the* chosen representative of Christ on earth in apostolic succession, who is held to have an enduring and unfailing relationship with God. In Bacon's garden of earthly pain we are presented with the symbolic representative of the one hope that might redeem our base lot. And how is the pope presented to us? Enthroned, alone, almost caged, his indistinct, white hands gripping the edge of the armrests, his mouth wide open in horror, screaming, as the dark pain all around bleeds into the foreground, runs down his face and almost blinds him. There is no salvation, no relief, no redemption from the horror. And what kind of attitude does Bacon recommend to his jaundiced vision of the world? A passive acceptance which constitutes a refusal to recognise or aspire to the things which could make such a condition bearable. Pain is our lot and this we should accept. No more and no less. In certain ways Bacon's vision is a humiliation of humanity, an attempt to reduce us to raw embodied appetites and feelings, self-consciousness only serving to heighten our pain by dint of self-awareness. We are diseased, corrupt, repulsive and plastic of form. It is no wonder that Bacon gave rise to such condemnation at the same time as giving rise to great praise. Bacon's is a vision of humanity which, morally speaking, we should reject. Yet at its best his painting is amongst the best of the latter half of the twentieth century. It pulls one back time and time again.

Forbidden knowledge

The value of a work depends partly on the quality of the experience the work affords and the insight or understanding it conveys to us. Many works enhance our understanding in terms of getting us to perceive the world aright or getting us to respond as we should. None the less, some works are both intelligible and insightful despite, or sometimes because of, the ways in which they get us to see or respond to things we would not actually deem to be right, good or true. The core thought is that, as in Bacon's work, we are sometimes prepared to suspend our actual moral judgements because of the potentially insightful rewards engaging with a morally problematic work might bring. Where a work yields up such rewards, it is valuable in part due to its morally defective aspect. The claim depends upon the assumption that, for creatures such as ourselves, experience is a primary means of understanding. We come to discriminate, appreciate and grasp many things on the basis of experience. Not only does this extend to the moral sphere but we also require comparative experience. We must have experienced, in some sense, the bad in order to understand the good. Someone whose life is utterly charmed, who has never experienced betrayal, deceit, tragedy or failure, may be able to appreciate many things, but it is unlikely they will really know certain things about friendship, love, morality or great art. They might be unable to see how friendships could be open to betrayal, how people can be easily tempted into doing the wrong thing or the myriad ways in which art works can turn out to be crass, vulgar or deeply mediocre. A true appreciation of such things requires an understanding of the ways in which they can go wrong. This applies not only to being subject to morally bad experiences but to being implicated in them in morally problematic ways. It is one thing to find out by experience that some people like fighting; it is another to find out that you too could derive pleasure from the infliction of violence upon others, a far more unsettling insight by far. Similarly it is one thing to know that some view humanity as corrupted, diseased, blindly animated meat; it is another to see how one could come to view humanity as such oneself. One needn't actually be drawn into actual physical violence or actually believe humanity to be such to find these things out about oneself; there are more indirect means. One of the most powerful is art.

I remember first seeing Bacon's *Three Studies for Figures at the Base of a Crucifixion* (1944) as a child and being transfixed with horror, revulsion and fascination. Even now the effect is undiminished and the fascination endless. It is a mark of Bacon's artistic success, rather than failure, that it yields up such appreciation despite its morally problematic nature. This is because there is something about Bacon's vision which is intelligible to us. It is not wholly false, just a peculiarly partial conception falsely generalised. Bacon is a permanently bleak painter. But we all know what such a mood is like – from time to time the world seems bleached of humanity; it strikes us that we are driven by base appetites and humanity itself is dirty, wicked, corrupted. Hence we respond to Bacon's expression of such a mood, which he smears over the entire world. We are more than this. But Bacon's general conception does rest on recognising a truth about particular aspects of our human nature – something from which we often shrink or self-deceivedly push to the back of our minds. We can be good, altruistic and driven by noble feelings, and appreciate refined sentiments. But part of us does remain revolted and fascinated by the ways our brutish animal natures can flatten out our higher nature, thus leading us to be appalled at the horror of existence. In particular, though the human figure can be beautiful, we too can see it as a piece of meat, deformed flesh, animated by drives and desires devoid of human will. As a general conception of humanity, it is not only false but morally pernicious. But that cannot prevent the recognition that there is something important about ourselves we can come to recognise in Bacon's work or that we can and should respond to Bacon's work as solicited. For the intensity of that vision, its sincerity and the sheer mastery of paint which gives rise to its peculiar effects make it great art indeed. Bacon succeeds because he shows us a deeply intelligible conception of the world and we respond accordingly, even though in actuality we may take such a vision to be distorted, jaundiced and myopic. What matters can't be reduced to whether or not the vision and responses sought are, morally speaking, the right ones. It is whether an artist can get us to see, feel and respond to his vision as he intends us to. Bacon succeeds, at least for many, and in so doing we come to learn something about ourselves and the world. Despite its general falsity, we learn that we could come to see humanity's corporeality as a curse, react with disgust to the physicality of others and refuse to see altruism, finer feeling or nobility of attitude in anyone.

Someone may refuse to appreciate Bacon fully because they cannot or will not bring themselves to entertain radical differences in world-views. But such an inability doesn't automatically reflect a defect in Bacon's work. No doubt most of us respond to Bacon's work in ways which are at odds with what we take to be plausible and morally adequate regarding the human condition. But psychologically speaking we can entertain Bacon's view because it relies on something close to a mood we sometimes find ourselves in and because the artistry of the work is so vivid, intense and convincing. Bacon's artistry enables us to take up such a stance because it renders intelligible and psychologically close certain things we already incipiently entertain and think. The suspension of moral judgement, from what we actually believe, is no different from Coleridge's suspension of intellectual belief. We can and do appreciate both intellectually and morally problematic works. By default where a work is morally defective, other things being equal, its value as art will be lessened. But other things are not always equal. For we can learn from great works in virtue of the ways in which they are morally defective.[28] So the moralist's thesis is wrong. Immoral works, where they deepen our understanding, can be better rather than worse works of art for so doing. It is no accident that some of the greatest works of art not only deal with evil but are shocking because they solicit thoughts, attitudes and responses which are morally problematic. Great art, after all, can be deeply shocking indeed – because we have found things out about ourselves that we would rather not have known.

Obscenity, censoriousness and censorship

If the argument above is right, then it can't be the case that all great art civilises nor that great art is necessarily exempt from charges of prurience, immoralism or obscenity. But just what is it for a work to be obscene? For the notion to be an interesting one it can't just pick out works we think are particularly immoral or in very bad taste. If that were all that were meant then the term would be merely a rhetorical one. True, sometimes that's all that seems to be going on. People occasionally say things like 'displaying that work is obscene', as some claimed regarding Harvey's *Myra*, or 'to render beautiful the suffering of others is obscene', an occasionally made condemnation of works which aestheticise the forlorn, dispossessed and dying. But such uses of the term seem only loosely related. Nor is the notion directly tied to causal considerations. Obscenity is often assumed to concern the likelihood of inducing morally problematic attitudes and behaviour. Hence, for example, a lot of obscenity debates about pornography centre on whether the sexual objectification involved is likely to cause immoral attitudes and behaviour towards women. This can't be right. Even if we granted that there are causal links from obscene representations to immoral actions, the causal assumption would apply to many representations we wouldn't judge obscene. Many Klimts, Pre-Raphaelite works, paintings by Frederick Leighton, Alma-Tadema and Allen Jones represent women as dependent, empty, flighty, fantastical or sexually objectified. We might worry that where someone's artistic diet consisted solely of such works then *perhaps* they may cultivate morally dubious attitudes or behaviour with respect to women but we wouldn't automatically condemn such works as obscene. Moreover, certain works by the photographer

Joel-Peter Witkin, which invite a compulsive interest in the freakish and deformed, Jake and Dinos Chapman's circle of child mannequins, with genitals protruding in place of mouths and ears, or Rick Gibson's *Human Earrings* (1985), featuring real foetuses attached as earrings to the ears of a mannequin, would be considered obscene without assuming they would affect anyone's attitudes or behaviour with respect to the disabled, children or the dead. So whatever judging something to be obscene consists in, it is prior to and conceptually independent of causal concerns.

A clue to what this is can be found in the typical subject matter judgements of obscenity cluster around. Marks of the obscene involve certain kinds of subject matter, sex, violence, death and the corporeal, or certain kinds of objectifying responses, interests and attitudes, such as disgust, repulsion and curiosity. But this is not enough for something to be judged obscene. Monet's portrait of his dead wife, Cézanne's depiction of his dead child or Lucian Freud's work, for example, all solicit an objectifying interest in our corporeal nature, the folds and tones of flesh that constitute our bodily nature, but such works are not obscene. Obscenity is a matter of the *ways* in which such subject matter and interests are treated by representations – which is a question of the kinds of desires and attitudes a work speaks to concerning the subject matter.[29]

There are at least three distinct responses or attitudes obscene works seek to cultivate. The first concerns the indulgence of basic motivating desires deemed to be morally wrong, misdirected or excessive. Consider certain pornographic works by Schiele, with their explicit sexual interest and genital fixation in the representation of young girls. Sexual desire is not as such wrong, but where it is fixated on the very young it is misdirected. Desire for sexual power over, domination of and sexual congress with those who appear young is not that uncommon; consider the age and appearance of many younger supermodels. But some of Schiele's pornographic works are obscene since they evoke a sense of sexual excitement, desire and arousal towards the very young who, morally speaking, we should be prohibited from thinking of in that way. Similarly, with respect to certain representations of violence, suffering and death, a work may solicit responses that speak to desires to see others suffer or savour their annihilation. Consider a series of untitled photographs by Sue Fox (1996–97) of cadavers. We are presented with corpses in various stages of being cut open, examined and left after autopsies. There is nothing wrong with examining corpses in a dispassionate way. This is what doctors themselves must do in seeking out the cause of death, and clinicians must distance themselves from their normal human reactions in order to realise their goal of discovering the cause of death. But in Sue Fox's work we are presented with dismembered, butchered corpses for the sake of aesthetic delight. We are to savour the colours, the hollowed out chest cavities, the folded, sunken in flesh, and tonal contrasts of red, white and yellow for our aesthetic pleasure. What does the work here is the thought that we are witness to the destruction of a body, which we cannot help but think of as some person. To solicit delight, for its own sake, in the destruction and annihilation of the human body in this way is morally problematic. It is something we ought not to be encouraged to do (in the same way we would worry about someone who sought out medical pictures of the diseased, crippled and deformed to delight in). Similarly Peng Yu's *Curtain* (1999), which uses more than 1,000 lobsters, grass-snakes and bull frogs pierced through their guts and strung up to die, solicits contemplation of and delight in suffering. Again such desires and the capacity to delight in them are common enough. Given the opportunity to actually fulfil such desires a morally decent person would not act on them, would feel overwhelmingly repulsed by witnessing such actions and would feel no excitement at the prospect of so doing. But the force of moral prohibition slackens when confronting mere representations and it is easier to feel the pull of the desires spoken to.

The second kind of response obscene works often speak to concerns the desire to be morally transgressive or to delight in feelings of repulsion and disgust. It is a common enough aim in contemporary art to seek to shock, repel or disgust. This is insufficient for something to be an obscene work. But one of the ways in which such shock and horror can be achieved is by moral transgression. So the aims of the works cited above may not just be to get us to delight in pain, annihilation or misdirected sexual desire. Part of the aim could also be to solicit excitement, interest and delight in moral transgression as such. No doubt many people find such an appeal delightful, since the desire to break free from the fundamental moral norms and mores we standardly take to be binding is not uncommon. We are not attracted to do so in real life because of the high moral costs to oneself and others and the likely prudential costs. But such costs are far less with respect to representations which indulge such desires but do not obviously involve harm to anyone. Hence, again, a work may successfully solicit the pull of morally prohibited desires in us.

The third kind of response concerns the attraction of cognitive interests such as curiosity or fascination. The work of the photographer Joel-Peter Witkin, for example, foregrounds an interest in the freakish, deformed and mutilated bodies of persons. Our attention is focused on their deformations and in some cases the recognition of them as individual persons is blocked off by their wearing masks. Such curiosity is not uncommon – as testified to down the ages from Plato's characterisation of Leontion in *The Republic*, who delighted in the appearance of executed corpses, through to the fascination of many for the death, disaster and car crash television programmes that attract high audience ratings.

Obscene works elicit or commend to us, in repulsive ways, morally prohibited responses which we none the less find attractive for some of the reasons articulated above. It is important to emphasise here that many works which might appear to be obscene aren't. The charge of obscenity is often too quickly and easily made. For example, take Tierney Gearon's photographs depicting her six-year-old daughter and four-year-old son. Her partly naked son urinates in the snow in one and, in the other, they are both looking at the camera, wearing nothing but theatrical masks. The depiction of the children, and the responses called upon, are in no way morally problematic. It is perhaps understandable why people may mistakenly judge them to be obscene, since they look very similar in some respects to the kind of photograph someone interested in indulging sexual desires for young children may take an interest in. No doubt they could be looked at in such terms – just as clothing catalogues could be looked at by such people in sexual terms. But that they could be misused in such ways doesn't make them obscene.

Context and purpose make a difference. If photographs like Gearon's were grouped together on a paedophilia collage or web-site they might become obscene, for they would be being grouped together in order to arouse sexual desires for pre-pubescents. The same may be true of medical photographs of diseased bodies or cadavers. Individual photographs may not be obscene in any way but where a collage of such photographs is arranged to delight in the pain, suffering or death represented, then they may become so. In a similar light consider the Body Worlds exhibition, put on in Brick Lane, London, in 2002 and previously displayed all round Europe. The exhibition consists of anatomical displays of real, dead human bodies, and various other animals which have been preserved using the technique of plastination developed by Dr Gunther von Hagens. From cross-sections of the brain or lungs, anatomical displays of the different layers of the body through to the fibrous, tendril-like patterns of arterial circulatory systems, the exhibition was fascinating, in parts beautiful and educative. Part of the exhibition is potentially disturbing. For example, a woman lying prone in a pose reminiscent of art historical portraiture has a cross-section of her belly removed to display a foetus in her womb. No doubt some found this upsetting. But the purpose of the display is not to delight in the annihilation of persons but to marvel at the nature, complexity and beauty of the human body – of which we are all made and yet think and know so little about. So the purpose and context makes a difference and we should be careful to pay attention to such matters before being moved to condemn representations as obscene. Some might be tempted to say such considerations exonerate Sue Fox's photographs from the charge of obscenity, since they too are presented in the context of an art world for artistic appreciation. Yet whereas Gearon's photographs do not themselves solicit sexual attention towards the children represented and von Hagens' anatomical displays do not solicit delight in the thought of the death of others, Fox's photographs seem to draw the viewer in to savour the annihilation of persons. *If* that's right, then they are indeed appropriate objects of judgements of obscenity.

The recognition that works may be immoral or obscene in character does not provide grounds for censorship. The denial that works can have such a character is often driven by well-meaning concerns that the floodgates barring censorship would otherwise be overwhelmed. For the censorious amongst us would happily prohibit the display of many works deemed to be deeply offensive. But this is really an act of intellectual cowardice. It amounts to a tacit concession that the case against censorship can't successfully be made if we openly acknowledge that works can be deeply immoral, obscene and offensive. But nothing could be further from the truth.

One of the classical liberal arguments against censorship, stemming from John Stuart Mill, relies on the harm principle: the idea that unless something constitutes a harm it should not be prohibited.[30] Mill's argument emphasises that we are fallible creatures who may be mistaken about what is the case or fail to appreciate why something is true. Hence banning the articulation of views which are offensive can only serve to stifle understanding in the service of truth. Only where more harm than good is likely to result, in a manner which involves the infringement of more fundamental rights of others, should the expression of a view be prohibited in a particular case. It is not the view as such that is banned, since it may be articulated elsewhere or in another form where harm is unlikely, but what is prohibited is its articulation in scenarios where there is likely to be provocation of harm to others. Thus an extreme fascist speaker may be banned from speaking in the East End of London on a particular occasion, since it is judged the likelihood of violence being inflicted on others will be high, though the views as such should not be prohibited.

Mill's view has two components. First, that freedom of expression is premised on the articulation or representation of views serving truth and understanding and, second, that only in particular instances may this be overridden owing to considerations from harm. Now in the case of many art works that are deemed deeply offensive, it's far from clear that they involve the articulation of views or opinions which are in the service of truth or understanding. At least, views that could not otherwise be articulated in ways deemed to be less offensive. For example, Harvey's *Myra*, displayed at the Royal Academy's Sensation exhibition, may be artistically interesting, in virtue of the way it is constructed from the handprints of children, but it doesn't obviously add anything to the debate about how and why someone like that could come to participate in the murder of children or what the right response to Myra Hindley's punishment should be. So it is not clear that such a work is protected under Mill's characterisation of freedom of expression in the service of truth and understanding. We could try to suggest that this is a mistake. This work and others like it do in some way add to our knowledge of ourselves and others, along the lines articulated in chapter 3. But this would already be to concede too much – as if the non-censorship of art works *depended* upon whether they enhanced our understanding. Let's just assume that some such works do not.

Now it is often claimed that works constituting a deep affront to others may constitute a harm.[31] Why? The first reason is that things found to be morally disgusting give rise to fundamentally unpleasant emotions of abhorrence, loathing, repulsion and anger. Not only is the nature of what is displayed found morally loathsome but sometimes there is a sense of someone's deepest personal commitments and identity being attacked. The thought is that we have a right to be protected from unpleasant feelings and attacks on our identity, just as we have a right to be protected from the unpleasantness and vulnerability that results when someone is harassed, stalked or intimidated. Notice that the claim is not that we have the right to have our morality respected as such; rather it is the right to be protected from an offence which makes us feel vulnerable and deeply disturbed.

But the appeal to deep offence is no good. It's not the case that everyone finds feelings of disturbance and vulnerability threatening. If this were the case then it would be nigh unintelligible as to why so many people go to horror movies, or enjoy mountain climbing, roller coaster rides or literary works which challenge, confront or threaten their feelings, assumed views and identities. Some people enjoy the thrill of fear and others embrace the opportunity to entertain possibilities their beliefs are fundamentally at odds with. Why should such people be prevented from doing so merely because some people find them disturbing and unpleasant in ways they find difficult to cope with? No one forces them to go to galleries, read books, watch horror movies or go mountain climbing. More importantly, even if a work does disgust nearly everyone, this is still insufficient reason to ban it. Why do such feelings of repulsion arise in the first place? As a result of moral, social or aesthetic judgements of the vile nature of an image or its represented attitude. But the frustration of desires concerning what others ought to say, do and think is based on a moral, social or aesthetic judgement. And no one has the right to impose their conception of the right, good and beautiful on others. This is not to say that we cannot be profoundly mistaken. We can. But the point of a liberal society is to protect and honour the individual autonomy of its citizens – and that includes the right to make, and the responsibility for, one's own mistakes, as long as the rights of others are not so infringed. And the display of deeply immoral works in no way does so – as long as it is made clear what is being exhibited so people can choose to avoid it or engage with it as they wish.

A distinct but related thought construes deep offence as public indecency.[32] Perhaps it's not the Myra Hindley image as such which is so offensive but its presentation in a public exhibition by the Royal Academy. Public indecency is a matter of displaying an image or committing an act in public that should essentially be considered private. Hence the display of highly explicit sexual images is typically regarded as indecent. However, this view itself depends upon a particular moral conception of the nature of sexual activities and relations. Matters should be organised or regulated such that those likely to be offended by exhibition material are not readily exposed to it against their will, yet this is not the same thing as censorship. Deep offence is a function of moral qualms about images, attitudes or public display. But moral judgements as such have no business influencing what is or is not permissible in a liberal state. The function of the law is to protect and honour our capacity to lead our lives as we choose – and that of necessity includes the possibility of choosing to display, engage with or create works which are obscene or immoral. It is a matter of individual responsibility. This is true even if, in particular cases, doing so may be a bad thing.

Chapter Five | The Truth in Humanism

Where we are now

What has much of contemporary art got to do with the art of the past? The last hundred years or more seem marked by the propensity to experiment, break free from art's past, explore new media, materials and technology. Duchamp's ready-mades, Christo's cloaking of buildings and landscapes in material, Tony Cragg's sculptures made from discarded plastic, the video installation pieces of Bruce Nauman, to name but a few, can all seem worlds away from the preoccupations of traditional visual art. Yet is this really so?

Take Gillian Wearing's *Signs That Say What You Want Them to Say and Not Signs That Say What Someone Else Wants You to Say* (1992–5). It's made up of a series of photographs of people holding up placards of what they were thinking, an example being a smooth, city slicker type whose sign reads 'I'm Desperate.' Wearing approached the individuals, who were complete strangers,

and asked if she could photograph them with something they chose to write on the blank placard which reflected something about themselves. The contemporary nature of the piece is made up of a variety of elements. For example, there's the medium, photography, the incorporation of random elements – Wearing must have had little idea what the people would write on the placards before they did so – and the *apparent* artlessness involved: the photographs seem as if they were taken with a complete lack of interest in their formal elements. What, we might ask, could such a work possibly have in common with more traditional works involving painterly technique and an eye for structural composition?

Yet we should pause to think what Wearing is striving for. One of the striking things about this series is the way it highlights how difficult it is to read off from people's expressions, appearances and manner the type of thoughts they have. In a very simple way it reminds us with psychological force of the depth of people's inner lives. It is the incongruity between what we expect of the people photographed, based on assumptions about their appearance and demeanour, and the nature of their self and self-represented situations which does the work. We naturally tend to categorise, stereotype and overgeneralise people's characters far too quickly. The incongruity, the immediacy of the photographic medium and the artificial artlessness involved combine to underline in a forceful way how we glibly make assumptions about the inner lives of others and how hard it is really to know what someone is really thinking or feeling.

How radically different is the underlying artistic concern in Wearing's piece from that to be found in more traditional visual

Gillian Wearing, *Signs*, *I'm Desperate* © Gillian Wearing/Maureen Paley Interim Art

artists? Remember the characterisation in the first chapter of Vermeer's *The Little Street* (1657–8)? The painterly technique, the artful use of structural composition and play of light, shadow, colour and proportion all conform to a more traditional conception of the means of visual art. But what are these means to? The odd female figures going about their daily activities, the barred or slightly gaping shutters, the blank windows of the house to the right, all intimate the recognition that inner lives cannot be read off from the world of appearances. The means may be very different, yet both the Vermeer and the Wearing are designed to foreground very similar insights in our appreciation of them. The underlying concerns in contemporary art more often than not share a commonality with more traditional visual art, even though the means may be radically different. This shouldn't be surprising. In general, though the forms taken may differ radically, there are basic human concerns ranging over the whole of human experience from death, destruction, loss and love to knowledge, that we are naturally interested in and motivated by. It should be unsurprising that, despite the disparate means involved, contemporary art should continue to explore the kinds of themes more traditional art was so preoccupied by.

It was in the Renaissance that art, music, literature and architecture truly began to flourish outwith the walls of religion. The new architecture changed the landscape to a human size, manifesting the guiding ideal of mankind's moral dignity. Through artists like Alberti, and pre-eminently Michelangelo, the body was transfigured from a vessel of shame to the expression of noble, human and thus Godly perfection. Indeed, as Kenneth Clark once observed, 'the most profound thought of the time was not expressed in words, but in visual imagery'.[1] Thus it was that the

Renaissance gave birth to humanism. Religious works came to emphasise the humanity of Christ instead of his distant divinity and the glorification of the Church was entwined with or even replaced by the glorification of secular patrons. Wholly secular works, ranging from portraiture to the revival of ancient Greek and Roman myths and landscapes, began to flourish. The conceptual breach between art and religion severed once and for all the notion that art should be in the service of religious devotion. So began a radical shift not just in the arts, which came to be created and appreciated primarily for their artistic qualities, but in Western culture as a whole. Humanity itself was to discover or provide the foundation, knowledge and rational order governing the world. The importance of the visual arts in such a self-conception grew, since art works represented the ideals, and expressed the attitudes and responses mankind was to live up to and judge itself by. The purpose of art was to provide a meaningful experience indeed.

As Western culture transformed itself through the Reformation, the Enlightenment and the Industrial Revolution, despite the darker underbelly of Romanticism, faith in humanism held firm. But with the brutal onset of the twentieth century, humanism found itself in crisis. For some this was a tragic though inevitable end. Inevitable, since humanity's disavowal of God could not but lead to disaster; tragic since a return to the Divinity seemed beyond us. This is the kind of sentiment we find in Matthew Arnold's image of the receding sea of faith or in Eliot's conception of the wreckage of Western culture faintly echoing the mute stones of ruined cathedrals. Yet for others this was just as much a liberation as humanism itself had originally proved to be. The illusion of humanistic order and universal values had been shown up for what it was: a distorting myth serving the purposes of the powerful. In the late twentieth century, much commonplace or cultural criticism concerning visual art favoured the latter response. That which had been held in high esteem was a function of class interests or socio-cultural bias. The idea that certain works were in and of themselves great, rather than reflecting particular subjective preferences, was thought to constitute unjustifiable elitism. These two reactions, at opposite ends of the spectrum, represent two sides of the same coin. For they both assume the failure of humanism: the collapse of the idea that there are values, standards and principles we can justify which should govern our judgements and help us discriminate the good from the bad and mediocre. But the collapse of humanism is itself a myth. For humanism explains precisely how and why we can discriminate between the good, the beautiful and the ugly. To think otherwise is to perpetuate the most vicious kind of elitism there is. But on what basis can we hold that there can be disputing tastes? In trying to pursue an answer to this question 'art' will be used in a more descriptive sense in this chapter – no longer meaning 'good or great art' – since we'll be discussing the possible under-lying basis for discriminating between good, mediocre and bad art.

A standard of taste?

If we look at contemporary culture, both down the sweep of ages and cross-culturally, it seems that tastes vary radically. Some people like the carefully constructed crisp lines and geometric colour blocks from Mondrian's middle to late period, whilst for others his work is too clean, pure and abstracted. Certain groups of people tend to go for conceptual art whilst others can't see the appeal at all. In the recent past Victorian architecture was held to be hideous, repulsive and ugly, yet now we do all we can to save what are regarded as some of the remaining architectural glories from that period. The tussle between neo-classicism and Romanticism in the late eighteenth and early nineteenth centuries oscillated between the historic grandeur and compositional formality of artists like David and the much greater emphasis on individual artistic expression we see in artists like Delacroix and Turner. Paragons of female nudes down the ages come in multiple shapes and forms, one age apparently favouring Rubenesque women, fleshly, curved and substantial, whilst a different age, for example the 1930s, favoured a more angular, androgynous, waif-like look as the height of female beauty. The more one concentrates on such radical divergences in judgements the more they seem to proliferate.

Such considerations are often adduced as if they constituted proof that our evaluation of art works can be neither universal nor objective. Hence, for example, Pierre Bourdieu argues that we should take Kant's theory as the articulation of a certain, particular aesthetic ideal which presents itself, falsely, as a universal account of all things beautiful.[2] It is, or so one might think, the aesthetic preferences of a certain class, from a specific time, located in a particular culture glossed with the illusion of universality. Thus, it's thought, aesthetic ideals really are just expressions of one's particular social background rather than judgements which could meaningfully strive for objectivity and universality.

We should not be tempted into concentrating too heavily on the diversity of aesthetic judgements. Disagreement as such shows nothing. People disagree in science but it doesn't follow there isn't a truth of the matter. A particular account of aesthetic judgement or particular aesthetic judgements emerge from specific times, cultures and classes but this may show only that certain conditions have enabled people to appreciate things properly. Of course it's true that, as we develop, our taste changes because we do. Our circumstances change; the nature of our affections, desires, aspirations and even changes in identifying groups or classes all have an influence on the kinds of things we come to like and appreciate. None the less, we recognise that people's discrimination and understanding can come to be more or less finely developed. Indeed if we consider our own development, at least in some instances where our taste has changed, it seems to be attributable to developments in our discrimination and capacities. The appeal of things we liked ten or fifteen years ago is sometimes diminished because we come to see certain things we failed to see before. Conversely we come to like certain things we hadn't appreciated before, since we come to be in a position to understand them better. This is true whether one is talking about coffee, wine or art. Someone who has never tasted coffee before is not in a good position to know whether the coffee they've been served is a good one, whether it's instant or not, whether arabica beans have been used or whether the beans have been burnt or not. In judging good coffee, as with art works, it's no doubt true that certain backgrounds favour appreciation more than others. Backgrounds which give exposure to art, encourage critically reflecting on works, discussing responses to them, attending to the discriminations that can be made between colours, texture and tone will provide a huge advantage over those that do not. And this is why it's criminal that in our culture from an early age many people are not given the proper chance to come across, engage with and react to art in interesting and stimulating ways. Background shapes where one starts from; it doesn't determine taste. People from all walks of life can and do come to appreciate great art and it is easy to lose sight of the fact that there is much agreement, at least regarding central cases. Was Picasso a great artist? Matisse? Turner? Caravaggio? Michelangelo? No one seriously disputes these judgements. Disagreement tends to rage over more marginal cases or more contemporary artists. Indeed evaluating contemporary art is harder precisely because we are so near to it. It's very difficult to know whether we value something because it merely expresses attitudes or ways of seeing the world we are sympathetic to or because it really constitutes a worthy artistic achievement. In the case of older works it is easier, though not to say easy, because we may be at one or several removes from the attitudes concerned. But all this shows is that sometimes one is in a difficult position to know what the right judgement is to make, not that there isn't a right judgement to be had.

When we truly appreciate a work, we appreciate its pictorial composition, the arc of the lines, the shading, foreshortening, the ways in which the artistry shapes and guides our responses. In one sense then artistic appreciation, and thus judgement, is subjective: it arises from the ways we are disposed to respond to a work. But it in no way follows that there is no disputing tastes. People's tastes can be better or worse, undeveloped, refined, coarse or indiscriminate. Hume, rather than Kant, seems to offer the most straightforward account of how this is so.[3] He starts off by thinking of artistic judgements in a manner akin to judgements of perceivable qualities like colour. They too are subjective in that we can't be mistaken about whether or not we have the sensation of seeing a certain colour such as blue. But we can be mistaken about whether we really are seeing blue. How come? The lighting conditions might be atypical. If we look at a piece of red paper under non-standard lighting conditions, it appears to be a different colour. In cyan light, red looks black and under sodium street lighting red looks brown. Alternatively, the conditions might be right but there might be something wrong with us; for example some people are colour blind or perhaps we are ill and hallucinating. Similar considerations apply to physical taste: if someone is running a high fever food often tastes very salty even though it's not.

None the less there is a crucial difference between ordinary perceivable qualities and the case of artistic judgement. Ordinary perceivable qualities are fixed in terms of what standard human nature is able to pick out under normal conditions. But in the case of artistic discrimination, there is the further matter of delicacy or refinement of taste. So Hume introduces the case of Sancho's kinsmen from *Don Quixote*. A cauldron of wine is being enjoyed by a group of villagers, yet two 'expert' characters complain about it. According to one, the wine is marred by an undercurrent of iron and, for the other, the taste of leather ruins the overall flavour. The villagers taste nothing wrong and ridicule them for contradicting one another. Yet when the cauldron has been drunk, at the very bottom lies a rusty iron key attached to a leather thong. So here we have a case where two characters could pick out elements of the wine's taste which no one else could. Their superficially contradictory discriminations are no such thing, just accurate judgements which are less than complete in different respects. We are familiar enough with wine tasting to know that those whose palettes are refined through experience and heightened sensitivity can pick out elements of a wine that, to the untutored palette, remain indiscernible. By analogy the same is true with respect to artistic discrimination and judgement. Consider how, in the case of music, an untutored ear cannot pick out different instruments, distinguish the harmony from the melody or hear the musical symbiosis in good free jazz. Similarly in the case of visual art. Devoid of visual experience, we would be unable to pick out the structure of the pictorial composition, the effects of foreshortening, contrasting colours or shading, the significant allusions or associations. This is something we can develop by looking at different art works, listening to those whose appreciation is more refined than our own or reading good art critics.

To take one example, I can remember a time when I thought Picasso *the* artistic genius of the twentieth century. Matisse, who is often held up as Picasso's equal, was, I thought, a good artist. Yet what I had seen of Matisse's work inclined me to think he was a great colourist but not much more. Then, in the 1990s, I was lucky enough to see the most complete exhibition of Matisse's work that I am ever likely to see. My conception of Matisse was transformed forever. I had always found his fauve period compelling; the vivid intensity of the colours, the freedom from naturalistic description and the substantial treatment of shadows and reflections, as if possessed of the solidity of objects, is stunning. But I'd failed to appreciate just how radical Matisse's experimentation with colour, pictorial structure and composition was. After his fauve period, Matisse developed an abstract formal style, flattening pictorial planes and depth as can be seen in *The Dance* (different versions, 1909–10) and *The Music* (1910). The sense of rhythm and movement in both pictures is tangible and the planes indicating depth are flattened out to such a degree that the two-dimensionality of the paintings is foregrounded, whilst none the less asserting depth in terms of the relations and demarcation between the figures represented. After 1916, whilst living in Nice, Matisse moved on to concentrating on studies, still lives and landscapes. Again we have his preoccupation with colour but the emphasis on the two-dimensional flatness of his earlier canvases has gone. As Robert Hughes puts it:

> Nice gave him a different light from that in Paris – a high, constant effulgence with little gray in it, flooding broadly across sea, city and hills, producing luminous shadows and clear tonal structures. It encouraged Matisse to think of space (in particular, the space of the hotel rooms where he worked, overlooking the promenade des Anglais) as a light-filled box, full of reflections, transparencies and openings. Shutters filter the light, and their bars are echoed in the stripes of awnings or rugs; light is doubled by mirrors that break open the space of the room, and discreetly splintered in the gleam from silk, pewter or furniture.[4]

And then we move on through to works like *Pink Nude* (1935).

The two-dimensionality of the canvas is emphasised once more with linear demarcations marking out depth, the heightened colour and exaggeratedly simplified form being used to evoke mood, attitude and character. Our appreciation of the intense subtlety of the picture is enhanced if we see the much more naturalistic portrait Matisse started from, producing a series which grew ever more abstracted until he achieved the interpenetration of colour, line and flatness he was after. Later, the culmination of his life's work, the paper cut outs, were brought about because the debilitating, crippling pain in his hands meant he could no longer paint. His prints for *Jazz* (1943) developed into the cutting out of shapes from highly coloured paper, putting the flat forms together and constructing elegies to folk tales, the circus and fugues of colour. The most immediately striking thing in his late works is the colour relations – the ways in which the blocks of colour immediately leap

Henri Matisse, *Large Reclining Nude* (also known as *The Pink Nude*) (1935). © Succession H Matisse/DACS 2004. Courtesy of The Baltimore Museum of Art: The Cone Collection, formed by Dr. Claribel Cone and Miss Etta Cone of Baltimore, Maryland. BMA 1950.258

out as distinct forms, figures and patterned wholes. But what really makes them work is the sense of weight, mass and tangible solidity. They are light, but a lightness born of a grasp of the solidity of things rather than an unreflective concern with shape alone. Picasso is indeed a great artist – more obviously so since both the shifts and the achievements of his artistic preoccupations are often easier to perceive. It takes more time, experience and refinement to see that Matisse was truly his equal as perhaps no one else was.

Despite the recognition that our tastes can be cultivated there remain some pressing questions. How do we know if our tastes are being cultivated in the right way? How do we know if our judgements are right rather than reflecting our own inadequacies? How can we settle critical disagreements? In the tale from *Don Quixote* the wine tasters had proof; they could point to the key and leather as causing the flavours they'd picked out in the wine. But in art works there seems to be nothing we can point to in this way. Hume's strategy for answering these questions adverts to the notion of ideal critics. He's not claiming that there are such people; the notion is a theoretical one which we can only imperfectly realise. But the basic idea is simple enough. Ideal critics are those whose sensitivities are appropriately refined and discriminating, who possess delicacy of imagination and breadth of experience, and can set themselves apart from the vagaries of fashion or their age. The appropriate evaluation of a work is the evaluation that such an ideal critic would come to. He even goes on to suggest that there is a kind of proof available to us, one provided by the test of time. Works which appeal to many refined people across different ages and epochs, of different cultures or attitudes, are ones we have most reason to believe truly are great art works. For despite the myriad differences in temperaments, attitudes and fashions, refined humanity has none the less found them to be deeply rewarding. Hume's picture enables us to see how disagreements might be resolved. Disagreements will often come about not just because someone's sensibility is insufficiently developed or they lack the right kind of experiences, matters which can in principle be remedied, but often because someone is too closely wedded to particular beliefs, attitudes or assumptions of their time. When the post-impressionists first exhibited, they were met with cries of incomprehension, derision and accusations of degeneracy from both academic and public circles. People remained so tightly wedded to a classical conception of beauty and art that they could not engage with the works on their own terms. They were blind to the artistic challenge artists as diverse as Matisse, Derain and

Gaugin had set themselves. It is true that we should never confuse unpopularity or shock value with real artistic value: there are many things that cause a fuss, are shocking or nigh unintelligible, which are and remain artistically negligible. But disagreements often do come about because we remain, perhaps unknowingly, in the grip of assumptions about the conversation of art which, with a little more imagination, we would come to see are false.

Hume's picture does have a certain plausibility about it. That we appreciate the works of Michelangelo, Caravaggio, Goya, Rembrandt or Vermeer hundreds of years after they were created stands testimony to their power and greatness. We can also see why works by artists highly acclaimed in their time are consigned to the outer reaches of historical memory. For example, Frank Brangwyn's artistic skills are not in doubt, but his murals, panels and paintings depicting the ethic of industry, God and Empire are often two-dimensional. Many of his contemporaries perhaps thought no such thing, since they tacitly assumed something of the attitudes represented, thus remaining blind to their static, laboured nature. But the distance we have from such attitudes enables us to examine them afresh, and in this case we find the work wanting where once it was celebrated because its appeal seems to rest upon attitudes particular to their time. Similarly Sir Lawrence Alma-Tadema's skilful, sensuous representation of the ancient world is sentimental, fantastical and disingenuously erotic. Beautiful though many of his paintings are, given our less romanticised view of the ancient world we are inclined to see the vision embodied in his work as clichéd. So the reputations of artists can rise high amongst their contemporaries, whilst waning rapidly thereafter, because they depend as much upon attitudes of their time as real artistic merit. In fact one can see this in accelerated form in the twentieth century. The dizzying shift of movements, conjoined with the vagaries of the market place, culminated in the 1980s to the 1990s with the hyperbolic talking up of artists, from Jean-Michel Basquiat and Julian Schnabel to Tracy Emin. Hume didn't claim that works which didn't stand up to the test of time were no good. It's just that if a work turns out to be consistently admired across different times and cultures then we have sufficient reason to hold that it's likely to be good and worth appreciating. If it doesn't then it's hard to sift out whether or not a work was appreciated in virtue of its being good or merely because it chimed with the attitudes and peculiarities of its time.

Ideal art critics and actual motivation

It has been argued, for example by Jerrold Levinson, that the real problem of Hume's Standard of Taste, if not quite the problem that Hume himself attempted to resolve, comes down to a motivational problem.[5] In essence, why should I care that my ideal art critic rates Picasso above Dalí? My present aesthetic character, let's say, enjoys Dalí and gets little out of Picasso. I may find the latter hard work, a less pleasurable experience and more tedious than Dalí's paintings which I find to be compulsive, richly dark and affecting. Assuming that Picasso is better than Dalí, though Dalí is no slouch when measured against the aesthetic standard, I should in some sense strive to become such that I begin to appreciate Picasso more than Dalí. But given my present aesthetic character, what motivation do I actually have to do so?

In an attempt to answer this problem Levinson characterises ideal art critics as those who fully appreciate the master works of art. The term appreciation here is important since it marks out a more demanding requirement than merely identifying, approving of or judging appropriately great art works. Ideal art critics, in addition, are able to understand, explicate and interpret such works. This presumably marks out their capacity to do so in virtue of their possession of certain capacities (standard human nature plus perfect delicacy of taste, discrimination, imagination, etc.), knowledge (all relevant knowledge concerning the nature of the work, etc.) and freedom from distorting idiosyncrasies (e.g. prejudices of cultural fashion). Master works are those that survive the test of time, factoring out appreciation due to peculiar differences. The test of time anchors the characteristics or marks we identify ideal art appreciators by as non-arbitrary. Ideal art appreciators will thus be good guides to art value generally conceived of in terms of the most rewarding kind of experiences.

We can set aside questions concerning the relativity or convergence of judgement of such ideal art critics. To make clear that the focus of the problem being dealt with here is the motivational one, rather than the universality or relativity of aesthetic judgement, we will just assume that for any person there is an ideal art critic of their type. This allows for the possibility of there being at least a number of distinct types of ideal art appreciators whose judgements may or may not converge whilst none the less maintaining the shape of the proposed solution. Where the experience of a master work is preferred by an ideal art critic to the experience afforded by another work – Picasso say is preferred to Dalí – this is indicative of its providing an experience more worth having. Levinson at this point invokes John Stuart Mill's test: 'the best, and possibly the only, evidence of one satisfaction or experience being better than another is the considered, ultimate, "decided" preference for the one over the other by those acquainted with and appreciative of both'.[6] Given ideal art critics can compare the rewards of your present aesthetic experiences with those available to them, they are in the best position to judge which will yield the most rewarding experience.

Ideal art critics are thus held to be our best guide to artistic value. At least assuming that we are interested in aesthetic appreciation, we all have a defeasible motivation to track the kind of appreciation and judgement of our ideal art critics. Why? Our doing so is likely to yield greater experiential rewards in our art appreciation.

It's important, if only to pre-empt certain worries, that three features of this kind of account are foregrounded:

1   That the ideal art critic of your type prefers one work to another only affords you a motivation for trying it. You may, after all, have other non-aesthetic motivations for not doing so. This rules out worries about devoting oneself to art appreciation at the expense of other aspects of one's life.

2   The motivation afforded is defeasible since present states of affairs such as your present incapacities may be relevant. The ideal art critic of your type may delight in certain colour field paintings but this may provide you with no motivation for trying them if you're colour blind.

3   This way of presenting and answering the motivational problem turns the pronouncements of the ideal art critic into probabilistic empirical predictions. We should be motivated to make the effort required to come to appreciate what the ideal critic appreciates as being more worthwhile because it's likely that we too will then have more rewarding aesthetic experiences than we presently do.

We should think of this kind of approach along the lines of an advice model. As parents might advise their children to try certain kinds of food rather than others, so too the ideal art critic of someone's type may advise them to try Picasso rather than Dalí. The response to even the most petulant 'why?', in both cases, is 'you'll likely find the experience more rewarding'.

Despite the apparent attractiveness of this approach there are some general questions we might ask which give rise to a sense of unease. Is such idealised abstraction, embodied in the notion of the ideal art appreciator, at too far a remove from any or most of us? Can the question of the relativity of taste be so easily set aside? Might not many works be more valuable as art whilst yet affording less rewarding experiences? On what basis can it be said that someone's type of ideal art critic could meaningfully compare the experiences I actually have with those that, hypothetically, he or she is capable of? I think these kinds of questions can be captured more precisely by the following particular worries. In working through them it will turn out that there is something fundamentally wrongheaded about raising the problem, and answering it, in this way.

Let's start by reflecting on the fact that even small changes in our capacities and discrimination can radically affect our experience and appreciation of works. Think back to the first chapter when I was describing how I came to re-evaluate Mondrian's work. At one time I thought of his middle to late period as an example of good painterly graphic design. Yet after seeing an exhibition of his I suddenly came to see that underlying his drive towards abstraction was an attempt to represent somehow the idea that beneath the world of appearances lay a more fundamental structuring order to the universe. Thus not only was my experience of Mondrian's work transformed, so too was my appreciation and evaluation of it. But given this is so, it's hard to see how we could possibly get a good fix on which works are better, since it would be nigh impossible to narrow down how things may look after small but ever increasing changes in my capacities and discrimination.

The point can be pressed another way. Why should we assume that the test of time is a defeasibly sufficient indicator of artistic worth? The assumption seems to be that aesthetic appreciation works along a continuum, becoming ever finer and more sophisticated. Yet we're familiar enough, from our own experience, with the recognition that artistic appreciation often isn't like this – it's often a case of radical readjustment and reconfiguration. Here's an analogy. Looked at from a certain distance and without my glasses, part of the impressionist painting in front of me looks as if it represents a tree. I put my glasses on and it comes more clearly into focus and it still looks as though it represents a tree. I walk nearer and nearer, the painting comes ever more into focus, and it still looks as if it represents a tree. Yet when I suddenly reach the right viewpoint I suddenly realise it represents a water lily and the configuration of the entire shape changes. Why might not the works that stand the test of time stand to artistic value as my impression of the shape representing the tree stand to its representation of a water lily? It looks like a bad inductive assumption to presume that works standing the test of time must be more or less right, given the recognition that our aesthetic experience and appreciation can radically reconfigure.

The fundamental problem may lie in trying to find an explicit motivational justification with respect to artistic value, in terms of 'if I judge this way, I'll be happier'. For the reasons given, this appears somewhat dubious. A more plausible (and, possibly, a more

Humean) approach is to see such self-interest as the justification for the overall practice of art appreciation, but then to see the practice as taking off under its own steam with its own inherent logic which may lead to conclusions that are not themselves justified in these terms. That is, we come to have aesthetic values, and these will lead us to value things for themselves – not just as a means to happiness – so the motivation is there (motivation requires a *motive*, not necessarily a pragmatically justifiable motive). Then if a question is asked as to why we should do such valuing, a number of answers are possible: e.g. 'we just do', 'we have a love of pattern etc. which serves us well in other spheres', 'we find this valuing pays off in other ways', 'the system of valuing enables us to get on intersubjectively in various ways'.

Here's a different way of putting the point. We should distinguish between genetic norms, the norms which explain how and why the practice of making and appreciating art comes about, and internal norms, the norms which are integral to the practice once it has taken off. Consider an analogy. Why play soccer? Perhaps the answer is to be given in terms of various benefits like you'll be healthier, make friends, learn to co-operate with people and so on. These are questions about how this kind of thing fits into our practical lives. But, where someone is involved in the sport, we don't then ask why they should be motivated to defend, try and score goals, learn to pass and so on. Moreover, the answer to such a question at that level should certainly *not* be because you'll be healthier or learn to make friends. Indeed, it had better not be, since scoring a particular goal may cost you friends or playing on during a particular game may injure you. The same may be said of art. Creating and appreciating art may be a good thing for all sorts of reasons tied in with our practical lives: it makes for more rewarding experiences, it cultivates our emotions, enables us to engage in fellow feeling and discourse with others and so on. So, why be interested in aesthetics at all? The answer is because you'll be better off in all these ways and more. However, why be interested in this rather than that work? That's a matter of the reasons we have to value one work over the other, whatever they are, reasons which are internal to the practice of art creation and appreciation. The advice model gets things the wrong way round. It presents matters as if we acquire motivation through thinking what our ideal art appreciator would say. Rather, we're *already* motivated to be better appreciators (if we're interested in aesthetics at all) and that's why we pay attention to those whose tastes seem related to our own and whose discrimination we respect.

Blameless differences and relativity

Hume's argument has much in its favour. Amongst other things, our tastes can be more or less developed, we can lack imagination, delicacy of sensibility, the right kind of experiences, and we are often more influenced than we would like to think by the market, fashion and the cultural zeitgeist. So we can dispute tastes because often our judgements are clouded by factors which obscure a work's true merits. People can be and often are mistaken about why they like particular art works. Hume thinks his argument establishes the standard of taste. All ideal critics, according to Hume, will naturally converge in their judgements. They will come to agree in virtually each and every case. Yet Hume's argument can't establish the kind of objectivity he claims.

Interestingly Hume does allow for two sources of legitimate, blameless disagreement: 'The one is the different humours of particular men; the other the particular manners and opinions of our age and country.'[7] Thus someone in their twenties might prefer romantic or expressionist artists, from Delacroix to Nolde, whilst someone much older might have a more classical bent towards Raphael and Poussin. The differences in preference may be blameless since they're not attributable to defects or lack of sensitivity in the persons concerned. Rather they merely reflect blameless differences in attitudes towards the world: the exuberance of youth and the solace found in order of those aged by experience. Neither attitude is faulty or unjustified. So too, we find differences in epochs and cultures. One epoch or culture may favour works which emphasise the life of the emotions whilst another may incline towards works which emphasise the rational unity, order and balance of the world. We are familiar with such differences on an individual level. The favourite artist of a friend of mine is Poussin and I can see why. It reflects something of his judicious, rationally ordered attitude towards the world. Yet, whilst I can recognise that Poussin is a great artist, his work fails to do as much for me when compared to Michelangelo, Caravaggio, Goya, Matisse or Bacon. Assuming that this isn't a result of deficiencies in nature or sensibility, or the result of incomplete, partial judgements, the divergences in preferences reflect blameless differences in character. Such an explanation strikes a chord with why we think the kind of art someone likes reflects something deep about themselves. They are the outward mark of the particular bent, shape and character of the kind of person they are. Hence looking at the collection of art books, novels and records someone has often reveals much about them.

The trouble is, once Hume rightly allows for this kind of relativity, it is hard to see why we should grant the assumption that ideal critics will, even for the most part, converge. The manifold potential differences in temperament, attitude, emotional lives and biographical history suggest that far from there being one set of judgements agreed by ideal judges, there will be many distinct groupings. The distinct groupings may overlap to a larger or lesser extent, but we have no reason to assume we will get full-scale agreement. To push the point further, there's reason to think that blameless differences don't just consist in distinct reactive psychological attitudes. One of the fundamental assumptions Hume makes concerns the fixity of human nature. Yet blameless differences can sometimes arise from variations even at this level. Take just two examples. The eyesight of Australian Aborigines is standardly far more powerful than that of an average European Caucasian. A likely explanation for this is an evolutionary one. Australian Aborigines needed to develop more discriminating eyesight over greater distances so they could pick out shapes indicating the presence of animals. The vast distances of the plains and the scarcity of prey were environmental factors which meant good object recognition over vast distances was highly adaptive. The differences in the European environment meant that such a highly developed capacity was not so adaptive. Hence Caucasian eyesight tends to be worse in this respect. There are other differences which aren't apparently evolutionarily adaptive (though they may be by-products of things that are). The number of taste buds people have on their tongues varies from individual to individual, as does our capacity to process certain flavours. For example, Brussels sprouts taste sweet to one half of the average population whilst they taste bitter to the other half, the reason being that only one half can taste a particular chemical.

Recognising that human nature is indeterminate within certain parameters, open both to evolutionary development and individual processing differences, doesn't entail that there is no such thing as human nature or that it fails to provide the anchor for our responses to art works. But it does show that there is not one standard against which all our responses to art can theoretically be measured. Human nature, from the basic levels of processing and appetites up, allows of many disambiguations. And within those disambiguations there are many further distinct possibilities emerging from differences in history, culture, society, through to the emotional and psychological histories of individuals. Indeed, this is compounded by something we noticed in the previous section; that appreciation isn't just the finer development of discrimination along a continuum but often consists in radical breaks, something which is unsurprising given the cognitively rich, emotionally divergent and historically complex attachments bound in to art appreciation. None the less, although we cannot establish the kind of objectivity Hume was after, it doesn't follow that there is no disputing tastes. We can retain the recognition that tastes can be better or worse, more or less well developed, inchoate or regularised, whilst simultaneously embracing the idea that there may be many distinct types of more idealised aesthetic characters. To pick up on an analogy Hume himself was fond of, we may differ markedly about the kinds of friends we keep, owing to blameless differences in our characters, but it doesn't follow from this that there's no disputing whether or not someone constitutes a good friend. We can meaningfully aim to regularise reflectively our own artistic attachments, tastes and appreciation, whilst recognising that works we don't appreciate may none the less be appreciable by those of a different aesthetic type, and this is all the surety that humanism needs.

Counsels of despair

The start of the last century ushered in artistic developments that would dominate the frenzied fissures of artistic movements for the next seventy years. Impressionism, from which modernism is typically dated, gave way to Cézanne, Braque, Picasso, Matisse, Gaugin and Derain, to name but a few, who rapidly reworked the art of the past, throwing down challenges which, taken up, would branch out rapidly to form new artistic problems and possibilities which in turn were enthusiastically taken up. Post-impressionism, fauvism, cubism, futurism, vorticism, Russian constructivism, the Blue Rider and The Bridge groupings, loosely identified as expressionism, Bauhaus, colour field and action painting, pop art and conceptual art all derive their lineage from the first ten years of the twentieth century – their artistic ideals, aspirations and experimentation are all incipiently there.

There is a story about Picasso which symbolises the hope, glory and hubris of this artistic period. Around 1905–6 he agreed to paint a portrait of Gertrude Stein, who had to sit for him for hours on end and wasn't allowed to see it. Stein complained constantly, but to no avail. Much later when he finally finished the painting Stein and others were stunned. The painting, she complained, looked nothing like her. To which Picasso famously retorted, 'The point is, Ms. Stein, it will come to.' Here we have both the recognition that the artistic experimentation of the time was just that, hence the painting wasn't seen to resemble Gertrude

Stein, and the self-assured confidence of one who, rightly as it turned out, assumed that the experiment would be a success. Later artistic developments would ensure that we would come to see the ways in which Stein's portrait does indeed capture something about her. This is a familiar enough pattern in the development of art history; the sketches of Constable, the later works of Turner and the works of the impressionists were all greeted by contemporaries as unfinished, manifesting an inability to paint and resembling nothing short of a mess. Yet we now see them as works of artistic greatness, showing us the flickering contrasts and play of light, shadow and colour. Truly great art is often ahead of its time, hence it is sometimes greeted with derision and only later with acclaim.

A short story by the French writer Honoré de Balzac, *The Unknown Masterpiece*, is fascinating in this light. It features three artists; Poussin, Pourbus and Frenhofer. The first two are loosely based on actual painters, the intellectual classicist Nicholas Poussin and the late mannerist Franz Pourbus. But Frenhofer is an entirely fictional creation. The story is set in early seventeenth-century Paris and concerns both the nature of erotic love and the aspirations of painting. Frenhofer, acknowledged as an artistic master by the other two, has been secretly working on a painting for years. He won't allow anyone to see it, partly we are to infer because it depicts his mistress naked, but he cannot finish it since he is now without his mistress. In exchange for his being allowed to use Poussin's mistress, Gillete, as a model to complete his work, he is then forced to reveal it to the others. When it is finally unveiled Frenhofer is carried away in an ecstatic reverie, characterising his work in terms of the perfection of form, colour, line and the illusion of reality brought to life. The reaction of the other two, however, is rather different;

'Do you see anything?' Poussin whispered to Porbus.

'No. Do you?'

'Nothing'

[. . .]

'The old fraud's pulling our leg,' Poussin murmured, returning to the so-called painting. 'All I see are colours daubed one on top of the other and contained by a mass of strange lines forming a wall of paint.'

'We must be missing something,' Pourbus insisted.

Coming closer, they discerned, in one corner of the canvas, the tip of a bare foot emerging from this chaos of colours, shapes, and vague shadings, a kind of incoherent mist; but a delightful foot, a living foot! They stood stock-still with admiration before this fragment which had escaped from an incredible, slow and advancing destruction. That foot appeared like the torso of some Parian marble Venus rising out of the ruins of a city burned to ashes.[8]

It becomes apparent to Frenhofer that his fellow artists can see nothing in the painting and, unlike Picasso, his reaction is one of dismal failure culminating, later that night, in his suicide.

One possibility here is that Frenhofer was so far ahead of his contemporaries that they couldn't yet see the painting as it should be seen. And that is the way we have come to think of the derisory reactions of contemporary audiences to the work of artists like Van Gogh, Manet, Matisse and Picasso. But another possibility is that, artistically, there really is nothing there to see at all. Perhaps Frenhofer, in his pursuit of freedom from the conventionality of painting, has ended up abstracting away the very artifice that makes engaging with painting worthwhile. Since time immemorial the human form has been a perennial subject for painting. But in seeking to free painting from the artifice of representing a three-dimensional figure in two dimensions, Frenhofer's painting seems to consist solely in the indiscriminate arrangements of lines, striations of paint and blotches of colour. This kind of problem is often associated with the very nature of abstraction – absence of representation. But this cannot be right, for abstraction admits of degrees. Even the most realistic, figurative duplication of the human form manifests a minimal degree of abstraction. The distortion, accentuation or schematisation of scale, proportionality or detail is itself an abstraction. And minimally abstract works can be poor paintings because they are too life-like – merely detailed two-dimensional visual replicas of what they are not. One way of viewing Frenhofer's work, then, is in terms of a dilemma – how to avoid mere life-like representation whilst avoiding meaningless abstraction. The problem is that the story is ambiguous between Frenhofer's work being an achievement ahead of its time and a complete failure. In the latter case, perhaps nothing really ever could be seen in the picture. On this interpretation, all that remains, yet to be abstracted is the vivid fragment of the foot, a relic serving as a reminder of the achievements of artifice in the service of artistry.

There are those who think of contemporary art in this way. Roger Scruton, the Carlyle of our times, argues that modernism's attempt to mark off high culture has degenerated into the very kind of kitsch fakery it sought to distance itself from. The disciplined drive towards abstraction resulted in routine modernist gestures, thereby losing the interest of the audience. Modernism thus transmuted itself into the deliberate, ironic production of kitsch which referred to, used or parodied ordinary objects, ready-mades or quotable images requiring little discipline and no real emotional engagement. In Scruton's view this artistic degeneration has been compounded by the vagaries of the market place, in particular the adoption of attitudes and techniques exploited in advertising. For what contemporary visual art has become is the selling of product, the marketing of the artist as a brand, independently of any true artistic achievement, and thus a grand pretence that commodity value in some way reflects artistic merit. A pretence, moreover, that is self-perpetuating, since the artists, galleries and buyers must buy into it to avoid the recognition that anyone could have faked the installations, images and paintings glorified in the hyperbolic terms of commerce:

> The result might be called cultural 'pre-emptiness': not a new form of art, but an elaborate pretence at art, a pretence at appreciation, and a pretence at criticism. And this story shows something about our cultural situation. You will not perceive modern high culture correctly, it seems to me, if you do not see that much of it – perhaps the major part of it – is a pretence.[9]

For Scruton, then, not only does the emperor of contemporary visual art have no clothes, there is no emperor, just the inanimate mannequin of fashion.

This kind of condemnation of contemporary visual art is not uncommon and has been echoed by, amongst others, Brian Sewell, Julian Stallybrass and Anthony Julius. Julius identifies the originating breach with Manet, in particular with his *Jesus Mocked by Soldiers* (1865) and *The Dead Christ and Angels* (1864). The shock value of these works lies in the way they unadulteratedly secularise these two paradigmatically religious scenes, where we are presented with pitiless mockery or mortality without any sense of redemption, ennoblement or transfiguration. We are to dwell on suffering and death alone. Julius then traces the trajectory of modern art as a series of transgressions, against the conventions of artistic practice, moral and social taboos, and political assumptions or beliefs. But, Julius argues, the history of twentieth-century art has culminated in a rather hopeless state of affairs. For, in the relentless and indiscriminate pursuit of ever more ways to shock, we have been reduced to an art which is exhausted, pointless and mundane:

> We may conclude that the indefatigable energy of the transgressive enterprise . . . its commitment to the breaching of every boundary, one that is both relentless and undiscriminating, has had mixed consequences for the making of art works. Of the adverse consequences, a certain triviality has come to characterize much contemporary transgressive art. It has tended to be both insignificant and to articulate a nihilism falsely presented as something liberating, and should make way for an *anti*-transgressive art, one committed to the construction of criteria rather than the breaking of taboos (to appropriate Susan Sontag's judgement on quotidian avant-garde art).[10]

There is perhaps something to much of this kind of analysis of the contemporary visual arts. The commodification of art is by no means new and is no different from the way in which people increasingly lay down wine, collect medals or buy property for investment purposes. But there is something peculiar about the giddy heights reached by the 1980s, with works of barely emerging artists starting to go for dizzying sums. The odd feature is the way in which the contemporary art market became shot through with a kind of psychological presentism conjoined with an incessant search for artistic revivals. In part this reflects a more general cultural trend. Endless polls of the greatest historical figures, films or pop musicians show just how extreme our tendency now is to favour, or rather be heavily prejudiced towards, the present and recent past. Part of the story involves a lack of education and underappreciation of the past but it's also a function of market pressures. The drive for increased turnover and capital return provides the impetus for characterising each emerging artist as the next best thing or for new artistic developments as providing *the* key to contemporary art. The more convincing one can be that each novelty is a must-buy, the more works can be sold. These pressures also converge with the fact that there are more people training, working and promoting themselves as artists than ever before. And what could be an easier route to success than promoting oneself as an artist doing something new, which can easily be identified as such by those whose knowledge of art history stretches back only twenty or thirty years and requires little real thought or emotional engagement to appreciate. Hence the successes of the Julian Schnabels, Jeff Koons, Damien Hirsts and Tracy Emins of the art world, since they can churn out multiple works easily, quickly and without little real artistic effort. At its best such art can only set up expectations, then proceed to shock, grandly gesture or ironically savour and fulfil them in expected ways. But the mark of good art is that it abstracts, exaggerates and subverts expectations in unanticipated ways, which are themselves found to be worthwhile. Irony, shock value or grand gestures are themselves futile if they provide the end purpose. Their value is parasitic on there being an underlying point or purpose to such attitudes and stances. Carravagio's *Salome Receives the Head of St John the Baptist* (1607–10), Goya's *Disasters of War* series (1810–14) or Picasso's *Guernica* (1937) were all driven to shock in the service of a point worth making. And the artistry involved in bringing the point home through shaping the viewer's experience is disciplined, hard won and effective. But the ease with which some conceptual art, installation art or ready-mades can be used to highlight or question in all too familiar ways – queries about what constitutes art say – provides an accommodating home for the artistically feckless and mediocre. If we concentrate on such art we are naturally led to think that, far from making things new, we are faced with the endless recycling of the already recycled.

The renewal of humanistic art

Intelligible as parts of it may be, this counsel of artistic despair is misconceived and ill judged. The view rests on a partial mischaracterisation of contemporary art, a conception that is itself a victim of the very phenomena decried, and a misevaluation of what our attitudes towards contemporary art should be. One thing such an analysis fails to realise, in claiming that we are being deceived by modern art, is that the risk of pretence and fraudulence is partly characteristic of certain kinds of modern art. Many contemporary artists lie quite deliberately, either by the digital manipulation of visual media responses or even in terms of the performance of anarchic gestures, as a kind of test of the viewers' assumptions. It's true that every time we engage seriously with such art we run the risk of being deceived. But part of the threat comes from the way in which such works can implicate ourselves – the risk involved is one which threatens to reveal our own responses, 'fine' art discriminations and judgements as themselves fraudulent.[11] In some cases it may be a case of not so much the new emperor wearing no clothes but of the 'wise' onlooker being exposed. Indeed, especially if we take to heart Greenberg's point about competence in artistic judgement requiring familiarity with the ongoing development of artistic traditions, this may explain just why the denunciations of much contemporary art emanating from the quarter of Scruton, Sewell *et al.* are so fierce and shrill. They manifest just such an anxiety.

The despairing view is motivated in part by a misleading contrast between the start of the last century and the present. If we look back a hundred years or more we can pick out the works of Cézanne, Picasso, Matisse and many others as constituting great artistic achievements. When compared to the litany of minimal, conceptual, neo-expressionist, politically 'radical' and shocking works that the despairing claim closed out the last century and ushered in the new, it may seem as if we have reached the point of artistic exhaustion. But even if the contrast is representative, it doesn't follow that our situation is peculiarly hopeless. It is perverse to think that most art at any given time ought to be exceptional. Such artistic epochs, from the Renaissance to the emergence of modern art, are rare. It is more common for the art produced at any given time to be fairly mediocre. The flowering of great artistic revolutions is understandably atypical. So even if we agreed that contemporary art is generally lacklustre, with some notable exceptions like David Hockney, Frank Auerbach or Jeff Wall, this puts us in no worse position than most other periods in art history. Nor should we be so quickly moved to sneer at the putative failure of contemporary art to produce works of deep originality.

Artistic progress may look as if it consists in a series of starbursts, the light from one great period diminishing until the next explodes apparently from nowhere, but the appearance is misleading. The dazzling shifts and reworkings of artistic traditions partly depend upon the work of many less gifted artists who create work that, if not great, is good enough, who keep traditional media alive and explore new ones by constantly testing, developing or refining the traditions from which they emerged. Michelangelo's *Pietà* would not have emerged without the Low Countries artists who developed that very genre. Perhaps without the example of Richard Wilson, the first British landscape painter, Turner would have been deprived of the tradition within which he came to experiment formally, to such luminous effect, with light, atmosphere and movement. And the Barbizon school, an association consisting of French landscape painters such as Rousseau, Daubigny, Troyon, may have helped to provide the impetus for the later rejection of academic painting by the impressionists. Ideas, experiments, concerns pursued by the good enough often provide the background, impetus or stimulation for the truly great. Human progress generally, from philosophy or science to art, depends upon artistic foot soldiers as much as it depends upon individual works of genius. And artistic foot soldiers only have to be good enough. So even if we accept the contrast, it doesn't tell us that the art of the present is uniquely impoverished, only that it is, more typically, not an age of artistic genius. And no artistic period should be condemned for that, nor should we despair at it. Works are still being made which are interesting, rewarding and enjoyable to look at, without which there wouldn't be the requisite background against which a future age of artistic greatness could emerge.

We should also wonder at the assurance with which it is pronounced that contemporary art is exhausted. Why should we accept the judgement that contemporary art is somewhat spent and lacklustre? The certainty involved assumes that we are in a good position to make such a judgement. Yet both reason and art history tell us that the artistic period we have most reason to be tentative about is our own. It is a myth that all great artists have been mis-understood in their time – from Michelangelo to Joshua Reynolds, many artists have been rightly celebrated from early on in their careers. Yet it is true that great artists have sometimes been ignored or contemptuously dismissed by their contemporaries. Just before his death in 1906 Cézanne was registering in the consciousness of British art circles but only as a confused, clumsy and simplistic painter. At the same time as the work of artists like Lawrence Alma-Tadema, Charles Leighton and other talented but derivative works of Victoriana were still highly celebrated, the Cézannes exhibited in the Durand-Ruel exhibition of 1905 at Grafton Galleries were almost wholly ignored. Yet slowly, in large part owing to the work of Roger Fry and the Bloomsbury set, Cézanne came to be seen as the lynchpin for the revival of modern art rather than signalling its degeneration into brutalism. One reason why such misjudgements can easily arise can be seen if we return to Hume, who pointed out that our judgements are often overly influenced by the vagaries of fashion, critical prejudices or socio-cultural beliefs and attitudes. There is a constant danger of over- or underestimating the quality of works because they speak to, or grate against, our prejudices. Not only is this generally true, but it is more likely to be viciously so when considering the art of the present. A somewhat different and more sophisticated reason is given by Clement Greenberg.[12] What constitutes competence in artistic appreciation, in particular with respect to contemporary art, requires one to have submitted to and grasped the kinds of pressures, developments and aims of the kind of art one is judging. Devoid of such education and understanding, one's appreciation and judgement will have little to recommend it. It's not that there's something wrong with such a person's eye-sight or indeed delicacy of taste or imagination. It's just that they can't be in a good position to appreciate certain kinds of work, such as abstract art say, if they fail to grasp the pressures and concerns involved in that kind of development of artistic taste.

Our culture is obsessed by celebrity status, fame and notoriety. Hence it is part of the fashionable zeitgeist to be interested in what particular celebrities look like, their public and private faces and what they are up to. It's not even a conscious matter so much as an unconscious disposition to notice such things, take an interest in them and derive pleasure from so doing. Even those who decry such a state of affairs often find themselves taking an interest, such is the extent to which our culture is in thrall to celebrity aspirations and schadenfreude. In this context it is much more difficult to be critically judicious about art which itself is concerned with or portrays the objects of such an interest. In 2001 there was an exhibition at the National Portrait Gallery in London, which subsequently toured internationally, of portraits by Mario Testino. Testino is highly regarded as a fashion photographer, having worked for *Vogue*, Versace and Gucci to name but three of his more prestigious clients. The show consisted of portraits of the rich and famous from supermodels like Kate Moss, music stars like Madonna and actresses like Gwyneth Paltrow to Diana, Princess of Wales. His photographs often use informal poses, a sense of colour and fairly well structured compositional elements, and their glossy finish enhances the sense that this world is one of effortless beauty, success and fun. It is unsurprising that the exhibition was met with some gushing reviews of rather hyperbolic proportions. But what is interesting, despite the hype, is that Testino has neither a distinctive photographic style nor anything that rewards the eye beyond the immediately obvious. By contrast, if you know their work, it is easy enough to pick out photographers such as Man Ray, Blumenfeld, Irving Penn, Cartier-Bresson, Bill Brandt or Martin Parr.

Take Penn's distinctive *The Harlequin Dress (Lisa Fonssagrives-Penn)* (1950). The voluminous folds of the dress billow out, drawing attention to the tucked-in waist; the contrasting textures and tones of the black and white add depth and the mask-like face with accoutrements backgrounds the sitter so that it is the dress that is the real subject of the photograph. The pictorial composition and use of the model in this way is part of what is distinctive of Penn's photography. Alternatively consider a radically different kind of photographer like Martin Parr. Parr is one of the most influential present-day photographers, whose election to the Magnum photographic agency was highly controversial. Cartier-Bresson famously opposed his election on the grounds that he took Parr's documentary style, in particular his work from the 1980s, to reflect a nihilistic strand in contemporary society. This is rather hard to see in his early work. Parr's portraits of northern England, specifically the intimacy of working- and lower-middle-class communities, have a gentle, sometimes wry, poignant air of traditional forms of life slipping away. We see black and white photographs of groups of men, families, friends, gathered together in faded village halls, weather-beaten sports grounds or village fêtes. But in the 1980s Parr shifted towards colour photography, unsparingly documenting the social movement of the working classes in Britain towards consumerism.

The Last Resort (1985), for example, Parr's series of photographs from New Brighton on the Wirral, shows holiday makers amongst the detritus of a decaying seaside resort, individuals sun tanning whilst ignoring their infants, girls parading for beauty pageants or masses of individuals swarming in an ice-cream parlour greedily stuffing themselves whilst unaware of the people next to them. It's easy to see why this shift in Parr's work appalled so many, though we might perhaps reflect on whether what is really so appalling is what Parr's photography documents rather than the work itself. It's not obvious that his work is unaffectionate since it is often so wryly observed and gently humorous. None the less, what's distinctive about Parr's style is the sharply defined, harshly lit nature of the images, gained by using a 6 × 7 cm camera and daylight flash. A wide-angle format allowed him to capture the dynamic social interactions of groups and individuals whilst maintaining a sense of being tightly up-close and personal. If we look at one of the photographs from an ice-cream parlour, see p. 244, with the serving girl, hand on hip, facing the camera, we can see what distinctive effects this enabled him to achieve. The light, sharpness and flatness of the photograph all enhance the sense of a frozen moment, each individual lost in their own thoughts and actions. The cones piled up on the left are ready to serve the ever insatiable demands of the never-ending customers pushing towards the counter and reaching for or busy with ice-creams. The small boy on the left stretches out, eager to be served, an early version of the adolescent boy who's acquired a handful of ice-creams and is now fixated by the serving girl's breasts, one appetite overruling the other. The little girl, food in mouth, looks at the camera in an echo of the serving girl she might become. The counter girl herself looks deadpan into the camera with emotionless disdain. The visual language Parr

Martin Parr, *The Last Resort, Girl in Ice-Cream Parlour* (1985) © Martin Parr/Magnum Photos

developed enabled him to capture the appetitive aspirations and alienation of a class now preoccupied not with the preservation of traditional communities but with the delights of consumption.

Now contrast the kind of thing we might say about Penn or Parr with what seems appropriate to Testino's portraits. Compare Testino's work with other decent photographs from the pages of various high-fashion magazines and you can't tell them apart. Looking at them, you're immediately struck by just who the photograph is of, Meg Ryan, Kate Moss, Liz Hurley, the artificiality of the informality, the studied nature of expensive elegance. And that's it. No interesting juxtapositions of line, colour, expression or pose, except for the more tasteful superficialities of Athena-like posters, and no insight, understanding or depth of character. The subjects are themselves intersubstitutable. The photographs are mute paeans to the superficial glamour they depict. One is left with the impression not so much of a photographer slickly sliding over the surface of things as of one who is all surface. The point is, we can see why Testino's photography is overestimated because his subjects, and manner, are the epitome of the celebrity glamour to which so many people are currently in thrall. That is why perhaps many fail to see that his photographs are not as good as is often claimed. And just as other people have blind spots, because of their interests, attitudes and aspirations, so too do we. We can critically reflect on whether such things are likely to be infecting our own artistic judgement, and so become more critical, but it is harder with things that are psychologically nearer to us than with those that are distant. Hence we are in a much better position to estimate the worth of a painter who did much the same thing a couple of hundred years ago.

Joshua Reynolds was, as Testino now is, a much sought after portraitist of the great, good, notorious and glamorous of his time. He was the first English painter sought after instead of Europeans, the first truly to master the grand style, and he was deeply informed by the art of the past. We may not know the Marlborough family (c. 1788), nor care much for them, but the interlocking composition of eight figures with dogs is constantly varied, complex and dynamic. The gestures, poses, expressions convey much about the familial relationships, the authority of the parents, the mischievousness of the children and the ties which bind them together. Aside from the formal portraits, his more informal work reveals a depth of insight into the character of his subjects. But in years to come, when people will neither have heard of nor care about many of the people in Testino's portraits, it is not obvious that they will gain much from them.

Artists are just as easily overlooked because they fail to conform to the prejudices of their time. Throughout much of the twentieth century, and still dominant in this, the standard characterisation of modern art's development started with Cézanne, through cubism, leading to painterly abstraction, pop art and conceptual art. The underlying rationale is the assumption that the original developments in twentieth-century art, identified with the avant-garde, are to be understood in terms of the drive towards abstraction. In part this is because of America's importance after the waning of Paris, and this story is held to give the most coherent explanation of the development of American art thereafter. But note that abstraction here is thought of as the deconstruction of the traditional elements of painting and art, or the visual appropriation of everyday objects. Indeed, Arthur Danto's celebrated end of art thesis holds that the progress of art in the twentieth century consisted in the transformation of the art object from works with mimetic or expressive qualities to objects, such as Duchamp's ready-mades or Warhol's Brillo boxes, transformed into art in virtue of the theory and art world institutions with which it came to be surrounded.[13] The trouble is that this kind of narrative, and the notion of artistic value involved, tends to be too internal to the art world, its institutions and 'official' histories. Against this background it is easy to see how a stereotypical history of British art in the last century goes. The Bloomsbury group, so enamoured of the post-impressionists, gives way to the St Ives group and Ben Nicholson's clean, abstract reliefs, and the 1960s work of artists like Anthony Caro, Richard Hamilton, Bridget Riley; the Art and Language movement of the 1970s runs through to the likes of Gilbert and George, Sarah Lucas, Damien Hirst and the Chapman brothers. No wonder British art in the twentieth century is often considered a weak cousin to the developments across the Atlantic. Apparent oddities from vorticists like Wyndham Lewis to Paul Nash, Stanley Spencer, Walter Sickert, Henry Moore, Francis Bacon, David Hockney or Frank Auerbach have been either given little credit or thought to stand alone. Given such critical preconceptions it is unsurprising that a number of truly great British artists have, at least in the recent past, been vastly underestimated. Their work fails to fit in or sits uncomfortably with the favoured narrative of twentieth-century art.

A case in point is Frank Auerbach. An immigrant child from Berlin in 1939, he studied at Borough Polytechnic, where he was taught by David Bomberg, then at St Martin's, where he met Leon Kossof, and finally at the Royal College of Art. In the 1970s his work formed part of an exhibition of figurative artists, alongside painters like Freud, Bacon, Kossof and Kitaj, the last himself choosing the paintings and dubbing the group the 'School of London'. The idea that these artists formed a tight school is misleading since the differences between the artists are multiple and varied. But one can see why, in the art world of the 1970s, they would seem to be a coherent association engaged in the same artistic conversation. For here was a group of artists swimming against the tide by pursuing the figurative tradition, albeit with distinct concerns, totally at odds with all that was deemed progressive, interesting and original. Auerbach's work was, and remains, almost sculptural, with thick layering of paint piled, scratched and scraped layer upon layer. His subject matter revolves around a group of people, some of whom have sat for him for over thirty years, and the cityscapes of London.

The mainstay of his working process as it evolved involves the project of abstraction. Starting from more detailed sketches or

Frank Auerbach, *3 Sketches from Titan's 'Bacchus and Ariadne'* (1970–1). Copyright the artist, courtesy Marlborough Fine Art, London. Photos © Tate, London 2003

Frank Auerbach, *Bacchus and Ariadne* (1971). Copyright the artist, courtesy Marlborough Fine Art, London. Photos © Tate, London 2003

painterly characterisations of his subject, Auerbach would then focus on the underlying rhythms, sense of movement and defi-nition, starting the process over again to render the representation in ever more basic lines, tones and shading. He took to translating his painterly methods into his drawings, scouring, smudging and overdrawing in a similar manner.

The essence of Auerbach's artistic process has much in com-mon with the process of abstraction we saw earlier when discussing the Matisse series which led up to his *Pink Nude* or Mondrian's early to middle period prior to his flight into pure geometry. The difference lies in the sheer tactile physicality of the paint, jutting, dripping, protruding and smeared across the canvas, its density and luminosity accreting as Auerbach wiped the canvas down, painting the next more abstracted version on to the same canvas over the previous layers of paint. The three-dimensionality of the stratified layers of paint helps to explain their sculptural quality. Initially it can be difficult to see the figurative features in the paintings or the pose of the subject in some of his works, but close attention to the strong lines, whorls of paint and visual planes brings the subject into focus. And as you become attuned to doing so, those works which seemed like undecipherable visual puzzles emerge more clearly defined. Seeing the figures emerge from the canvas, perceiving how the simple, dense delineations of paint relate different features to one another, foregrounds the physicality of the paint, the act of looking at a virtually two-dimensional canvas, whilst at the same time having an experience as of seeing a three-dimensional subject with distinct features and characteristics. The success of Auerbach's work in part depends upon showing us how the visual system can come to make sense of, and round out, the most basic patterns of colours, lines and texture into fully formed figures. The disciplined, hard-won precision is devoted to pene-trating our experience with a sense of the subject's distinctness through the physicality of the paint whilst foregrounding the medium itself. The visual oscillation between subject and surface, the ways they come to frustrate, surprise and interpenetrate, is an achievement indeed. And yet for all that, certainly up until the later 1980s, Auerbach was considered an artistic oddity, cultivating the artistic dead end of traditional painterly concerns and the figurative tradition. As Robert Hughes points out, a not untypical case, in 1986, was 'the critic Stuart Morgan [who] assured the readers of *Vogue* that Auerbach was "the ultimate pig-headed Englishman", condemned by his own narcissism to do the thing over and over again'.[14] Auerbach's work had no obvious links to the well-regarded art of his time, the flat colour field paintings, the ironies of pop art, the radical conceptual concerns of Art and Language or the explosion of interest in electronic and mass media. Latterly, in part owing to the championing of Robert Hughes amongst others, Auerbach has come to be properly recognised as a seriously good painter, culminating in his Royal Academy show in 2002. But for much of his artistic career he was condemned to a kind of critical exclusion. It is understandable why this was so – given the intellectual and critical fashions prevalent in the art world. His is a prime case of the worth of an artist being underestimated owing to the critical prejudices of much of his time.

In the particular case of British art, there is much good work that's been underestimated because it fails to conform to the archetypal modernist story about the developments in twentieth-century art. In particular this explains why those who've tended to work within the landscape and figurative traditions have been all too easily overlooked. By contrast, work which reflects certain interests of the cultural zeitgeist, from our preoccupation with celebrities to the critical overestimation of much minimalist, conceptual and ready-made work, explains the exaggerated claims made for works which strive for relevance without necessarily realising artistic worth. The counsel of despair not only fails to recognise this but is itself a victim of the very phenomenon adverted to. For in discussing contemporary art, the despairing focus almost exclusively on those works which have tended to generate the most publicity. And we have seen why we have good reason to be sceptical of the assumption that the most worthwhile work being produced now is necessarily that which gets the most coverage. Furthermore, glib generalisations are made concerning the paucity of all contemporary conceptual, transgressive or less traditional art forms. It's as if the impoverished nature of particular works is taken to reflect the inherent inadequacies of all multimedia, conceptual or ready-made art. This betrays a failure to set prejudices aside and look sympathetically for the realisation of artistry, since there are works being produced in these forms which are highly valuable. The despairing are as myopic as those who would celebrate as great the achievements of any contemporary art that is transgressive, shocking or conceptual. For they take at face value a highly distorted and selective characterisation of contemporary art. The only difference is that one bemoans what the other eulogises.

Yet, in terms of both contemporary British and world art, the works of Tony Cragg, Richard Long, Andres Serrano, Bridget Riley, Sean Scully, Patrick Caulfield, Jeff Wall, Bruce Nauman, Cindy Sherman or Gillian Wearing, to name but a handful, all fit into the characterisations of contemporary art proffered by those who decry its parlous state. And yet it is difficult to see how serious critical reflection could deny their artistic worth. Conversely, the despairing rarely talk about artists like Frank Auerbach, David Hockney, Howard Hodgkin, Anish Kapoor or Eric Fischel, whose work is deeply serious and rewarding, no doubt because they do not fit neatly into the caricature of contemporary art that passes for knowledge and understanding. There is something to the notion that certain aspects of contemporary art are playing themselves out, fatigued into the weak mimicry of played-out signs, ideas and banal disgust. But we should be careful not to overexaggerate the present state of affairs. Contemporary art is much more diverse and vigorous than we are led to believe. The favoured narrative backdrop against which contemporary art is made sense of, by both its defenders and its detractors, is misguided. Contemporary art is not in a desperate state nor best seen as a further playing out of anti-traditional artistic concerns. Nothing could be further from the truth.

The ultimate test of art lies in what reasons we have to value a work. Is a work original, expressive of distinctive qualities of mind, engaging, beautiful, insightful? Does it repay close study? Is it compelling time after time? These kinds of questions constitute the most basic test of how good a work is. Our understanding and experience of a work seeks to track such reasons. But not just any old experience will do. Amongst other things, one has to be open to and understand what the artist is trying to do; one has to be in a position to know what references and allusions are being made, to have developed through experience the capacity to make the right kind of discriminations. Striving for delicacy of taste is a never-ending process, akin to moral discrimination and understanding, which is impelled by a deep sense of curiosity and appreciation of the riches that art can bring to one's life conjoined with the humility to recognise that there is always more one could appreciate, be challenged and surprised by. This is as true for those striving to be artists as it is for those who appreciate art. The recognition that there are different levels of understanding is not elitist. It is the straightforward recognition that the richness of experience depends upon what one brings to it. Without embarking on such a journey, and the will to pursue it, we leave ourselves bereft of a primary means of rendering ourselves articulate and enabling us to make sense of our selves and the human condition. Travelling through the imaginative landscapes of art, and the experiences afforded, is a powerful aid to cultivating our inner lives.

Notes

Chapter One   Originality and Artistic Expression

1   Walter Benjamin, 'The Work of Art in the Age of Mechanical Reproduction', 1936, as excerpted in Charles Harrison and Paul Wood (eds), *Art in Theory 1900–1990: An Anthology of Changing Ideas* (Oxford: Blackwell, 1992), p. 515.

2   André Malraux, *Le Musée imaginaire*, which is vol. I of his *The Psychology of Art* (New York: Pantheon Books, 1949–50).

3   Roger Scruton claims that photography cannot be an independent representational art on this basis. See his 'Photography and Representation' and 'Fantasy, Imagination and the Screen', both reprinted in his *The Aesthetic Understanding* (London: Methuen, 1983) and his 'The Photographic Surrogate', reprinted in his *The Philosopher on Dover Beach* (Manchester: Carcanet, 1990).

4   See Bill Jay, Nigel Warburton and David Hockney, *Brandt* (London: ipublish.com, 1999) and Nigel Warburton's 'Individual Style in Photographic Art', *British Journal of Aesthetics* 36, no. 4, 1996, pp. 389–97, reprinted in Alex Neill and Aaron Ridely (eds), *Arguing about Art*, 2nd edn (London: Routledge, 2002).

5   See Saul Kripke, *Naming and Necessity* (Cambridge, MA: Harvard University Press, 1980), pp. 110–15.

6   See David Davies, *Art as Performance* (Oxford: Blackwell, 2004), who argues that our rejection of fakes and forgeries shows that artistic value can't be wholly reduced to the value of the experiences art works afford. For further elaboration of this line of thought see his 'Against Enlightened Empiricism' in Matthew Kieran (ed.), *Contemporary Debates in Aesthetics and the Philosophy of Art* (Oxford: Blackwell, 2005). I am indebted to a long and engaging correspondence with David, which included discussion of the Van Meegeren forgery case and the achievements of cubism, which influenced my views on this matter.

7   As the foremost empiricist philosopher it is no surprise that Hume held this view: 'all the general rules of art are founded only on experience, and on the observation of the common sentiments of human nature', p. 138. See his 'Of the Standard of Taste', originally published 1757, included in his *Selected Essays* (Oxford: Oxford University Press, 1993). More contemporarily we have Malcolm Budd claiming that 'a perspicuous elucidation of the concept of artistic value is possible

in terms of what I shall call "the experience a work of art offers"'. (from his *Values of Art: Pictures, Poetry and Music* (London: Allen Lane, 1995), p. 4). George Dickie also holds this kind of view, as articulated in his *Evaluating Art* (Philadelphia: Temple University Press, 1988) and his *Art and Value* (Oxford: Blackwells, 2001). I once held a similar view, as articulated in my 'Value of Art' in Berys Gaut and Dominic McIver Lopes (eds), *The Routledge Companion to Aesthetics*, 1st edn, (London: Routledge, 2001). I was once tempted to think that a form of enlightened empiricism could relate all artistic achievements, even if only indirectly, back to the value of the experiences afforded. For remarks which suggest something like a form of enlightened empiricism see Jerrold Levinson, 'Pleasure and the Value of Works of Art' in his *The Pleasures of Aesthetics* (Ithaca: Cornell University Press, 1996), and his 'Evaluating Music' in P. Alperson (ed.), *Musical Worlds* (College Park, PA: Penn State Press, 1998). Now I consider this view to be mistaken. No doubt some of the achievement and meaning properties of a work could be captured in terms of the experiences afforded to a suitably informed spectator, but certainly not all nor in the right kinds of ways. For further elaboration see my modified version of 'Value of Art' in the second edition of *The Routledge Companion to Aesthetics* (London: Routledge, 2005).

8 See Robert Stecker, *Artworks: Definition, Meaning and Value* (University Park: Pennsylvania State University Press, 1997), pp. 247–68.

9 Nigel Warburton, 'Is Art Sacred?' in Ben Rogers (ed.), *Is Nothing Sacred?* (London: Routledge, 2004).

10 R. G. Collingwood, *Principles of Art* (Oxford: Clarendon Press, 1928), p. 336.

11 See Aaron Ridley, *R. G. Collingwood: A Philosophy of Art* (London: Orion Books, 1998), for just such a sympathetic reading.

12 Gordon Graham, 'Expressivism: Croce and Collingwood' in Berys Gaut and Dominic McIver Lopes (eds), *The Routledge Companion to Aesthetics* (London: Routledge, 2001), makes this point whilst going on to argue that this evacuates expressivism generally of any of its distinctive content as a general account of all art.

13 Nick Zangwill, 'Art and Audience', *Journal of Aesthetics and Art Criticism* 57, no. 3, 1999, pp. 315–32, discusses artistic sketches amongst other things in order to suggest the much more extreme view that 'there should be no reference to an audience in a theory of the nature of art'. I am not claiming there should be no such reference but rather that such reference cannot capture everything that is always valuable about art works.

14 I'm indebted here to Albert E. Elsen's 'Drawing and a New Sexual Intimacy: Rodin and Schiele' in Patrick Werkner (ed.), *Egon Schiele: Art, Sexuality, and Viennese Modernism* (Palo Alto: The Society for the Promotion of Science and Scholarship, 1994).

15 The importance of Mondrian's beliefs and intentions in understanding his work shows that the narrowly formalist approach to his work, though often highly illuminating, as exemplified by Yves-Alain Bois's *Painting as Model* (Cambridge, MA: MIT Press, 1990), cannot be wholly adequate. See Daniel A. Herwitz on Mondrian's beliefs in *Making Theory/Constructing Art* (Chicago: University of Chicago Press, 1993).

16 Michel Foucault's 'What is an Author?' for example characterises the notion of the author or artist as an ideological construct we would best do away with. For we should be indifferent to or unconstrained by whatever meaning or expression the originating author took his work to have. See Paul Rabinow (ed.), *The Foucault Reader* (New York: Pantheon, 1984), pp. 101–20.

17 As quoted in Ian Chilvers, Harold Osborne and Dennis Farr (eds), *The Oxford Dictionary of Art* (Oxford: Oxford University Press, 1988), p. 384.

18 See Judy Chicago, *The Dinner Party* (New York: Penguin, 1996) for a thorough detailing of the history of the making and reception of the work, with many photographs which give a sense of the piece.

Chapter Two   Beauty Resurrected

1 Barnett Newman, 'The Sublime Is Now', 1948, as excerpted in Charles Harrison and Paul Wood (eds), *Art in Theory 1900–1990: An Anthology of Changing Ideas* (Oxford: Blackwell, 1992), p. 573.

2 Henri Matisse, 'Notes d'un peintre', *La Grande Revue*, Paris, 25 December 1908, quoted from the translation 'Notes of a Painter', as excerpted in Harrison and Wood (eds), *Art in Theory 1900–1990*, p. 76.

3 André Breton, *Surrealism and Painting*, 1928, as excerpted in Harrison and Wood (eds), *Art in Theory 1900–1990*, p. 445.

4 Immanuel Kant, trans. James Creed Meredith, *The Critique of Judgement* (Oxford: Oxford University Press, 1952), Pt I, Bk I, Sections 3–5, pp. 44–50.

5 *Ibid.*, Section 9, p. 58.

6 In essence this constitutes what Kant terms the four moments (i.e. conditions) that constitute aesthetic judgement and take up the first book of the first part of *The Critique of Judgement*, Pt I, Bk I, Sections 1–22 pp. 41–89.

7 Remarks of this kind can be found, for example, in Gordon Graham, *Philosophy of the Arts*, 2nd edn (London: Routledge, 2000), pp. 179–82, and Marcia Meulder Eaton, 'Kantian and Contextual Beauty', *Journal of Aesthetics and Art Criticism* 57, no. 1, 1999, pp. 11–15, written as part of the 'Symposium: Beauty Matters' edited by Peg Brand for the journal.

8 Clive Bell, *Art*, 2nd edn (London: Chatto and Windus, 1949), p. 25, orginally published 1914.

9 Kant, trans. Meredith, *The Critique of Judgement*, Pt I, Bk I, Sections 16–17, pp. 72–80.

10 *Ibid.*, Section 5, pp. 48–50, for the recognition that all may give rise to delight but distinguishing them requires distinguishing their grounds; Sections 16–17, p. 74, for confusing free and dependent judgements of beauty; and Section 16, pp. 72–4, for the requirement to get the relevant concepts right in judgements of dependent beauty.

11 Note that many who would subscribe to sophisticated aestheticism as characterised needn't subscribe to the details or substantive claims of Kant's account of aesthetic judgement except with respect to the separation of cognitive and aesthetic values along these lines, with only the aesthetic ones figuring in a work's value as art. For one of the most sophisticated and inclusive characterisations of this kind of approach see Peter Lamarque, 'Cognitive Values in the Arts: Marking the Boundaries' in Matthew Kieran (ed.), *Contemporary Debates in Aesthetics and the Philosophy of Art* (Oxford: Blackwell, 2005).

12 Noël Carroll's *A Philosophy of Mass Art* (Oxford: Oxford University Press, 1998), chapter 1, esp. pp. 89–109, constitutes an interesting diagnosis and critique of the Kantian influenced dismissal of mass art, from movies to pulp literature and comics.

13 I think the original source for these objections in contemporary analytic philosophy is Marshall Cohen, 'Aesthetic Essence' in M. Black (ed.), *Philosophy in America* (Ithaca: Cornell University Press, 1965), pp. 115–33.

14 See Edward Bullough, 'Psychical Distance', *British Journal of Psychology* 5, 1912, pp. 87–118 and Jerome Stolnitz, *Aesthetics and Philosophy of Art Criticism* (Boston: Houghton Mifflin, 1960).

15 The classic and still the best source for this objection is George Dickie, 'The Myth of the Aesthetic Attitude', *American Philosophical Quarterly* 1, no. 1, 1964, pp. 56–65.

16 Noël Carroll has in recent years been developing an argument along just these lines. See, for example, his 'Aesthetic Experience: A Question of Content' in Kieran (ed.), *Contemporary Debates in Aesthetics and the Philosophy of Art*.

17 In this tradition of conceiving of perception as a kind of hypothesis-driven schema formation and application see, for example, E. H. Gombrich, *Art and Illusion*, 5th edn, (Oxford: Phaidon, 1977), part IV, esp. pp. 246–79, originally published 1960; R. L. Gregory, 'Perceptions as Hypotheses', *Phil. Trans. Roy. Soc. Lond.*, B290, 1980, pp. 181–97; and Semir Zeki, 'Art and the Brain', *Journal of Consciousness Studies* 6, 1999, pp. 76–96.

18 See, for example, Mary A. McCloskey, *Kant's Aesthetic* (London: Macmillan, 1987), chapter 14, esp. pp. 142–7, where Kant's account of art is characterised as being superior to Collingwood's on the grounds that Kant's theory is tightly linked to perceptual form in this way, and Malcolm Budd, *Values of Art* (Harmondsworth: Penguin, 1995), chapter 1, pp. 27–31 and 34–5, where in interpreting Kant emphasis is placed on the perceived form of the object or art work.

19 Kant, trans. Meredith, *The Critique of Judgement*, Pt I, Bk II, Sections 45–9, pp. 166–82.

20 See, for example, Monroe Beardsley, *Aesthetics* (New York: Harcourt, Brace and World, 1958),

Section 24, pp. 456–70, and his 'On the Generality of Critical Reasons', *Journal of Philosophy* 59, no. 18, 1962, pp. 477–86.

21 Kant, trans. Meredith, *The Critique of Judgement*, Pt I, Bk II, Section 48, p. 173.

22 C. R. Leslie, *Memoirs of the Life of John Constable*, 1843, chapter 17.

23 Kant, trans. Meredith, *The Critique of Judgement*, Pt I, Bk II, Section 48, pp. 173–4.

24 Richard Hülsenbeck, 'First German Dada Manifesto (Collective Dada Manifesto)', as excerpted in Harrison and Wood (eds), *Art in Theory 1900–1990*, pp. 254–5.

25 William Shakespeare, *Twelfth Night* (1601), Act 3, Scene 1, line 159.

26 For the origination of this line of argument, and a fuller treatment, see Matthew Kieran, 'Aesthetic Value: Beauty, Ugliness and Incoherence', *Philosophy* 72, no. 281, 1997, pp. 383–99.

27 Plato, *The Republic*, trans. D. Lee, 2nd edn (Harmondsworth: Penguin, 1974), Bk IV, pp. 215–16, lines 439e–440a. The italics are my own to emphasise that Leontion delights in the sight of the corpses.

28 John Ruskin, *The Stones of Venice* (London: Smith, Elder and Co., 1874), vol. III, chapter III, section XV, p. 121.

29 *Ibid.*, section XVI, p. 121.

30 Robert Hughes, 'Art and Money' in his *Nothing If Not Critical* (London: Collins Harvill, 1990), pp. 387–404.

31 See, for example, Bill Beckley and David Shapiro (eds), *Uncontrollable Beauty* (New York: Allworth Press, 1998); Elaine Scarry, *On Beauty and Being Just* (Princeton: Princeton University Press, 1999); Peg Zeglin Brand (ed.), *Beauty Matters* (Bloomington: Indiana University Press, 2000); and Arthur C. Danto, *The Abuse of Beauty* (Chicago: Open Court, 2003).

32 Scarry, *On Beauty and Being Just*, esp. pp. 93–118.

33 Danto, *The Abuse of Beauty*, chapter 4.

34 Danto, 'The Artworld', 1964, as excerpted in Alex Neill and Aaron Ridley (eds), *The Philosophy of Art: Readings Ancient and Modern* (New York: McGraw-Hill, 1995), p. 209.

35 In this respect see Kendall Walton, 'Categories of Art', *Philosophical Review* 79, 1970, pp. 334–76, for an elegant argument to the effect that aesthetic properties of a work don't depend wholly on those properties perceivable by the senses but also on the categories it is appropriate to consider the work in relation to.

Chapter Three   Insight in Art

1 Paul Auster, *Moon Palace* (London: Faber and Faber, 1989), p. 170.

2 Vincent van Gogh, Letter no. 404, 30 April 1885, *The Complete Letters of Vincent van Gogh* (New York: New York Graphic Society, 1958), quoted by Rosemary Treble in *Vincent: The Paintings of Van Gogh* (London: Hamlyn, 1989), p. 32.

3 See Theodor Adorno, *Aesthetic Theory*, ed. Gretel Adorno and Rolf Tiedemann, trans. C. Lenhardt (London: Routledge & Kegan Paul, 1984), originally published in German, 1970, and *Brecht on Art and Politics*, ed. and trans. Tom Kuhn and Steve Giles (London: Methuen, 2003).

4 This is a point made by Noël Carroll in his 'Art, Narrative and Moral Understanding' in Jerrold Levinson (ed.), *Aesthetics and Ethics* (Cambridge: Cambridge University Press, 1998).

5 Plato, *The Republic*, trans. D. Lee, 2nd edn (Harmondsworth: Penguin, 1974), pp. 430–1, Book X, lines 601e–602b.

6 This is the gist of an attack on the cognitive value of art articulated in contemporary terms by Jerome Stolnitz, 'The Cognitive Triviality of Art', *British Journal of Aesthetics* 32, 1992, pp. 191–200.

7 Martha Nussbaum, for example in her *Love's Knowledge* (New York: Oxford University Press, 1990), esp. pp. 125–67, argues this holds for literature with respect to moral knowledge. See Berys Gaut, 'Art and Knowledge' in Jerrold Levinson (ed.), *The Oxford Handbook of Aesthetics* (Oxford: Oxford University Press, 2003), for a detailed classification of the different ways in which cognitivists think that art may afford knowledge.

8 Frank Jackson, 'Epiphenomenal Qualia', *Philosophical Quarterly* 32, 1982, pp. 127–36 and 'What Mary Didn't Know', *Journal of Philosophy* 83, no. 5, 1986, pp. 291–5.

9 See Peter Lamarque and Stein Olsen, *Truth, Fiction and Literature* (Oxford: Oxford University Press, 1994) and Bernard Harrison, *Inconvenient Fictions* (New Haven: Yale University Press, 1991) for different ways of making this kind of claim out.

10 The view that truth matters but is only one of a range of cognitive virtues (or one aspect of understanding) which can be or is relevant to artistic evaluation is a position common to many cognitivist approaches to artistic value. See, for example, my 'Art, Imagination and the Cultivation of Morals', *Journal of Aesthetics and Art Criticism* 54, no. 4, 1996, pp. 337–51; my 'Value of Art' in Berys Gaut and Dominic McIver Lopes (eds), *The Routledge Companion to Aesthetics*, 1st edn (London: Routledge, 2001); Gordon Graham, *Philosophy of the Arts* (London: Routledge, 1997); and Berys Gaut, 'Art and Cognition' in Matthew Kieran (ed.), *Contemporary Debates in Aesthetics and the Philosophy of Art* (Oxford: Blackwell, 2005).

11 Tony Godfrey, *Conceptual Art* (London: Phaidon, 1998), p. 383.

12 Sol Le Witt, 'Paragraphs on Conceptual Art', first published in *Artforum* 5, no. 10, 1967, pp. 79–83, as excerpted in Charles Harrison and Paul Wood (eds), *Art in Theory 1900–1990: An Anthology of Changing Ideas* (Oxford: Blackwell, 1992), p. 834.

13 James Shelley, 'The Problem of Non-perceptual Art', *British Journal of Aesthetics* 43, no. 4, 2003, pp. 363–78, argues that art objects needn't be perceivable by means of our senses to be appreciated as art works, but goes on to characterise our appreciation of such mental objects in terms of more traditional notions of beauty and the aesthetic. Whilst I am sympathetic to this line of thought I don't think it's the only way in which conceptual pieces can be valuable as art.

14 As quoted in Toby Clark, *Art and Propaganda in the Twentieth Century* (London: Weidenfeld and Nicolson, 1997), p. 120.

15 A by now classic source of this objection is Richard Wollheim, *Art and Its Objects*, 2nd edn (Cambridge: Cambridge University Press, 1980), but see Gary Kemp's 'The Croce–Collingwood Theory as Theory', *Journal of Aesthetics and Art Criticism* 61, no. 2, 2003, pp. 171–93, for a very thorough and sympathetic account.

16 Dominic McIver Lopes's *Sight and Sensibility: Evaluating Pictures* (Oxford: Oxford University Press, 2005) is a rare exception to which I am indebted. Lopes argues that part of the value of painting as an art lies in its development of our epistemological character through the process of engaging our visual systems.

17 See Michael Baxandall, *Patterns of Intention* (New Haven: Yale University Press, 1985) for a rich characterisation of Chardin's painterly preoccupations with vision articulated in relation to his *A Lady Taking Tea*.

Chapter Four   Art and Morality

1 Kathryn Moore Heleniak, *William Mulready* (New Haven: Yale University Press, 1980), p. 158.

2 Jean-Louis Ferrier, editor in chief, *Art of Our Century: The Chronicle of Western Art 1900 to the Present* (New York: Prentice-Hall, 1988), p. 136.

3 Anthony Burgess, 'What Is Pornography?' and George Steiner, 'Night Words: High Pornography and Human Privacy' in Douglas A. Hughes, ed., *Perspectives on Pornography* (New York: St. Martin's Press, 1970); Joel Feinberg, *Offense to Others* (Oxford: Oxford University Press, 1985), chapter 11; and Jerrold Levinson, 'Erotic Art' in Edward Craig, ed., *The Routledge Encyclopedia of Philosophy* (London: Routledge, 1999).

4 Roger Scruton, *Sexual Desire* (Manchester: Phoenix, 1994), p. 318.

5 See Kenneth Clark's testimony to Lord Longford's committee on pornography as represented in *Pornography: The Longford Report* (London: Coronet, 1972), pp. 99–100. A similar thought is implicit in some remarks made by Jerrold Levinson, 'Erotic Art' in Craig, ed., *The Routledge Encyclopedia of Philosophy*.

6 Scruton, *Sexual Desire*, pp. 138–9.

7 *Ibid.*

8 I have discussed this in more detail in my 'Pornographic Art', *Philosophy and Literature* 25, no. 1, 2001, pp. 31–45.

9 Classic sources for this kind of feminist worry about artistic representations of women, and about art more generally in relation to the gendered gaze, are Laura Mulvey, 'Visual Pleasure and Narrative Cinema', *Screen* 16, no. 3, 1975, pp. 6–18, included in her *Visual and Other Pleasures* (London: Macmillan, 1989), and Griselda Pollock, *Vision and Difference: Feminity, Feminism and the Histories of Art* (London: Routledge, 1988).

10 Laura Mulvey, 'You Don't Know What Is Happening, Do You, Mr. Jones?', quoted from Rozsika Parker and Griselda Pollock (eds), *Framing Feminism* (London: Pandora Press, 1987), p. 131, and originally published in *Spare Rib* 8, 1973, pp. 13–16.

11 Oscar Wilde, 'The Critic As Artist' in his *Intentions*, 8th edn (London: Methuen, 1913), pp. 190–2, first published 1891.

12 Nietzsche, *Twilight of the Idols*, originally published 1888, trans. Duncan Large (Oxford: Oxford University Press, 1998), Bk IX, section 24, p. 55.

13 For a particularly good articulation of sophisticated aestheticism see Peter Lamarque, 'Cognitive Values in the Arts: Marking the Boundaries' in Matthew Kieran (ed.), *Contemporary Debates in Aesthetics and the Philosophy of Art* (Oxford: Blackwell, 2005).

14 I used to think that something like this cognitivist line of thought led directly to the claim that a moral flaw in a work, where it was part of the imaginative understanding prescribed, lessened a work's artistic value. See my 'Art, Imagination and the Cultivation of Morals', *Journal of Aesthetics and Art Criticism* 54, no. 4, 1996, pp. 337–51. For reasons which will become apparent I no longer hold this to be the case.

15 Nietzsche, *The AntiChrist*, originally published 1888, trans. A. M. Ludovici (London: Russell & Russell, 1964), section 47, p. 196.

16 See Aristotle's *Poetics*, chapter 25, trans. S. Halliwell (London: Duckworth, 1986) and Noël Carroll, 'Moderate Moralism', *British Journal of Aesthetics* 36, no. 3, 1996, pp. 223–38.

17 David Hume, 'Of the Standard of Taste', originally published 1757, included in his *Selected Essays* (Oxford: Oxford University Press, 1993), pp. 151–2.

18 Berys Gaut, 'The Ethical Criticism of Art' in Jerrold Levinson (ed.), *Aesthetics and Ethics* (Cambridge: Cambridge University Press, 1998), p. 182, and his *Art, Emotion and Ethics* (Oxford: Oxford University Press, 2005).

19 Mary Devereaux, 'Moral Judgements and Works of Art: The Case of Narrative Literature, *Journal of Aesthetics and Art Criticism* 62, no. 1, 2004, pp. 3–11.

20 John Ruskin, *The Stones of Venice* (London: Smith, Elder and Co., 1874), vol. III, chapter III, section I–II, p. 112.

21 Peter Fuller, 'Nature and Raw Flesh: Sutherland v. Bacon', p. 135, in his *Modern Painters: Reflections on British Art*, ed. John McDonald (London: Methuen, 1993).

22 David Hume, 'Of the Standard of Taste', originally published 1757, included in his *Selected Essays*, p. 150. Much more recently Wayne Booth's *The Company We Keep* (Berkeley: University of California Press, 1988) argues for moral criticism on the basis of the analogy to friendship, and in 2001 I responded to a paper by Anne Eaton, 'Reading Titian through Hume: The Intersection of Morality with Artistic Beauty' at the annual American Society of Aesthetics meeting which had this kind of thought at its core.

23 Hume, 'Of the Standard of Taste', p. 152.

24 This is just as true of Booth's line of thought since his neo-Aristotelian conception of full friendship is highly moralistic. See Booth, *The Company We Keep*, esp. pp. 170–4.

25 As quoted by Lionel Lambourne, Caricature (London: HMSO, 1983), p. 40.

26 Joseph Addison, 'Uses and Abuses of Ridicule', Essay no. 249 for *The Spectator*, in John Foftis (ed.), *Addison: Essays in Criticism and Literary Theory* (Northbrook, IL: AHM Publishing, 1975), p. 28.

27 Although I remain unconvinced for the reasons given, an interesting paper which draws attention to the problem and attempts to show how moral criticism might get round this objection is Katherine Thomson's 'Aesthetic and Ethical Mediocrity in Art', *Philosophical Papers* 31, no. 2, 2002, pp. 199–215.

28 Daniel Jacobson's 'In Praise of Immoral Art', *Philosophical Topics* 25, 1997, pp. 155–99, is a rich paper which was the first to challenge moralists drawing a tight connection between merited

responses to art works and moral responses. He argues for a piecemeal approach to such evaluation in his 'Ethical Criticism and the Vices of Moderation' in Kieran (ed.), *Contemporary Debates in Aesthetics and the Philosophy of Art*. As I suggest in this section, however, I think a more reasoned theoretical basis can be given for holding that a work can be valuable as art partly in virtue of its immoral character. See my 'Forbidden Knowledge: The Challenge of Cognitive Immoralism' in S. Gardner and J. Bermúdez (eds), *Art and Morality* (London: Routledge, 2002), pp. 56–73, for a more detailed explication of much of the argument in this section.

29 See my 'On Obscenity: The Thrill and Repulsion of the Morally Prohibited', *Philosophy and Phenomenological Research* 64, no. 1, 2002, pp. 31–56.

30 John Stuart Mill, *On Liberty* (Harmondsworth: Penguin, 1982), esp. pp. 59–108.

31 *The Williams Report: Report of the Committee on Obscenity and Film Censorship*, ed. Bernard Williams (London: Cmnd. 7772, 1979), p. 99, suggests that certain deep offences of this kind may constitute a harm.

32 For a more detailed discussion of offence construed as a harm in terms of deep offence or public indecency, and its incompatibility with liberal assumptions, see Anthony Ellis, 'Offense and the Liberal Conception of the Law', *Philosophy and Public Affairs* 13, 1984, pp. 1–23, and his 'Censorship and the Media' in Matthew Kieran (ed.), *Media Ethics* (London: Routledge, 1998).

Chapter Five   The Truth in Humanism

1 Kenneth Clark, *Civilisation* (London: BBC and John Murray, 1969), chapter 5, p. 126.

2 Pierre Bourdieu, *Distinction: A Social Critique of the Judgement of Taste*, trans. Richard Nice (London: Routledge & Kegan Paul, 1984).

3 David Hume, 'Of the Standard of Taste', originally published 1757, included in his *Selected Essays* (Oxford: Oxford University Press, 1993), p. 149.

4 Robert Hughes, 'Henri Matisse in Nice' in *Nothing If Not Critical* (London: Collins Harvill, 1990), p. 172.

5 Jerrold Levinson, 'Hume's Standard of Taste: The Real Problem', *Journal of Aesthetics and Art Criticism* 60, no. 3, 2002, pp. 227–38, and his 'The Real Problem Sustained: Reply to Wieand', *Journal of Aesthetics and Art Criticism* 61, no. 4, 2003, pp. 398–400.

6 Jerrold Levinson, 'Hume's Standard of Taste: The Real Problem', *Journal of Aesthetics and Art Criticism* 60, no. 3, 2002, p. 234.

7 David Hume, 'Of the Standard of Taste', p. 149.

8 Honoré de Balzac, *The Unknown Masterpiece*, trans. Richard Howard, intro. Arthur Danto (New York: New York Review of Books, 2001), pp. 40–1.

9 Roger Scruton, *An Intelligent Person's Guide to Modern Culture* (London: Duckworth, 1998), p. 88.

10 Anthony Julius, *Transgressions: The Offence of Art* (London: Thames and Hudson, 2002), pp. 220–1.

11 See in particular Stanley Cavell's 'A Matter of Meaning It' in his *Must We Mean What We Say?*. (Cambridge: Cambridge University Press, 1976).

12 See, for example, Clement Greenberg, 'Towards a Newer Laocoon', *Partisan Review*, July/Aug. 1940, as excerpted in Charles Harrison and Paul Wood (eds), *Art in Theory 1900–1990: An Anthology of Changing Ideas* (Oxford: Blackwell, 1992).

13 See Arthur Danto, *The Philosophical Disenfranchisement of Art* (New York: Columbia University Press, 1986).

14 Robert Hughes, *Frank Auerbach* (London: Thames and Hudson, 1990), p. 10.

Bibliography and Suggested Reading

General collections

There are many good general collections which contain articles by different authors addressing issues in this book. Among the best are:

Alperson, Philip (ed.), *The Philosophy of the Visual Arts* (New York: Oxford University Press, 1992)

Gaut, Berys, and Dominic McIver Lopes (eds), *The Routledge Companion to Aesthetics*, 2nd edn (London: Routledge, 2005)

Hanfling, Oswald, (ed.), *Philosophical Aesthetics* (Oxford: Blackwell, 1992)

Kelly, Michael (ed.), *Encyclopedia of Aesthetics*, 4 vols. (New York: Oxford University Press, 1998)

Kieran, Matthew (ed.), *Contemporary Debates in Aesthetics and the Philosophy of Art* (Oxford: Blackwell, 2005)

Kivy, Peter, *The Blackwell Guide to Aesthetics* (Oxford: Blackwell, 2003)

Lamarque, Peter, and Stein Olsen (eds), *Aesthetics and the Philosophy of Art: The Analytic Tradition* (Oxford: Blackwell, 2003)

Levinson, Jerrold (ed.), *The Oxford Handbook of Aesthetics* (Oxford: Oxford University Press, 2003)

Neill, Alex, and Aaron Ridley (eds), *The Philosophy of Art: Readings Ancient and Modern* (New York: McGraw-Hill, 1995)

Neill, Alex, and Aaron Ridley (eds), *Arguing about Art: Contemporary Philosophical Debates*, 2nd edn (London: Routledge, 2002)

Turner, J. (ed.), *The Dictionary of Art* (London: Macmillan, 1996)

References and further reading

Addison, Joseph, 'Uses and Abuses of Ridicule', Essay no. 249 for *The Spectator*, in John Foftis (ed.), *Addison, Essays in Criticism and Literary Theory* (Northbrook, IL: AHM Publishing, 1975)

Adorno, Theodor, *Aesthetic Theory*, ed. Gretel Adorno and Rolf Tiedemann, trans. C. Lenhardt (London: Routledge & Kegan Paul, 1984), orig. publ. in German, 1970

Anderson, James, and Jeffrey Dean, 'Moderate Autonomism', *British Journal of Aesthetics*, vol. 38, 1998, pp. 150–66

Aristotle, *Poetics*, trans. S. Halliwell (London: Duckworth, 1986), orig. from approx. 367–322 BC

Auster, Paul, *Moon Palace* (London: Faber and Faber, 1989)

Balzac, Honoré de, *The Unknown Masterpiece*, trans, Richard Howard, intro. Arthur Danto (New York: New York Review of Books, 2001)

Baumgarten, Alexander, *Aesthetica* (Frankfurt, 1750/58)

Baxandall, Michael, *Patterns of Intention* (New Haven: Yale University Press, 1985)

Beardsley, Monroe, *Aesthetics: Problems in the Philosophy of Criticism* (New York: Harcourt, Brace and World, 1958)

Beardsley, Monroe, 'On The Generality of Critical Reasons', *Journal of Philosophy*, 59, no. 18, 1962, pp. 477–86

Beardsley, Monroe, *The Aesthetic Point of View* (Ithaca: Cornell University Press, 1982)

Beckley, Bill, and David Shapiro (eds), *Uncontrollable Beauty* (New York: Allworth Press, 1998)

Bell, Clive, *Art* (London: Chatto and Windus, 1914)

Benjamin, Walter, 'The Work of Art in the Age of Mechanical Reproduction', 1936, as excerpted in Charles Harrison and Paul Wood (eds), *Art in Theory 1900–1990: An Anthology of Changing Ideas* (Oxford: Blackwell, 1992)

Bois, Yves-Alain, *Painting as Model* (Cambridge, MA: MIT Press, 1990)

Booth, Wayne, *The Company We Keep* (Berkeley: University of California Press, 1988)

Bourdieu, Pierre, *Distinction: A Social Critique of the Judgement of Taste*, trans Richard Nice (London: Routledge & Kegan Paul, 1984)

Brady, Emily, and Jerrold Levinson (eds), *Aesthetic Concepts* (Oxford: Clarendon Press, 2001)

Brady, Emily, *Aesthetics of the Natural Environment* (Edinburgh: Edinburgh University Press, 2003)

Brand, Peg Zeglin (ed.), *Beauty Matters* (Bloomington: Indiana University Press, 2000)

Brecht, B., *Brecht on Art and Politics*, ed. and trans. Tom Kuhn and Steve Giles (London: Methuen, 2003)

Breton, André, *Surrealism and Painting*, 1928, as excerpted in Charles Harrison and Paul Wood (eds), *Art in Theory 1900–1990: An Anthology of Changing Ideas* (Oxford: Blackwell, 1992)

Budd, Malcolm, *Values of Art* (London: Penguin, 1995)

Bullough, Edward, 'Psychical Distance', *British Journal of Psychology*, 5, 1912, 87–118

Burke, Edmund, *A Philosophical Enquiry into the Origin of Our Ideas of the Sublime and Beautiful* (London, 1757)

Carroll, Noël, 'Art, Narrative and Moral Understanding', in Jerrold Levinson (ed.), *Aesthetics and Ethics* (Cambridge: Cambridge University Press, 1998)

Carroll, Noël, *A Philosophy of Mass Art* (London: Routledge, 1998)

Carroll, Noël, *The Philosophy of Art* (London: Routledge, 1999)

Carroll, Noël, 'Art and Ethical Criticism: An Overview of Recent Directions of Research,' *Ethics*, 110, 2000, pp. 350–87

Carroll, Noël, 'Moderate Moralism', *British Journal of Aesthetics*, 36, no. 3, 1996, pp. 223–38

Carroll, Noël, 'Aesthetic Experience: A Question of Content' in Matthew Kieran (ed.), *Contemporary Debates in Aesthetics and the Philosophy of Art* (Oxford: Blackwell, 2005)

Cavell, Stanley, *Must We Mean What We Say?* (Cambridge: Cambridge University Press, 1976)

Chicago, Judy, *The Dinner Party* (New York: Penguin, 1996)

Chilvers, Ian, Harold Osborne and Dennis Farr (eds), *The Oxford Dictionary of Art* (Oxford: Oxford University Press, 1988)

Clark, Kenneth, *Civilisation* (London: BBC and John Murray, 1969)

Clark, Toby, *Art and Propaganda in the Twentieth Century* (London: Weidenfeld and Nicolson, 1997)

Cohen, Marshall, 'Aesthetic Essence' in M. Black (ed.), *Philosophy in America* (Ithaca: Cornell University Press, 1965)

Collingwood, R. G. *The Principles of Art* (Oxford: Oxford University Press, 1958)

Currie, Gregory, *An Ontology of Art* (London: Macmillan, 1989)

Danto, Arthur, 'The Artworld,' *Journal of Philosophy*, 61, 1964, pp. 571–84

Danto, Arthur, *The Transfiguration of the Commonplace* (Cambridge, MA: Harvard University Press, 1981)

Danto, Arthur *The Philosophical Disenfranchisement of Art* (New York: Columbia University Press, 1988)

Danto, Arthur, *The Abuse of Beauty* (Chicago: Open Court, 2003)

Davies, David, 'Artistic Intentions and the Ontology of Art', *British Journal of Aesthetics*, 39, 1999, pp. 148–62

Davies, David, *Art as Performance* (Oxford: Blackwell, 2004)

Davies, David, 'Against Enlightened Empiricism' in Matthew Kieran (ed.), *Contemporary Debates in Aesthetics and the Philosophy of Art* (Oxford: Blackwell, 2005)

Devereaux, Mary, 'Moral Judgements and Works of Art: The Case of Narrative Literature', *Journal of Aesthetics and Art Criticism*, vol. 62, no. 1, 2004, pp. 3–11

Dewey, John, *Art as Experience* (New York: G. P. Putnam, 1934)

Dickie, George, 'The Myth of the Aesthetic Attitude', *American Philosophical Quarterly*, 1, 1964, pp. 55–65

Dickie, George, *Evaluating Art* (Philadelphia: Temple University Press, 1988)

Dickie, George, *Art and Value* (Oxford: Blackwell, 2001)

Eaton, Anne, 'Reading Titian through Hume: The Intersection of Morality with Artistic Beauty', paper delivered to the Annual Conference of the American Society of Aesthetics, 2001

Eaton, Marcia Muelder, 'Kantian and Contextual Beauty', *Journal of Aesthetics and Art Criticism*, 57, no. 1, 1999, pp. 11–15, written as part of the 'Symposium: Beauty Matters' edited by Peg Brand for the journal

Eaton, Marcia Muelder, *Merit, Aesthetic and Ethical* (Oxford: Oxford University Press, 2001)

Ellis, Anthony, 'Offense and the Liberal Conception of the Law', *Philosophy and Public Affairs*, 13, 1984, pp. 1–23

Ellis, Anthony, 'Censorship and the Media', in Matthew Kieran (ed.), *Media Ethics* (London: Routledge, 1998)

Elsen, Albert E., 'Drawing and a New Sexual Intimacy: Rodin and Schiele' in Patrick Werkner (ed.), *Egon Schiele: Art, Sexuality, and Viennese Modernism* (Palo Alto: The Society for the Promotion of Science and Scholarship, 1994)

Feinberg, Joel, *Offense to Others* (Oxford University Press: Oxford, 1985)

Ferrier, Jean-Louis (editor in chief), *Art of Our Century: The Chronicle of Western Art to the Present* (New York: Prentice-Hall, 1988)

Fuller, Peter, *Modern Painters: Reflections on British Art*, ed. John McDonald (London: Methuen, 1993)

Gadamer, Hans, *The Relevance of the Beautiful and Other Essays*, trans. N. Walker (Cambridge: Cambridge University Press, 1986)

Gardner, S., and J. Bermúdez (eds), *Art and Morality* (London: Routledge, 2003)

Gaut, Berys, 'Art and Knowledge' in Jerrold Levinson (ed.), *The Oxford Handbook of Aesthetics* (Oxford: Oxford University Press, 2003)

Gaut, Berys, 'The Ethical Criticism of Art', in Jerrold Levinson (ed.), *Aesthetics and Ethics* (Cambridge: Cambridge University Press, 1998)

Gaut, Berys, *Art, Emotion and Ethics* (Oxford: Oxford University Press, 2005)

Godfrey, Tony, *Conceptual Art* (London: Phaidon, 1998)

Goldman, Alan, *Aesthetic Value* (New York: Westview, 1995)

Gombrich, E. H., *Art and Illusion* (Oxford: Phaidon, 1960)

Goodman, Nelson, *Languages of Art* (London: Indianapolis University Press, 1968)

Graham, Gordon, *Philosophy of the Arts*, 2nd edn (London: Routledge, 2000), orig. publ. 1997

Graham, Gordon, 'Expressivism: Croce and Collingwood' in Berys Gaut and Dominic McIver Lopes (eds), *The Routledge Companion to Aesthetics* (London: Routledge, 2001)

Greenberg, Clement, 'Towards a Newer Laocoon', *Partisan Review*, July/Aug. 1940.

Gregory, R. L., 'Perceptions as Hypotheses', *Phil. Trans. Roy. Soc. Lond.*, B290, 1980, pp. 181–97

Guyer, Paul, *Kant and the Claims of Taste* (Cambridge, MA: Harvard University Press, 1979)

Harrison, Bernard, *Inconvenient Fictions* (New Haven: Yale University Press, 1991)

Hegel, G. W. F., *Introductory Lectures on Aesthetics*, trans. B. Bosanquet (Harmondsworth: Penguin, 1993), orig. edited in 1835 and revised in 1842 for the posthumous edition of Hegel's collected works

Heleniak, Kathryn Moore, *William Mulready* (New Haven: Yale University Press, 1980)

Herwitz, Daniel A., *Making Theory/Constructing Art* (Chicago: University of Chicago Press, 1993)

Hopkins, Robert, *Picture, Image and Experience* (Cambridge: Cambridge University Press, 1998)

Hughes, Douglas A. (ed.), *Perspectives on Pornography* (New York: St Martin's Press, 1970)

Hughes, Robert, *Frank Auerbach* (London: Thames and Hudson, 1990)

Hughes, Robert, *Nothing If Not Critical* (London: Collins Harvill, 1990)

Hülsenbeck, Richard, 'First German Dada Manifesto (Collective Dada Manifesto)', as excerpted in Charles Harrison and Paul Wood (eds), *Art in Theory 1900–1990: An Anthology of Changing Ideas* (Oxford: Blackwell, 1992)

Hume, David, 'Of the Standard of Taste', included in his *Selected Essays* (Oxford: Oxford University Press, 1993), orig. publ. 1757

Hutcheson, Francis, *An Inquiry into the Origin of Our Ideas of Beauty and Virtue* (London, 1725); 4th edn (London, 1738)

Jackson, Frank, 'Epiphenomenal Qualia', *Philosophical Quarterly*, 32, 1982, pp. 127–36

Jackson, Frank, 'What Mary Didn't Know', *Journal of Philosophy*, 83, no. 5, 1986, pp. 291–5

Jacobson, Daniel, 'In Praise of Immoral Art,' *Philosophical Topics*, 25, 1997, pp. 155–99

Jacobson, Daniel, 'Ethical Criticism and the Vices of Moderation', in Matthew Kieran (ed.), *Contemporary Debates in Aesthetics and the Philosophy of Art* (Oxford: Blackwell, 2005)

Jay, Bill, Nigel Warburton and David Hockney, *Brandt* (London: ipublish.com, 1999)

John, Eileen, 'Artistic Value and Opportunistic Moralism', in Matthew Kieran (ed.), *Contemporary Debates in Aesthetics and the Philosophy of Art* (Oxford: Blackwell, 2005)

Julius, Anthony, *Transgressions: The Offence of Art* (London: Thames and Hudson, 2002)

Kant, Immanuel, *The Critique of Judgement*, trans. James Creed Meredith (Oxford: Oxford University Press, 1952), orig. publ. 1790

Kemp, Gary, 'The Croce–Collingwood Theory as Theory', *Journal of Aesthetics and Art Criticism*, 61, no. 2, 2003, pp. 171–93

Kieran, Matthew, 'The Impoverishment of Art', *British Journal of Aesthetics*, 35, no. 1., 1995, pp. 15–25

Kieran, Matthew, 'Art, Imagination and the Cultivation of Morals', *Journal of Aesthetics and Art Criticism*, 54, no. 4, 1996, pp. 337–51

Kieran, Matthew, 'Aesthetic Value: Beauty, Ugliness and Incoherence', *Philosophy*, 72, no. 281, 1997, pp. 383–99

Kieran, Matthew, 'In Defence of the Ethical Evaluation of Narrative Art,' *British Journal of Aesthetics*, 41, 2001, pp. 26–38

Kieran, Matthew, 'Pornographic Art', *Philosophy and Literature*, 25, no. 1, 2001, pp. 31–45

Kieran, Matthew, 'Value of Art', in Berys Gaut and Dominic McIver Lopes (eds), *The Routledge Companion to Aesthetics*, 1st edn (London: Routledge, 2001), 2nd edn, 2005

Kieran, Matthew, 'On Obscenity: The Thrill and Repulsion of the Morally Prohibited', *Philosophy and Phenomenological Research*, 64, no. 1, 2002, pp. 31–56

Kieran, Matthew, 'Art and Morality' in Jerrold Levinson (ed.), *The Oxford Handbook to Aesthetics* (Oxford: Oxford University Press, 2003)

Kieran, Matthew, 'In Search of a Narrative' in Matthew Kieran and Dominic McIver Lopes (eds), *Imagination, Philosophy and the Arts* (London: Routledge, 2003)

Kieran, Matthew, 'Forbidden Knowledge: The Challenge of Cognitive Immoralism' in S. Gardner and J. Bermúdez (eds), *Art and Morality* (London: Routledge, 2003)

Kivy, Peter, *Philosophies of the Arts: An Essay in Differences* (Cambridge: Cambridge University Press, 1997)

Kripke, Saul, *Naming and Necessity* (Cambridge, MA: Harvard University Press, 1980)

Lamarque, Peter, and Stein Haugom Olsen, *Truth, Fiction and Literature* (Oxford: Clarendon Press, 1994)

Lamarque, Peter, *Fictional Points of View* (Ithaca: Cornell University Press, 1996)

Lamarque, Peter, 'Cognitive Values in the Arts: Marking the Boundaries' in Matthew Kieran (ed.), *Contemporary Debates in Aesthetics and the Philosophy of Art* (Oxford: Blackwell, 2005)

Lambourne, Lionel, *Caricature* (London: HMSO, 1983)

Le Witt, Sol, 'Paragraphs on Conceptual Art', *Artforum*, 5, no. 10, 1967, pp. 79–83

Leslie, C. R., *Memoirs of the Life of John Constable* (London: 1843)

Levinson, Jerrold, 'Art, Value and Philosophy' (a critical review of Budd's *Values of Art*), *Mind*, 105, 1996, pp. 667–82

Levinson, Jerrold, 'Pleasure and the Value of Works of Art' in his *The Pleasures of Aesthetics* (Ithaca: Cornell University Press, 1996)

Levinson, Jerrold, *The Pleasures of Aesthetics* (Ithaca: Cornell University Press, 1996)

Levinson, Jerrold, 'Evaluating Music' in P. Alperson (ed.), *Musical Worlds* (College Park, PA: Penn State Press, 1998)

Levinson, Jerrold, (ed.), *Aesthetics and Ethics* (Cambridge: Cambridge University Press, 1998)

Levinson, Jerrold, 'Erotic Art,' in Edward Craig, ed., *The Routledge Encyclopedia of Philosophy* (London: Routledge, 1999)

Levinson, Jerrold, 'Hume's Standard of Taste: The Real Problem,' *Journal of Aesthetics and Art Criticism*, 60, no. 3, 2002, pp. 227–38

Levinson, Jerrold, 'The Real Problem Sustained: Reply to Wieand,' *Journal of Aesthetics and Art Criticism*, 61, no. 4, 2003, pp. 398–400

Longford (Lord), *Pornography: The Longford Report* (London: Coronet, 1972)

Lopes, Dominic McIver, *Sight and Sensibility: Evaluating Pictures* (Oxford: Oxford University Press, 2005)

McCloskey, Mary A., *Kant's Aesthetic* (London: Macmillan, 1987)

Mallaband, Philip, 'Understanding Kant's Distinction between Free and Dependent Beauty', *Philosophical Quarterly*, 52, 2002, pp. 66–81

Malraux, André, *Le Musée Imaginaire*, which is vol. I of his *The Psychology of Art* (New York: Pantheon Books, 1949–50)

Matisse, Henri, 'Notes d'un peintre', *La Grande Revue*, Paris, 25 December 1908; 'Notes of a Painter' as excerpted in Charles Harrison and Paul Wood (eds), *Art in Theory 1900–1990: An Anthology of Changing Ideas* (Oxford: Blackwell, 1992)

Mill, John Stuart, *On Liberty* (Harmondsworth: Penguin, 1982), orig. publ. 1859

Newman, Barnett, 'The Sublime is Now', 1948, as excerpted in Charles Harrison and Paul Wood (eds), *Art in Theory 1900–1990: An Anthology of Changing Ideas* (Oxford: Blackwell, 1992)

Mulvey, Laura, 'You Don't Know What Is Happening, Do You, Mr. Jones?', *Spare Rib*, 8, 1973, pp. 13–16

Mulvey, Laura, 'Visual Pleasure and Narrative Cinema', *Screen*, 16, no. 3, 1975

Mulvey, Laura, *Visual and Other Pleasures* (London: Macmillan, 1989)

Nietzsche, Friedrich, *Twilight of the Idols*, trans. Duncan Large (Oxford: Oxford University Press, 1998), orig. publ. 1888

Nietzsche, Friedrich, *The AntiChrist*, trans. A. M. Ludovici (London: Russell & Russell, 1964), orig. publ. 1888

Nussbaum, Martha, *Love's Knowledge* (New York: Oxford University Press, 1990)

Parker, Rozsika, and Griselda Pollock (eds), *Framing Feminism* (London: Pandora Press, 1987)

Plato, *The Republic*, trans. D. Lee, 2nd edn (Harmondsworth: Penguin, 1974), orig. written around 375 BC.

Pollock, Griselda, *Vision and Difference: Femininity, Feminism and the Histories of Art* (London: Routledge, 1988)

Rabinow, Paul (ed.), *The Foucault Reader* (New York: Pantheon, 1984)

Ridley, Aaron, *R. G. Collingwood: A Philosophy of Art* (London: Orion Books, 1998)

Ruskin, John, *The Stones of Venice* (London: Smith, Elder and Co., 1874)

Savile, Anthony, *The Test of Time* (Oxford: Clarendon Press, 1982)

Scarry, Elaine, *On Beauty and Being Just* (Princeton: Princeton University Press, 1999)

Scruton, Roger, *Art and Imagination* (London: Methuen, 1974)

Scruton, Roger, *The Aesthetic Understanding* (London: Methuen, 1983)

Scruton, Roger, 'The Photographic Surrogate', reprinted in his *The Philosopher on Dover Beach* (Manchester: Carcanet, 1990)

Scruton, Roger, *Sexual Desire* (Manchester: Phoenix, 1994)

Scruton, Roger, *An Intelligent Person's Guide to Modern Culture* (London: Duckworth, 1998)

Sharpe, R. A., 'The Empiricist Theory of Artistic Value', *Journal of Aesthetics and Art Criticism*, 58, 2000, pp. 321–32

Shelley, James, 'Hume and the Nature of Taste', *Journal of Aesthetics and Art Criticism*, 56, no. 1, 1998, pp. 29–38

Shelley, James, 'The Problem of Non-perceptual Art', *British Journal of Aesthetics*, 43, no. 4, 2003, pp. 363–78

Sibley, Frank, 'Aesthetic Concepts', *Philosophical Review*, 68, 19—, pp. 421–50

Sibley, Frank, *Approach to Aesthetics* (Oxford: Clarendon Press, 2001)

Stecker, Robert, *Artworks: Definition, Meaning, Value* (Pennsylvania: Penn State University Press, 1997)

Stolnitz, Jerome, *Aesthetics and Philosophy of Art Criticism* (Boston: Houghton Mifflin, 1960)

Stolnitz, Jerome, 'The Cognitive Triviality of Art', *British Journal of Aesthetics*, 32, 1992, pp. 191–200

Tanner, Michael, 'Morals in Fiction and Fictional Morality II', *Proceedings of the Aristotelian Society*, suppl. vol. 68, 1994, pp. 51–66

Thomson, Katherine, 'Aesthetic and Ethical Mediocrity in Art', *Philosophical Papers*, 31, no. 2, 2002, pp. 199–215

Tolstoy, Leo, *What is Art? and Essays on Art*, trans. Aylmer Maude (London: Duckworth, 1930), orig. publ. 1898

Townsend, Dabney, *Hume's Aesthetic Theory: Taste and Sentiment* (London: Routledge, 2001)

Treble, Rosemary, *Vincent: The Paintings of Van Gogh* (London: Hamlyn, 1989)

Walton, Kendall, 'Categories of Art', *Philosophical Review*, vol. 79, 1970, pp. 334–67.

Walton, Kendall *Mimesis as Make-Believe* (Cambridge, MA: Harvard University Press, 1990)

Walton, Kendall, 'Morals in Fiction and Fictional Morality I,' *Proceedings of the Aristotelian Society*, suppl. vol. 68, 1994, pp. 27–50

Warburton, Nigel, 'Is Art Sacred?' in Ben Rogers (ed.), *Is Nothing Sacred?* (London: Routledge, 2004)

Wilde, Oscar, *Intentions*, 8th edn (London: Methuen, 1913)

Williams, Bernard, *The Williams Report. Report of the Committee on Obscenity and Film Censorship* (London: Cmnd. 7772, 1979)

Wollheim, Richard, *Art and Its Objects*, 2nd edn (Cambridge: Cambridge University Press, 1980), orig. publ. 1968

Wollheim, Richard, *Painting as an Art* (London: Thames and Hudson, 1987)

Wolterstorff, Nicholas, *Worlds and Works of Art* (Oxford: Clarendon Press, 1980)

Zangwill, Nick, 'Art and Audience', *Journal of Aesthetics and Art Criticism*, 57, no. 3, 1999, pp. 315–32

Zeki, Semir, 'Art and the Brain', *Journal of Consciousness Studies*, 6, 1999, pp. 76–96

Index